Living in the Light

Living in the Light

A WALK THROUGH *1·2·3 JOHN*

Sam Gordon

AMBASSADOR

Belfast Northern Ireland **Greenville** South Carolina

Living in the Light
© 2001 Trans World Radio

ISBN 1 84030 103 1

Ambassador Publications
a division of
Ambassador Productions Ltd.
Providence House
Ardenlee Street
Belfast
BT6 8QJ
Northern Ireland
www.ambassador-productions.com

Emerald House
427 Wade Hampton Blvd.
Greenville
SC 29609, USA
www.emeraldhouse.com

Trans World Radio
11 St James Gardens
Swansea
SA1 6DY
United Kingdom

01792 483050

www.twr.org.uk

Trans World Radio
P O Box 8700
Cary
NC 27512, USA

1 800 456 7TWR

DEDICATION

to
Jan

*your editorial genius and passion for the
word of God is reflected on every page of
this volume and many others in the series*

*without the Lord, we can do nothing …
without you, it wouldn't have happened!*

Truth for Today

~ Mission Statement ~

*'To teach the entire Bible in a warm expository
style so that people's lives are influenced to such
a degree that they impact their world for Christ.'*

First Word

Reading through the epistles of John, one is impressed with the author's intensity. While John is probably best known as the apostle of love, you can rest assured, he was no starry-eyed doting grandfather, he was no spiritual softie; as a man of integrity and principle, a man whose life was anchored to biblical truth, he was intolerant of heresy. These seemingly opposing dynamics emerge in the first epistle on numerous occasions. Indeed, in John's actions, in his love for his 'little children' and in his condemnation of heresy, he is intense.

I once heard a friend say that when he was younger, there were many things of which he was certain, but as he grew in years and matured in his faith, the list of sureties became shorter. However, in considering the major doctrines of the faith, he became more convinced - more intense, if you will.

My friend, Sam Gordon, has the gift of driving home the truths of Scripture. I especially like his approach to the Johannine epistles. John's teaching is clear and forceful and Sam does a magnificent job in bringing to life the human author as he is enabled by the Holy Spirit. Reading Sam's book helped me understand the message our

Lord wanted John to convey, but Sam's unique style of communicating helped me to come away from these epistles feeling like I know the man John more personally.

The heartbeat of the ministry of Trans World Radio for the last 47 years has been preaching and teaching the word of God. Through the tool of super-power radio that God has given us, we are ministering today in almost 170 languages to people around the world - many of whom live in places where there is little or no opportunity to hear that God loves them and Jesus Christ died for them. Sam Gordon personifies the core of what we do and who we are in both his radio broadcast, *Truth for Today*, which is aired via TWR all across Europe, and in his writing ministry.

I wholeheartedly commend Sam's book, *Living in the Light*, to you. I guarantee that you will come away from this book with a better understanding of what it means to live in the light.

Dr Tom Lowell

President
Trans World Radio

September 2001

Second Thoughts

'I'm so glad I'm a part of the family of God!'

You may be familiar with those words - they were penned a few years back. I will let you into a secret, they mean so much to me!

There is nothing that thrills my heart more in my travels than when I meet someone else from within God's global family. The chances are we may never have met before and, if my experience is anything to go by, that does not pose any real problem, it is not even an issue; the fact is, nine times out of ten, there is an immediate rapport between us, we seem to hit it off for we have something in common.

It is true, we are strangers when we meet the first time but, when the time comes for us to part, we leave the very best of friends. To me, that is what makes the worldwide family of God quite unique and extra special.

It never ceases to amaze me, it does not matter where I minister throughout the world, there is frequently someone I meet with whom I share a mutual acquaintance. In such moments, people often say to me, with more than a hint of elation and surprise in their voice:

'My, it's a small world, isn't it!' Well, it may seem like that, but I like to think of it like this: it is not that the world is getting any smaller, it is just that the family of God is getting bigger!

In some ways, that is the default position of John's three epistles. The dedicated theme is an emphasis on family life. And, if we are living it to the full, we will be walking in the light as well as walking in love.

John pulls no punches when he underlines our responsibilities to one another and, when occasion demands it because some folks are not pulling their weight, he is not afraid to name names. I think John, in the brief compass of seven chapters, scratches where people are itching; he is answering the questions many people are asking!

Take heart, in a mixed up world where people have lost their sense of identity, we know who we are, we are the children of God; we know where we are going, we are destined for heaven. We also have the added bonus of a real sense of belonging; and, believe it or not, that unexpected perk is ours for one reason only ... we are family!

And, because we are family, we enjoy happy fellowship together as we share a common life and bond in the Lord Jesus; to me, that is a wonderful blessing, an incomparable blessing, a blessing that money cannot buy. It is a blessing worth so much more than acres of diamonds.

Sam Gordon

Contents

1 JOHN

1

Jesus ... no phantom of the divine opera!

An introduction

The epistle of 1 John is a fascinating book of five chapters, the kind of book we can easily read through in 15 or 20 minutes. It is all about the global family of God. At the same time, John also focuses on the joys and delights of Christian fellowship. He has a lot to say about love and light and life for these are the dynamics of a healthy and fruitful relationship with God. It is a book that shows us how to maximise our gifting and find our full potential realised in God.

John says, in a world of make-believe, in a world where absolutes are out of fashion, in a world of fantasy, in a world of shallow relationships, in a world of forty shades of grey ... be real, be authentic!

It seems to me that is a stirring challenge from the pen of an apostle who proved to be such a seasoned campaigner in the halcyon days of the early church. He was a pastor with a big warm heart; he was a man who was keenly interested in people; he was a person who wanted to bring out the best in you. That's John!

In fact, the historian Jerome tells us that when the aged apostle became so weak that he could no longer preach from the pulpit, he used to be carried into the congregation at Ephesus and he had to content himself with a brief word of exhortation. *'Little children,'* he would say, *'love one another.'* That was his only message. So far as John was concerned, there was no other!

That same, single-minded, no-nonsense approach to knowing God better is what gives his epistle a sharp cutting edge for John is scratching where people are itching. He is answering the questions which ordinary people are asking. He does not side-step the thorny issues; he faces every problem head-on. John knows how to get his message across. He excels in the fine art of good communication.

Martin Luther said about 1 John, *'I have never read a book written in simpler words than this one, and yet the words are inexpressible.'*

And for a man who spent the early part of his working life as a fisherman on the sea of Galilee, it just proves the point that when we follow Jesus Christ, he takes us the way that we are and he shapes us into the kind of people he wants us to be.

John's contribution to the New Testament is second only to that of the apostle Paul. He was profusely prolific with his pen. John gave us the Gospel that bears his name, we have the three epistles of 1, 2 and 3 John and we have the Apocalypse (the book of Revelation) which also carries his name as the human penman. Over the years, God used him in a very special way, not only to bless the local congregation in the city of Ephesus but to encourage the worldwide church.

We know from reading between the lines of history that John lived to a ripe old age. Irenaeus, the bishop of Lyons, confirms the traditional belief that John continued in fellowship with the church at Ephesus until the times of Trajan, which stretch from AD 98 to AD 117. He was probably the last of the apostles to leave this earthly life and that means this trio of letters may well be the last of those added to the canon of Scripture, probably during the decade AD 85-95.

An untraditional letter

When compared to other epistles in the New Testament, 1 John is not the normal, traditional kind of letter. It is more in the mould of the book of Hebrews which is itself a circular letter. It is not an apostolic letter addressed to an individual church such as Paul's letter to the Philippians; it is not written to a particular person such as the letter to Philemon; it is not a theological treatise such as the letter to the Romans. It is more of an affectionate, heart-to-heart letter penned to those whom John calls *'dear children'* as in 2:1 and 5:21. At other times, he refers to his readers as *'dear friends'* as in 3:2 and 4:7.

The letter is so intensely personal and so obviously Johannine that he does not even bother to sign his name to it! The people who read it will know straightaway that the source is John; it is 'the way he tells it' that shines through on every page! There is not the remotest chance that the author could be mistakenly identified as anyone other than John for his fingerprint is etched on every verse.

Written in response to a crisis

John put quill to parchment to counter a terribly sad situation that had arisen in some of the assemblies probably in Asia or what is now known as modern-day Turkey. We know there was a split in the church and that a number of people left because they thought their version of Christianity was an improvement on what the apostles taught. That much is inferred from John's incisive comments in 2:19.

When that happens in the life of any church fellowship, those who are left behind to pick up the broken pieces often end up on an elongated guilt trip. People become quite introverted when churches come apart at the seams and they often feel discouraged, dispirited and disheartened. They frequently need some kind of spiritual uplift as well as words of reassurance that they are still on the right track.

The problem was those who left did not walk out because they did not get their way over the colour of the carpet or because the church up the road had a more contemporary style of worship. The people who left had taken on board an early form of Gnosticism which is generally called Docetism. The word 'docetist' comes from the Greek word *dokeo* which means, 'I think', 'I seem', or 'I appear'. Paul employs this word when writing in 1 Corinthians 12:22 about the role of the members of the body.

These folks taught that Christ appeared to be a man but was not truly human. The Christmas story for them was not just a miracle, it was an impossibility. The Gnostic, which comes from the Greek word *gnosis* meaning 'knowledge' had similar views on many of these doctrinal issues. He was sure that the Christ spirit descended on the man Jesus at his baptism but then left him before the crucifixion. Hence, there was no real incarnation. In the view of the Docetist or Gnostic, the Word did not truly become flesh nor did the fulness of the Godhead dwell bodily in Jesus Christ.

When we take this view to its logical conclusion, it means that Christ was only play-acting when he ate a meal, when he drank some water, when he grew weary and slept. It means, he did not really suffer on the cross or die as a substitute for sinners! That was the gigantic problem they were wrestling with and that explains why John responded the way he did.

To clarify a point of doctrine

It is abundantly clear from 5:13 that John wrote to those who believed in the name of the Son of God in order that they might know that they possessed eternal life. In fact, the two Greek words for *'to know'* are found about thirty-eight times in John's three epistles. When all is said and done, these folks needed to know who was right and who was wrong. That is why John gave them three main tests so they could distinguish between truth and error:

- *test number one: the doctrinal test (4:2),*
- *test number two: the relationships test (4:20,21),*
- *test number three: the obedience test (2:3,4).*

That is why the epistle of 1 John is so vitally important in these days for it gives us guidance on what a real Christian is; it plugs the gap in our thinking and gives us adequate information whereby we can confidently test the claims of others. Someone has said and he is absolutely right, 'The first letter of John is at once a pastoral sermon and a theological tract aimed at those who thought you could separate them.' In other words, 1 John is all about striking a balance between our head and our heart in terms of spirituality and, at the same time, harmonising both our doctrine and our experience.

You see, real faith must be based on time-tested truth. Living in a multi-cultural, multi-faith society as we do, the tendency is for the people of God to almost apologise for their faith in the Lord Jesus Christ. We often dilute our message and blunt the impact of our evangelism because we dread being marginalised in the local community; we live in fear of being shunted into the siding in the workplace. We do not like being rejected, we want to be one of the lads. John's powerful argument is that we have nothing to be embarrassed about.

When we stand at the evangelical crease, we should be batting on the front foot as we remind a secular generation that the Lord Jesus Christ is staggeringly unique. He stands alone for he is the incomparable Christ!

From John's perspective, this form of Gnosticism was not just a radical evangelical movement that he was much too conservative or too old-fashioned to appreciate; it was a pernicious conspiracy of lies! It could not be tolerated and John was not prepared to give it any leg room; he would not, he could not, give it an ounce of credibility. Irrespective of the tight corner he was backed into, there is no way that he dare sanction what was going on.

The truth mattered so much to John that this gentle pastor, who above anybody championed love of the brethren, could when occasion demanded become a zealous inquisitor vigorously campaigning for the excommunication of heretics.

Building a spiritual staircase

The way John puts his case and advances his argument is fascinating. I have found the image of a spiritual staircase the most helpful in trying to get to grips with the intricacies of John's message. As we climb the central marble staircase in a royal palace or a stately home, we see the same exquisite objects, the hanging tapestries, the oil paintings and the portraits of a bygone era ... we see all of them from a different angle and often with a new appreciation of their beauty. We often hear people exclaim with more than a hint of finesse, 'I never saw it like that before!'

It is a bit like that with the great truths John is sharing with us in his letter. The overall view becomes more wonderful as we climb higher and the heavenly light shines more and more clearly until we reach the top. A four-point outline from David Jackman's commentary has helped me ascend the stairs:

- it is all about *walking in God's light* (1:1-2:14),
- it is all about *practising God's truth* (2:15-3:10; 4:1-6),
- it is all about *living in God's love* (3:11-24; 4:7-21),
- it is all about *sharing God's victory* (5:1-21).

Some aesthetically sensitive Bible expositors have jumped on the hermeneutic bandwagon and with artistic elegance they have compared 1 John to a musical score in which several motifs recur a number of times. For example:

- he raises the issue of *a right belief in Christ* in 1:1-4, and then returns to it in 2:18-27, and again in 5:5-12;
- he deals with *sin and obedience* in 1:5-2:2, and then returns to it in 2:28,29, and again in 3:3-10, and in 5:16,17;

- he raises the issue of *loving the brethren* in 2:7-11,
  and then returns to it in 3:11-18,
  and again in 4:7-5:3.

We can see what is happening. In each case the motif is developed a little more and the original idea is expanded; while in 3:21-23 the three motifs of belief, obedience and love are joined together in one harmonious whole where John says, '*We have confidence before God and receive from him anything we ask, because we obey his commands and do what pleases him. And this is his command: to believe in the name of his Son, Jesus Christ, and to love one another as he commanded us.*' Based on this line of approach, Warren Wiersbe suggests the following easy-to-remember outline:

- in chapters 1 and 2, *the tests of fellowship are based on the fact that God is light;*
- in chapters 3-5, *the tests of sonship are based on the fact that God is love.*

The triple test in each section is linked to obedience, love and truth. It is all about walking in the light, walking in love and walking in the truth.

A complementary touch

I mentioned earlier that John has a handful of volumes to his name: there is the Gospel of John, the Epistles of John and the Revelation. These actually complement one another in a beautiful way and they give to us a full picture of the Christian life.

- The emphasis in the Gospel of John is on salvation,
  the emphasis in the Epistles of John is on sanctification,
  the emphasis in Revelation is on glorification.

- The first deals with past history,
  the second deals with present experience,
  the third deals with future hope.

- The message of the Gospel narrative is that Christ died for us, the message of the trio of Epistles is that Christ lives in us, the message of the Apocalypse is that Christ is coming for us.

The final comparison puts the spotlight on the Word:

- In the Gospel we have the Word made flesh, in the Epistles we have the Word made real in us, in the Revelation we have a picture of the Word conquering.

His raison d'être

John leaves us in no doubt as to his motive and reason for putting pen to paper. His overall aim is stated quite clearly and explicitly on four separate occasions with his use of a keynote phrase incorporating the word *'write'*. For example:

> *'We write this to make our joy complete' (1:4),*
> *'My dear children, I write this to you so that you will not sin'(2:1),*
> *'I am writing these things to you about those who are trying to lead you astray' (2:26),*
> *'I write these things to you ... so that you may know that you have eternal life' (5:13).*

We can summarise it like this:

- the initial purpose is to promote joy in the heart of the Christian and that is exclusively based on our fellowship with God in Christ;
- the second purpose is to remind the people of their need to grow in grace daily and to challenge them to sin less today than they did yesterday;
- the third purpose is to protect the saints against those who would lead them astray;
- the final purpose is to provide assurance for the believer - we can know, with total certainty, we are saved because God has told us so in his word.

It seems to me, there is a tender pastoral touch to John's letter for he writes to counteract the confusion that these false teachers have sown in the minds of honest Christians.

For John, as he is now in the eventide of life, with the sun setting on a long and fruitful ministry, his carefully chosen words are well worth listening to. He writes from a huge reservoir of vast experience and his sagacious comments and astute insights are so incredibly profound!

Speaking personally, I find it so refreshing to discover someone who passionately believes in the primacy of knowing what he believes.

Doctrine matters

Biblical doctrine is of mega-importance! In fact, its value cannot be over-estimated! It is vital in the area of Christian morals! The fact is, our beliefs condition our behaviour, they colour the way that we think and act. But more than that, doctrine was essential to John in the realm of Christian unity. You see, if the church does not have a clearly defined confession of faith on which to build her common life, the inevitable happens for, sooner or later, she disintegrates into factions!

Doctrine was fundamental to John for the sake of evangelism and outreach in the wider world because doctrine is what makes Christianity distinctive. Our faith, with a capital F, is strangely unique! It rests on the solid rock of objective truth.

I have hinted at it already but doctrine was central to John's mindset because it is part and parcel of Christian assurance. It is an integral component of our belief system. The roguish impostors came along and infiltrated the church and undermined the simple faith of down-to-earth believers.

It is no exaggeration to say, these good folks were gutted, they were shaken to the core, they were devastated, they were like a spiritual football for they felt as though they were being kicked around all over the place; it was so bad, they did not know whether they were coming or going. That is supremely why John wrote what he did!

1:1

Eternally ... Jesus is real

When you cast your eye down the opening paragraph in John's epistle, you will be surprised and, presumably, amazed to discover there are no words of introduction! There is not a single word of greeting to anyone, anywhere. There are no niceties of small talk! He wastes no time, he pulls no punches, he launches straight into his subject. This guy cannot wait to start talking about Jesus! The inference from silence is that this letter is for God's people everywhere!

John starts off on a hugely positive note for he speaks about Jesus as the *'Word of life'*. You will be interested to know that John is the only writer in the entire New Testament who refers to Jesus Christ as the Word! He does it in the opening verse of his Gospel - that is one we are all familiar with - and he repeats it in Revelation 19:12,13 where he informs us that the name of the coming King is 'the Word of God'. And here in verse 1, we are introduced to him as *'the Word of life'*.

In today's hi-tech, media driven world, when we wish to convey a message to someone either verbally or electronically, we communicate with them through the medium of words. John, in a stroke of genius, is confirming that Jesus Christ is God's communication to us.

Jesus is the noun of God, Jesus is the verb of God, Jesus is the adjective of God!

That means, when we listen to Jesus, we are listening to God, for Jesus articulates God!

Jesus is revealed

John tells us that the Son was from the beginning but that he revealed himself in human history; he tells us, he is the one '... *which we have heard, which we have seen with our eyes, which we have looked at and our hands have touched.*' In other words, the apostles heard him, saw him and touched him. This was no figment of their imagination. They were not living in a dream world of spiritual fantasy.

These well-rounded individuals actually saw Jesus with their own eyes, they actually heard him with their own ears, they actually touched him with their own hands. This Jesus is real! He is no phantom!

The opening thought in verse 1 has subtle echoes of a similar phrase which John employed in his Gospel narrative. Here, he says, *'That which was from the beginning'*. In his Gospel, John says, 'In the beginning was the Word, and the Word was with God, and the Word was God' (1:1). I think you probably realise that is a mirror of the very first verse in the Bible where we read, 'In the beginning God created the heavens and the earth' (Genesis 1:1).

The implication is obvious. Go back as far as you will in your imagination, says the writer in Genesis, before time began, before the morn of creation dawned, and you will find God. He was there when nothing else was there! Go back to that same point, says John in the fourth Gospel, and you will find Jesus Christ with God, because he was God. He says, you will find him there in eternity past, he was there long before the world was made, he was there before the stars were hung and planets fashioned. The message is crisp and concise: God always has been, and in the same way, Jesus always has been!

The has been / is now Jesus

But the thought in 1:1 is not quite the same. The focus here is not creation, it is the incarnation! John wants to drive home the point that the Word, who was made flesh in the womb of the virgin Mary, was the same eternal Son of the Father who was before all time and who was the agent of all creation.

In other words, the Word of life did not merely come into existence at Bethlehem; he already existed from the very beginning with the Father. Bethlehem only hailed his arrival on planet earth in human form; he had been around for aeons of eternity before that!

The hymn writer refers to him as 'the everlasting Word'. He is; and by the same token, he is the one who became the man, Christ Jesus.

You see, there can be no separation between the two. It is gloriously true to say that there never was a time when the Word was not; it is equally true to say that there was a defining moment in time when that Word of life appeared in his humanity at the incarnation. Jesus, the man, was nothing less than God. In fact, he is the God-man!

And that is what makes Christianity different from every other religion in the whole world. This is the central tenet of the Christian gospel. This is the foundation of the Christian faith. Jesus Christ is real, and that statement can be documented eternally!

1:2a

Historically … Jesus is real

John reminds us of this world-shattering event in verse 2 where he says, *'the life appeared'*. Sure it did for that is precisely what transpired in the rural environs of Bethlehem in Judea two thousand years ago!

Ask the local shepherds ... their lives were impacted to such a degree that their tiny world was turned upside down. *Ask the wise men from the east* ... they fell down before him in adoring worship. *Ask the angels from on high* ... they danced with delirious joy in the courts of heaven. *Ask Joseph and Mary* ... they had no doubts that the one they cradled in their arms was Jesus Christ the Lord. *Ask the 'righteous and devout' Simeon* ... he died a happy and contented man because he had seen the 'Christ, the consolation of Israel'. *Ask eighty-four years old Anna ...* in a heart-stopping moment, she encountered the child Jesus in the temple. *Ask John and the other apostles ...* he was no Stranger of Galilee to them for they walked with him and talked with him as his devoted and dedicated disciples.

Oh yes, he appeared alright! These folks can vouch for that. To a man, theirs is a credible testimony, theirs is a believable story. As the old song says, 'They were there when it happened so they ought to know!' Here is the authentic apostolic witness to the advent of Jesus Christ. All that John says is guaranteed by personal experience. I have not seen Jesus and neither have you. John has! And so too have the other apostles. That is why John uses the word *'we'* in his prologue.

The Johannine 'we'

On that note, I think it is beneficial for us to recognise that John uses the first person pronoun *'we'* a lot in this letter. Generally speaking, it has a comprehensive feel to it for it is used to include the author with his readers. The thought is, 'look folks, we're in this together.' It has the idea of 'one in, all in!' Some of the best examples are found in 2:1 and 3:1.

But here, in his introductory comments, John is using the pronoun *'we'* in a significantly different way. He does not include himself with his readers; rather, he uses it to distinguish himself from them. The contrast here is not *'we'* as opposed to 'they', but *'we'* as opposed to 'you'. In other words, John is claiming a unique position within the church.

The *'we'* that John is using here with great effect in verses 1 and 2 is not the all-inclusive 'we' of Christian fellowship; it is more restrictive in that he narrows it down to the exclusive 'we' of apostolic privilege. Now, because of that, we have complete confidence in his testimony. What John says is extremely convincing; it makes a lot of good sense to the man on the street.

So far as John and the apostles were concerned, Jesus was a real man; a man who really lived, a man who really died, a man who really rose again from the grave. They saw him with their own eyes!

This was no optical illusion, this was no mystical vision, this was no magical trick, they beheld him in living reality. It did not happen once or twice, it was a regular occurrence, it was a consistent daily revelation.

They touched him with their own hands before he died on the cross at Calvary, they touched him physically after the resurrection on Easter Sunday morning. This was no spirit being dressed up for the day; this was no divine trickster disguised in a temporary human suit of clothes!

This was no ghost, it was no zombie from another planet. This was flesh and blood, this was the Word of life, this was Jesus Christ, this was the God of eternity who stepped into time and made his mark on history.

1:2b

Relationally ... Jesus is real

In the same verse, John uses a lovely phrase when he talks about *'the eternal life, which was with the Father'*. We know from elsewhere in Scripture that eternal life is more often than not depicted as an essentially vibrant relationship with an eternal person. The picture John gives here is that of a dynamic face-to-face relationship of ever-deepening intimacy. His point is emphasised because of his choice of tense and his use of a preposition in the phrase.

Here is someone unique, someone who shared eternity with God in a most extraordinary way. Yet, says John, without even pausing to catch his breath, he *'appeared'!* He stepped out on to the stage of history like a light bulb being switched on after being concealed in the darkness. We can put it like this: the one who was invisible and eternal became visible and touchable and, John says, *'we have seen him'*.

Jesus Christ as the Word of life is real - eternally, historically, and relationally!

1:3

Fellowship: we are in it together

John moves on in verses 3 and 4 to anchor these foundational truths concerning the perceived reality of Christ to everyday experience. There are serious implications surrounding these doctrines for every believer in the rough and tumble of normal life. The plain fact is, these fundamental truths are earthed to reality. There is a practical application ensuing from the apostolic testimony to the lives of his readers for learning and living are two sides of the same coin.

The main reason behind his proclamation of the truth about Jesus Christ is *'so that you also may have fellowship with us'*. John spells that out clearly in verse 3. His aspiration is to communicate to them, to contribute to them, to distribute among them, those deeper truths and precious experiences of our blessed Lord.

This is one of the great spin-offs of the Christian message, this is one of the many wonderful bonuses of the family of God: we can really enjoy open and intimate fellowship with each other!

A supernatural dimension

John gives the concept another dimension, he raises it to a higher plane when he informs us, *'And our fellowship is with the Father and with his Son, Jesus Christ.'* This is life as God intended it should be. Life, when lived to the full, finds its ultimate fulfilment in a meaningful relationship with another. There is nothing unusual about that for this is very much in keeping with the words of Jesus in his high-priestly prayer of John 17:3, 'This is eternal life: that they may know you, the only true God, and Jesus Christ, whom you have sent.'

Believing God's truth brings us into a living union with God. It brings us into a place of fellowship with the Father and the Son. We cannot know God without first of all knowing Jesus Christ. We cannot know fellowship without receiving the truth.

That is the fellowship the apostles knew and enjoyed; that is the fellowship we also benefit from because we know the unsurpassed joy of sins forgiven and the thrill of reconciliation to God. Our blessings are no less real because they rest on faith, rather than sight. Jesus implied as much in his twin-pronged comment to doubting Thomas in John 20:29.

The lesson is, faith is the door to fellowship!

A partnership

The word that John uses for *'fellowship'* in verse 3 is a most fascinating one. It is the Greek word *koinonia.* This particular word was used in classical Greek as a favourite expression for the intimate bond enjoyed by a couple in their marital relationship. It also conveys the idea of participation or sharing in a more general sense; it is a word that is particularly appropriate when used to speak of a business partnership or a joint tenancy of an apartment.

I suppose John could look back to his early days when he and his big brother James were shareholders in the family fishing business. It was their relationship to their father and so to each other in the family that gave them a common concern. In the best sense of the word, that is what fellowship is; it is a sharing together in the family! It means, we have something in common.

As sinners, men have absolutely nothing in common with a holy God. But God, in his mercy and grace, sent the Lord Jesus into the world to have something in common with men. Christ took upon himself a human body and became a man. Then he went to the cross and took upon that body the sins of the world as Peter says in 1 Peter 2:24. Because he paid the price for our sins, the way is open for God to forgive us and welcome us as adopted children into his family. When we trust Christ, we become partakers of the divine nature (2 Peter 1:4).

The term translated 'partakers' in Peter's epistle is from the same Greek root as the word translated *'fellowship'* in 1:3. What a tremendous truth that is! The new birth is the believing sinner's initiation into a brand new partnership with deity. Jesus Christ took upon himself the nature of man so that by faith we may receive the nature of God.

By any stretch of the imagination, that is fellowship with a capital F.

Two tiers of fellowship

Fellowship can be experienced on two levels:

* *level one* is horizontal, where we enjoy fellowship with kindred hearts and minds;
* *level two* is vertical, where we engage in fellowship with God in heaven.

No matter which level we choose to operate on, it has to be said that fellowship is something which is relational. It is not just a cup of tea or a mug of coffee after church on a Sunday morning. I have a good friend who often signs his letters, 'Yours, because his'. That just about sums up in a sentence, in a succinct way, this wonderful fellowship which we have with the Godhead and with each other.

Because we belong to him, we belong to one another.

1:4

Joy ... it gets better every day

There is a second consequence to taking on board the truth which John is proclaiming and that is summed up in verse 4 where John says, *'We write this to make our joy complete.'* What an inspirational stimulus that is to maintaining an animated relationship with the Lord. We have a joy that is constantly increasing! A joy we can never have enough of! A joy we cannot get too much of!

Ironically, this is the one and only appearance of the word *'joy'* in John's first epistle. The Greek word *chara* can easily be translated to read 'delight' or 'gladness'. It is a 'sweeps you off your feet' feeling of pleasurable emotion and exultation caused by the heightened expectation or realisation of some good thing.

It is worth noting that biblical scholars differ in how they deal with this particular text and their bias is reflected in the numerous translations of Scripture. For example, some read '*our* joy' while others favour '*your* joy'. For what it is worth, I think the former is the more likely rendition of the Greek, it is certainly the preferred option; having said that, both variants are true for this joy can be personalised in our individual experience.

We need to remember that a little while later John would write in his third epistle: '*I have no greater joy than to hear that my children are walking in the truth.*' The key question is, what greater joy could there be for his children too? I think the best way to answer that in as comprehensive a way as possible is to say:

- there is the conscious possession of eternal life,
- there is the daily enrichment of personal fellowship with the living God,
- there is a deep awareness that we are one with all God's people everywhere!

It seems to me, when we have these vital ingredients in our lives, our joy will be complete. The cup of our lives will be full and running over! The joy we are talking about here is a deep joy that no-one can drain. It is a full joy which nothing can quench, it is a joy which finds its focus in Jesus!

Joy ... even when we are not happy!

Quite frankly, it is seemingly quite incredible but three times in the upper room, with Calvary only a handful of hours away, Jesus spoke of the joy that awaited his disciples (John 16:20,22,24). The joy he was talking about was a total joy, an indestructible joy. The fact is, it came to them and it comes to you and me through the cross; it is ours because he gave himself with total dedication and maximum commitment to fulfil his Father's eternal plan and purpose.

We read in Hebrews 12:2 that he 'endured the cross' because of 'the joy that was set before him'. That kind of mindset is strangely out of vogue, it goes against the grain, it swims against the tide. And yet, that is what Jesus was willing to do on our behalf.

Today, because of his atoning work at Calvary, we enjoy the handsome benefits of warm Christian fellowship, we enter into the good of all that he attained and achieved on our behalf, for we have the status of sons and daughters in his global family. We experience a real sense of purpose in life, we are the recipients of his unfailing joy. There is all of this and so much more!

It was the German political philosopher Karl Marx who wrote, *'The first requisite for the people's happiness is the abolition of religion.'*

In marked contrast, the apostle John writes, 'Faith in the Lord Jesus Christ gives us a joy that can never be duplicated by the world. I have experienced this joy myself and I want to share it with you.'

I often think of the words of the old Puritan, Charles Simeon. He put it so well when he said, 'There are but two lessons for the Christian to learn: the one is, to enjoy God in everything; the other is, to enjoy everything in God.' I have a hunch that John would go along with that. I am fairly sure it is the kind of sentiment he would warmly endorse and to which he would say a hearty 'amen!'

1:5

God is light

In verse 5, John commences his letter proper by launching into one of the greatest theological statements of Scripture. He says, *'God is light'*. It is fascinating to note, even though John has his work cut out for him in terms of dealing with some of the tensions and crises in the early church, he does not start out by drawing up a lengthy list of ideological and personality related idiosyncrasies alongside a host of variegated problems - he begins with God! Surely that speaks volumes in itself.

We can read all about God's attributes in the biblical narrative stretching from Genesis through to Revelation. We see them powerfully revealed in his words and in his actions. What John does here is unique.

He seeks to expound the essence of the nature of God in a way that the ordinary man can understand. He directs his message not to those who are theologically trained but to those who are spiritually aware; not to those who have an intuitive feel for great truths but to those who have a big heart for God.

He uses everyday language and easy-to-grasp illustrations to convey the most unfathomable concepts. That is what makes John not only a wonderful theologian but a competent and skilful teacher. He has the knack of making the profound splendidly simple!

You will remember, it was he who recorded for us the teaching of Jesus to the sinner woman of Samaria. He informs us in John 4:24 that 'God is spirit'. He supplements that in this incredible first epistle when he adds that *'God is love'* (4:8). Light and love are the essence of God, just as 'spirit' is. They describe not his qualities nor his characteristics; rather, they portray his being.

It resembles a relay

John is not informing us of some exciting and breathtaking discovery he has made. This is not the result of long hours of careful and meticulous research, it is not even a guess or some bright idea he woke up with one morning. This insight has nothing to do with John's intellectual powers or prowess. On the contrary, all that John shares with us in this section is a message which he has received. He says, in verse 5, *'This is the message we have heard from him and declare to you.'*

The obvious question is, who did John get the message from? The answer is relatively straightforward: he received it from Jesus Christ. It is an unmistakably clear reference to him and it backs up two verses to verse 3.

It was the special task of John and the other apostles to announce and proclaim to others what they heard from the Lord, that was their primary role in the early church. They were to pass on the baton of truth to the next generation, and so on.

That means, there is an unbroken chain of witnesses to the truth of God as revealed in Christ and to the apostles from day one, right up to this moment in time. Two millennia down the road, the same awesome responsibility rests on your shoulders and mine.

John is at pains to emphasise the divine source of what he is about to share with us. The authority for his teaching lies in what he has heard in the historical revelation of God in Jesus Christ. The message has not been tampered with in any way; it has not been watered down; it has not been made more palatable; it has not been embellished in any manner; it has not been redefined or modernised or even updated!

We can read John's message with total confidence for what he says in the epistle is exactly the same as that which he received from the Lord. That means, quite simply, that God's revealed truth is not negotiable.

What he is, what he isn't

John's matter-of-fact statement is magnificently expressed in three single syllable words, *'God is light'*. No matter how we look at it, no matter what angle we view it from, that is a hyper-positive affirmation of who God is.

John pulls no punches, he is not playing with words for no sooner has the ink dried on the parchment when John reinforces it with an equally strong negative when he says, *'In him there is no darkness at all'*. John really drives home the point in the original language; this is what it says, *'God is light, and darkness, in him, no, not any at all!'* In other words, the two are utterly incompatible.

In the Greek, it is classed as a double negative. I am perfectly happy to concede, if I were a purist, it is almost unforgivable what John has done for it is appallingly bad English; however, it *is* excellent theology!

There is no imperfection whatsoever in God, there is no spot on the person of God, there is no blemish on the being of God, there is no dark side to his character, there are no shadows to his personality - he is light personified, he is light unsullied and undiluted, he is all light and nothing but light!

We read in 1 Timothy 6:16 that God 'lives in unapproachable light'. The 'otherness' of God's flawless nature is ably demonstrated by the prophet Habakkuk's conviction as stated in 1:13 where he says, 'Your eyes are too pure to look on evil; you cannot tolerate wrong.' When we are confronted with such an unbelievable representation of God's transparent nature, I think we can do no better than to sing with Thomas Binney,

> *Eternal Light! Eternal Light!*
> *How pure that soul must be,*
> *When, placed within thy searching sight,*
> *It shrinks not but, with calm delight,*
> *Can live and look on thee!*

When John says that God is light, he has in mind three wonderful truths:

The glory of God

As we carefully study the Bible, we notice that every time God comes on the scene, there is light. In Genesis 1:2 we are told there was 'darkness over the surface of the deep'. Then God said in verse 3, '"Let there be light," and there was light.' The God who creates begins with light for light is the primary expression of his eternal being. And it is from light that everything else grows and develops.

Without that light, there would be no plant or animal life; there would be no growth, no activity and no beauty. In an amazing way, all creation owes its existence and its sustenance to the God who is light. That light makes all the difference in the world and, at the same time, it makes a world of difference!

That is what the children of Israel discovered as they journeyed mile after mile through the desert en route to the land of promise.

We read in Exodus 13:21 that 'the Lord went ahead of them in a pillar of cloud to guide them on their way and by night in a pillar of fire to give them light, so that they could travel by day or night.' The light was a source of illumination and guidance to them.

The same can be said of the shekinah cloud in the tabernacle and in the temple. It was a symbol of the presence of God in the midst of his people. The light was a token reminder that God was in there with them. On a physical level, light represents the glory of God.

The knowledge of God

On an intellectual level, it is equally true to say, light represents the knowledge of God. The Bible explicitly states that God has all knowledge. He knows everything. There is nothing we can teach him. He never has a 'new' thought! There is nothing God can learn because he is omniscient.

The holiness of God

On a moral footing, light represents the holiness of God. This is the primary reference here for John is making an audacious statement about the character of God. He is saying that God is absolutely holy, he is totally moral. He is one hundred percent pure.

Such light scatters all our darkness. It is the truth against which all other claims must be tested. The light reveals the reality and while it effectively dispels darkness, we need to remember it also exposes what the darkness would hide. I think C S Lewis makes the point well when he says that we believe the sun has risen not because we see it, but because by it we see everything else. In that sense, there is no twilight zone in God's nature; he is peerless and unadulterated light.

Take your pick

If we choose to interpret verse 5 from a theological standpoint, John is saying, 'God is truth and error can have no place with him.' If we prefer to interpret it from an ethical perspective, John is saying, 'God is good and evil can have no place beside him.'

All these thoughts come together in the beautiful words of F W Faber's hymn,

> *My God, how wonderful thou art,*
> *Thy majesty how bright,*
> *How beautiful thy mercy-seat,*
> *In depths of burning light!*
> *How wonderful, how beautiful,*
> *The sight of thee must be,*
> *Thine endless wisdom, boundless power,*
> *And awesome purity!*

1:6,7

Making a claim

In verse 6, John is quite specific; he does not mince his words. There is no softly, softly approach to sin advocated or encouraged here. John is a realist and he knows how we try to justify our position when we fall for the devil's bait - hook, line and sinker. He comes straight out with it. He calls a spade, a spade! He knows only too well if we play with fire, we end up getting badly burned.

So far as John is concerned, it does not matter how agile or athletic we are, we cannot run with the foxes and hunt with the hounds at the same time. It is a non-starter, it is downright impossible!

We are only kidding ourselves if we think we can live some sort of compromise existence with one foot walking in the light with God and the other foot remaining in the darkness of the world.

I discovered many years ago when messing about in boats that you get seriously wet if you have one foot in the boat and the other foot on the river bank. John says, the spiritual splits are equally impossible!

The big problem in the early church was compounded by three false notions which were rampant in John's day and which are still around in our own. That is what John is focusing our minds on here in verse 6 and he does something similar in verses 8 and 10. On every occasion, he pulls the rug from under their feet. Each of these wrong attitudes or false assertions with which John now deals is prefaced with the same introductory phrase, *'if we claim'*.

A mix and match experience

John knows full well that the proof of the pudding is in the eating. That is why he says, *'If we claim to have fellowship with him yet walk in the darkness, we lie and do not live by the truth.'* He has already established that God is light; now he goes a step further by saying, if our life is in touch and in tune with the Lord, then we will be walking in the light. On the other hand, if our life is out of step with the Lord, we can talk until the cows come home, we can pull the wool over other people's eyes, but we cannot fool God.

The bottom line is, our lifestyle will reflect a breakdown in our relationship with God. It shows in our daily lives if we are, or if we are not, walking in harmony with the revealed will of God.

'Don't do as I do, do as I say' can never be a maxim for the child of God. There should never be a contradiction between what I profess with my lips and how I conduct my affairs in the real world. One should complement the other!

John says quite categorically, a person who persists in living in sin cannot be living in fellowship with God. It is a non-starter for the two states are mutually exclusive. They just do not tally; it is one of those classic situations where, try as we will, two and two do not make four!

Someone has coined the tongue-in-cheek phrase by arguing that 'you might just as well live in a coal pit and claim that you're developing a sun tan!'

It is crazy, the whole idea is preposterous, isn't it! It does not make a lot of sense. Therein lies the fallacy of their claim!

Getting along with one another

The contrast is patently obvious in verse 7 when John reminds us, *'But if we walk in the light, as he is in the light, we have fellowship with one another, and the blood of Jesus, his Son, purifies us from all sin.'* This is a wonderful truth which John is sharing with us for here he explains the basis of fellowship within the family of God. At the end of the day, it is all down to our walking in the light.

We need to understand that it is sin which mars and spoils our fellowship with God and, consequently, with the people of God. If we have a genuine spiritual experience of God in our lives, then we will truly enjoy and appreciate happy fellowship with others who have been born and brought into God's global family.

There is no place for spiritual lone rangers, there is no place for going it alone in the family of God. We see that clearly in verse 6 for the darkness which John is especially concerned about is the mindset which says, 'I can have fellowship with God without having fellowship with my fellow believers.' John knocks that one on the head!

Spiritual cloning

Let us be honest: we do not always agree with one another, we will not always see eye to eye with one another, but that is not the essence of Christian fellowship anyway. According to Paul in 1 Corinthians 12:12, we are all one but we are not all the same.

There is no hint of cloning in the church of Jesus Christ.

It is about loving one another; it is about valuing one another; it is about appreciating one another for who we are in Jesus.

And when we have a healthy attitude like that, we do not feel threatened for we can agree to differ and still find a delightful bond and depth in our Christian fellowship. Because we do get along with one another, that in itself pays an eloquent tribute to the fact that we are walking in the light! It means, we will be sensitive to the needs of other people and, at the same time, we will be very conscious of our own failings and shortcomings.

In his light

It seems to me, the nearer I come to the Lord and the closer I walk with the Lord, the more conscious I am of my own sin and rebellion. I suppose Paul is the classic example of that, isn't he. The greatest saints have often seen themselves as the worst of sinners. Paul writes along those lines in 1 Timothy 1:15.

How true it is, the more we contemplate the holiness of God, the more we realise we need a God who is not only holy, we need a God who is gracious too! Thank God, he is oozing with grace for he gave his only Son to be our Saviour and Redeemer. When we do fall by the wayside and yield in the moment of temptation, when we do stray into the darkness and fail to walk in the light of God, we can appropriate the cleansing of his precious blood in our lives.

It's there for the asking

The thought behind the word *'purifies'* is that it denotes a continuous action. In other words, he keeps on washing us clean and that means forgiveness is there for the asking! I am so grateful for the fact that it is not just for certain sins; John makes the point that his blood is effective and efficient in dealing with every sin.

To *'walk in the light'* means we keep short accounts with God; it means, there is no earth-born cloud between us and our Father in heaven; it means, the thread of communion has not been broken; it means, we are on speaking terms with our God.

I find it thrilling (and humbling) that Calvary covers it all: my sin in the past, my sin in the present, my sin in the future, is all under the blood of Jesus Christ. This is mind-blowingly great, it is stupendous!

For this, I have Jesus

Not only does the blood of Christ secure forgiveness for penitent sinners, but cleansing too! Not only is the guilt of sin atoned for, its power is broken! Not only is the sinner justified, he is sanctified!

According to John, we have a brand new nature, we have a grand new status, and we have a totally new direction.

Holiness is demanded by a holy God, but holiness is also provided by him.

The baseline is, no matter what kind of situation we find ourselves in, no matter how difficult the circumstances, no matter how dark the hour, no matter how fierce the opposition, no matter how severe the trial, for this and every changing season of life, we have Jesus. That is the confidence we have when we are walking in the light!

1:8-10

Inevitable, not inexcusable

The punchline in this section is that even though sin may be inevitable in each of our lives, by the same token, John argues, it is inexcusable when we do it.

That is our big problem, isn't it. As they say, we are caught between a rock and a hard place. When we fall into sin, it interferes in a huge way with our communion with the Lord and it seriously impairs our happy fellowship with the people of God. Sin throws the spanner in the works on two different levels: it ruins our fellowship with our heavenly Father on a vertical level and it spoils the rapport we share with one another on the horizontal plane.

It comes naturally

The tragedy is and we know this from painful personal experience, we cannot stop ourselves from sinning! We are commanded in the word of God to be sinless, but you know as well as I do that we are bound in sin. It is one of those hot-potato issues that is far too hot for us to handle on our own. It all seems to be too much like asking a blind man to see, a deaf man to hear, a lame man to walk, or a dead man to rise up and run!

The six-million-dollar question we are wrestling with is, how then do we deal with sin? John has pointed out in verse 6 that it is impossible to live a double life. We cannot spend our waking hours walking in darkness and expect to maintain, at the same time, some semblance of intimacy with the Almighty.

He progresses that thought even further when he contends with their self-justification. He exposes the ridiculous nature of their comments when he tries to lay their argument to rest. They were protesting their innocence on all matters sinful by arguing, 'But I'm not even a sinner!' It boils down to the fact that they were denying the sinful nature.

We read the gist of their philosophy in verse 8 where it says, *'If we claim to be without sin, we deceive ourselves and the truth is not in us.'*

It is a relatively simple fact of life that even in the early days of the third millennium there are a lot of people who are in the same sinking boat as those of John's day. It is incredible the number of people who believe that we are not born with a sinful nature; such folks subscribe to the view that we are born with glorious potential. It seems to me, one of the central truths of the Christian message is that every man, woman, boy and girl has been sinful from the day of conception.

The psalmist David was party to that particular view! We know that from his eye-opener of a testimony in Psalm 51:5 when he bared his heart and honestly confessed, 'Surely I was sinful at birth, sinful from the time my mother conceived me.' And the apostle Paul was another one who was totally committed to it as well. He writes in a similar vein in Romans 3.

John is caustic in his denunciation of such a foolhardy claim; it is outrageously absurd, he feels, especially when we follow it through to its logical conclusion. John frankly believes that these folks are having themselves on, they give themselves away, they shoot themselves in the foot. In the cold light of day, they are living in a spiritual fantasy world and, for all their religion, they are far from Jesus Christ.

Some things never change

There are none so blind as those who do not want to see! These folks are guilty of self-delusion, they have the blinkers on.

The plain fact is, if we shut our eyes to Hitler's gas chambers and the unthinkable horrors of the holocaust, if we pretend Stalin's purges did not happen, if we close our eyes to the crushed skulls of Cambodia's killing fields, then we may convince ourselves that there is no essential evil in modern man!

The harsh reality is, twenty-first century man is as brutal and selfish as man has always been!

Oh yes, modern man may be more enlightened and he may be better educated and he may live in a more ideal environment, but he certainly has not evolved into a more human (and humane) species.

And I hasten to add, utopia is not around the next corner! The people who think things are improving are living in a fool's false paradise. They are not living in the real world! It is a pathetic picture to watch someone caught up in this web of self-delusion.

I am every bit as convinced as John is that we are going down a cul-de-sac if we deny that we are sinners by nature! As John rightly says, we only deceive ourselves if we say we have no sin; the chances are, we probably deceive no-one else and we certainly do not pull the wool over God's eyes!

The domino effect

Let us skip over verse 9 (do not worry, we will come back to it) and move into verse 10 where John says, *'If we claim we have not sinned, we make him out to be a liar and his word has no place in our lives.'* This is tough talking from the apostle, it really is! In a sense, this is the darkest of the three false claims. This is the ultimate for the other two have been leading up to this one.

The false claim of verse 6 leads to the erroneous mindset of verse 8, which in turn leads to the foolish notion which is embraced and elucidated in verse 10. The difference in wording between verse

8 and verse 10 is highly significant. Here in verse 10 we move from the inward principle of the sinful nature to the outward symptoms that confirm the existence of the dreaded disease.

What I do on the outside shows what I am like on the inside. We can look at it like this: I am not a sinner because I do sinful things; I do sinful things because I am a sinner! There is no mileage gained when we put the cart before the horse.

Sin from a spin-doctor's perspective

The built-in tendency in human beings is for us to cover up and brush it all under the carpet. It happens all the time in our culture and, sadly, it infects our church life too. We no longer call sin, 'sin'. We call it by a host of other names. For example:

- *lying is a credibility gap or being economical with the truth,*
- *deceit is getting along in your business relationships,*
- *adultery is a harmless escapade or having an affair,*
- *stealing is helping yourself to the perks of the job,*
- *embezzlement is creative accounting,*
- *selfishness is me standing up for my rights.*

What happens is this: we no longer call sin what the Bible calls it, we dress it up in some designer label cloth and when we do that we put ourselves in the unenviable and untenable position of making God out to be a liar. We think we know better! When we go down that tortuous and serpentine road we have relegated his word to a place in our lives where it means little or nothing.

To all intents and purposes, we have sidelined God from his proper place in our hearts. The big problem is, we end up on a downward spiral where we are inclined to forget that the chickens hatched by such a syndrome always come home to roost!

Where confession is good for the soul

A lot has been written about sin but, thank God, that is not the end of the story! We find the good news in verse 9 where John tells us, *'If we confess our sins, he is faithful and just and will forgive us our sins and purify us from all unrighteousness.'* That is tremendous, isn't it! What an amazing verse this is! What a wonderful way forward!

We can make all kinds of claims but, at the end of the day, there is only one antidote or countermeasure for our terrible condition before a God who is light!

- Unlike the *antinomian*, the real answer to this massive problem treats the importance of sin ever so seriously.
- Unlike the *humanist*, it faces up to the age-old problem we all wrestle with for it treats the existence of sin honestly.
- Unlike the *perfectionist*, it does not fudge the issue or even hedge its bets; it looks the problem straight in the eye for it treats the power of sin realistically.

The remedy is not a false defence put forward by a clever legal team, it is not in making plausible sounding excuses, it is not in shifting the blame on to someone else or something else, it is not in a complacent shrug of the shoulders with the wry comment, 'Oh well, I can't help it, nobody's perfect.'

The only solution to the problem is found in confessing our sins before a holy God. The answer to denial is confession. If we have any doubts lurking in the front of our minds about that scenario, ask Peter the big fisherman-cum-apostle; he knows all about it, he's been there, he's done that!

The word *'confess'* in verse 9 is a fascinating word and it is also a word that is often misunderstood in today's spiritual climate where men are more inclined to treat God as some kind of best pal. Literally, it means, 'to say the same thing'. In other words, it is to agree with God against ourselves. The inference is that we ought to name our sins before God in a quite specific sense. There is no place here for a sweeping open-ended statement before God regarding our sin! We are not meant to generalise when we name our shortcomings before the Lord.

Don't beat about the bush!

John's proposition is: let us say I have been dishonest and I have told a lie to someone during the course of the day. John says that I need to be specific in my dealing with that incident before the Lord. It is simply not enough for me to get down on my knees before I jump into bed and say, 'Lord, I'm sorry for all the wrong things I've done today, please forgive me.'

During the awful tragedy of Nazi Germany, the eminent theologian Dietrich Bonhoeffer headed up a seminary of the German 'Confessing Church' at a little place called Finkenwalde. It was here that Bonhoeffer proclaimed in a truly memorable catch-phrase, *'In confession occurs the breakthrough to the cross.'*

How true that is! You see, according to verse 9, a true confession of sin asks for and anticipates forgiveness. I think it is good to remind ourselves, this benefit and blessing does not come to us on the grounds of the intensity of our repentance, but solely on the grounds of what Christ did when he died for our sins on the cross of Calvary. To put it simply, it is not what I have done, it is what he has done; that is what makes the radical difference.

The character of God

John handles this glorious truth in a wonderful way for he shows us how God responds to our sincere request for forgiveness. There are two strands woven into the fabric of verse 9 and when we place them side by side we cannot help but notice how they counterbalance the false claims we have been examining in this study.

- *Our God is one who is faithful and just - a confirmation of the divine nature.*
- *Our God is one who forgives and purifies - a confirmation of the divine actions.*

He does what he does because he is who he is!

We are introduced here to a couple of divine attributes: God is *'faithful'* and God is *'just'*. He is faithful to his own nature and that means it is impossible for him to act in any other way than is consistent with his moral perfection. He never betrays himself! He is faithful to his word. If he says it, he will perform it, he will do it! It is as simple as that! It is taking God at face value, it is believing God will accomplish what he says he will do. Actually, he cannot do anything else for that would be a slur on his faithfulness and a black mark against his integrity.

So when God promises to forgive us when we admit our sins before him, we can depend upon him to honour his word. We can rely on him to keep his word. And he will not let us down.

The other great attribute assigned to him is that he is just. It would be easy to water down this word and dilute it of its meaning. It means so much more than someone who is kind and merciful. The word has the idea of his inflexible righteousness enshrined in it. But in God's great scheme of things, this also guarantees our forgiveness. God's justice ensures that he will give to each of us what we deserve. Were it not for the sacrificial death of Jesus, we would tremble at that thought, we would be scared stiff, for the justice of God would rightly condemn us and banish us from the presence of God.

The old account was settled long ago!

But we have a Saviour who has died in our place and whose blood goes on cleansing us from sin ... he has turned away God's wrath. Having lived the perfect life that we failed to live, he died the death that we deserve to die. The fact that the penalty for our sin was paid by Jesus means that God will not demand a second payment. In Jesus Christ, the work is accomplished - once and for all - and we are forgiven.

The justice of God requires him to forgive because the debt has been fully met. What we deserve is God's judgment but this is just what he does not give us. Instead, we receive what we do not deserve and that is his mercy and pardoning grace. The old hymn says it all,

Because the sinless Saviour died,
My sinful soul is counted free;
For God, the just, is satisfied,
To look on him and pardon me.

Forgiveness plus

God freely and fully forgives us, but there is more, he purifies us. Forgiveness absolves us from the punishment of sin which we admittedly deserve. Cleansing frees us from the pollution of sin.

I think we can look at it like this: when God forgives us, he cancels the substantial unrepayable debt that we owe to him. He wipes the slate clean so that we can come before him as an acquitted people; the reality is, we stand before him as if we had never sinned. He does not stop there for he cleanses us, he purifies us, he makes the sinner holy.

- Because God is faithful ... it means, *he forgives us*;
- because God is just and righteous ... it means, *he cleanses us*.

This was gloriously true in your life and mine when we came to him the very first time and he delivered us from the kingdom of darkness and ushered us into the kingdom of his marvellous light. It is no less true today for he wants us to walk in the light with him and, wonder of all wonders, it will still be true tomorrow for 'his blood shall never lose its power, till all the ransomed church of God, be saved to sin no more!'

2

The real McCoy believer

2:1-6

I came across a great story the other day about Calvin Coolidge who was president of the United States away back in the 1920s. As a man, it has to be said, he was not the world's greatest conversationalist. He was renowned for never using an unnecessary word. He was a person who kept his counsel to himself.

One Sunday morning, as was his custom, he went off to church. When he came back someone asked him what the preacher had spoken about in his sermon. Coolidge replied, 'Sin!'

The frustrated questioner should have known better, but he went on to pass the comment, 'Well, well, that was it? What did the preacher say about it?' Mr Coolidge's response was typical of the man. He replied, 'He was agin' it!'

When we read the opening verses of this chapter, we discover very quickly that God and the Washington preacher are reading from the same script. They are both against sin! One of the noble aims which John has in writing this letter is to warn the people off regarding sin. The danger they faced, and the rest of us are in the same boat, is one of complacency arising from a comfortable and cushioned lifestyle. That explains why John expressed it in the manner in which he did.

- He says, *'My dear children, I write this to you so that you will not sin.'*
  John was a perfectionist!
- In the next breath, he says, *'But if anybody does sin.'*
  That makes John a realist!

The first one should be the aspiration felt in the hearts of all the people of God; the second one is our fall-back position when we know we have not quite made it. We will never attain a state of sinless perfection this side of heaven, but that should not deter us from making it our goal and our aim. By the same token, we should avoid becoming careless in our conduct and blasé about our behaviour as though sin did not matter.

It seems to me, there is a healthy tension between the two ideas put forward by John. What he has to offer is neither an excuse for sin nor a counsel of perfection. He offers to us a remedy specially designed by God to meet the real needs of sinners in a fallen world.

I often think of the thrilling story of John Newton, the boozy womanising sea captain who was heavily involved in the slave trade prior to his conversion experience. He went on to become a minister of the gospel and a great hymn writer. He spent a lot of time wrestling with the kind of problem John is tackling here in verse 1; he drew the various strands together when he wrote in his journal, *'I am not what I ought to be, but I am not what I once was. And it is by the grace of God that I am what I am.'*

I believe John Newton and the apostle John were living their lives on the same wavelength, for what we have recorded in the opening verses of chapter 2 are the distinctive marks of Christian reality.

2:1

A Christian knows who Christ is

The lovely story is told of John Wesley that, when he left home for the first time, his mother Susannah is said to have written some words in the flyleaf of his Bible. She penned, 'Sin will keep you from this book, but this book will keep you from sin!' That is sound advice!

The old man John had weathered many a storm, but down through the years he came to appreciate more and more the power of God's word to defend his people from the attacks of the enemy and to inspire them to holy living. That is why he picked up his quill and wrote such wise words on the parchment.

What John says here is an echo of Psalm 119:11 where we read, 'I have hidden your word in my heart that I might not sin against you.' John knows only too well the frailty of human nature; he has been around long enough to know his personal limitations, but he has also seen it in the lives of ordinary people. He is all too aware of the fact that sin is public enemy number one so far as the Christian is concerned. How we handle those moments when we fall flat on our face depends on our having a genuine knowledge of Jesus Christ and what he has done and what he is doing for us. We come face to face with him here as *'Jesus Christ, the Righteous One'*.

Jesus the man

The name *'Jesus'* is the earthly name of our Saviour. It is a name which anchors him in history as a real man. At the same time, it helps us to focus on the supreme reason for his coming into the world. We read in Matthew 1:21, 'Give him the name Jesus, because he will save his people from their sins.' That is it in a nutshell: Jesus is the one who rescues us from sin.

Jesus the Christ

John also refers to him as *'Christ'* and the thought here is of one who is the messiah or the anointed one. John often went to great lengths in his Gospel to clarify the precise role of the messiah. The mindset of the people in John's day led them to feel that the messiah was a warlike conqueror or a nationalistic super hero. They saw him as the ultimate figure when it came to freedom fighters!

The fact is, there was nothing overtly political about the arrival of Jesus Christ in the world and there was certainly nothing which would associate him with some kind of elitist private army of guerrilla soldiers. Nothing could be further removed from the eternal purpose of God for his Son.

It seems to me, the heart of the messianic secret lay in his claim to be not only David's son, but David's Lord. We read elsewhere that he is the 'root *of* David' and, by the same token, he has his roots *in* David. We find an allusion to those twin truths tucked away in Mark 12:35-37.

Let us face the facts, it was for this reason that he was crucified. I read somewhere recently that his identity as 'Christ' is so central to the early church's understanding of Jesus that *Christos* was used virtually as a proper name. We are right back to square one, we are back to what John was saying in the preamble to his epistle. Born at Bethlehem as a human child, he was nevertheless pre-existent with the Father. He is the Son of God! He is God the Son!

The two natures of Jesus Christ, his humanity and his deity, are brought together in a wonderful way when John describes him as *'the righteous one'*. We can look at it like this:

- *as to his eternal deity, he is righteous by definition, because he is God;*
- *as to his earthly life, he is also righteous, in contrast to sinful man.*

He was faced with many tough times of temptation, but never once did he succumb to the pressure the enemy put on him; never once did he yield to the power of the devil; never once did he have to backtrack because Satan waylaid him. He never had to apologise and say 'sorry'. The old devil threw every trick in the book at him, but Jesus remained resolute to the very end; he never flinched, he never wavered. He was buffeted from every side but, thank God, he came through unscathed.

That, according to John in verse 1, is what enables him and equips him to *'speak to the Father in our defence'*. He was sinless on the first day, he was sinless on the last day, and he was sinless every day in between! In life, and in eternity, he is perfection personified!

You see, he knows what makes us tick, he feels for us, he empathises with us. That is why he can plead our case effectively as our heavenly advocate. The Greek word used here by John is the word *parakletos* which means, 'one who is called alongside to help someone else'.

Actually, John describes the Holy Spirit by the same title in his Gospel where he uses the same Greek word a number of times in chapters 14, 15 and 16. Peter jumped on the same train of thought when he wrote in his first epistle in 3:18, 'For Christ died for sins once for all, the righteous for the unrighteous, to bring you to God.'

The chilling fact is, we have no leg to stand on! We are the guilty ones, we are unrighteous, we are in the wrong! That is the main reason why he chooses to act on our behalf as our defence lawyer. He is the righteous one, he is in the right, and he is in the know.

The great news is, as our advocate, he has not lost a single case yet!

2:2

A Christian trusts what Christ did

John says, *'He is the atoning sacrifice for our sins, and not only for ours but also for the sins of the whole world.'* The key duo of words here in the NIV translation is *'atoning sacrifice'*. If we check it out in the older translations such as the AV and the RV, they prefer to express it like this: 'he is the propitiation for our sins'. When the RSV came along, it opted for the word 'expiation'.

For what it is worth, I think the one used in the AV is a much better rendering of the original and I feel it is a great pity that many commentators deliberately shy away from the word 'propitiation'. It is a word that is rarely used these days in modern speech, but it is the one word, perhaps more than any other, which gets to the heart of what John is trying to communicate to the church in the first century.

The Greek word is *hilasmos* and it is used on only one other occasion in the New Testament and that is in 4:10 of this epistle. In the Septuagint, the Greek translation of the Old Testament, the term is used to translate the Hebrew word for 'sin offering' in Ezekiel 44:27. The prophet says, 'On the day he goes into the inner court of the sanctuary, to minister in the sanctuary, he is to offer a sin offering for himself, declares the Sovereign Lord.'

A diversionary tactic

We can see what is happening. The priest, a sinful human being, was to offer a sacrifice to enable him to enter into the presence of the righteous God. I think this helps us to envision what transpired at Calvary; it was there that the Lord Jesus offered himself on the cross on our behalf as an acceptable means by which punishment is diverted; it is changed to forgiveness and, at the same time, wrath is changed to mercy. That is the fundamental principle behind the word 'propitiation' for it includes the concept of turning away the wrath of God from the sinner to the substitute.

It is interesting and helpful to note that the word 'propitiation' in the Old Testament is 'mercy seat'. The mercy seat was the golden slab on the top of the ark of the covenant which held, among other things, the broken law of God. It was there that the blood of the sacrifice was applied as an atonement for the sin of the people.

The thought is simply this: we have an advocate on the basis of the blood poured out on the cross of Calvary. Because Jesus Christ is the propitiation for our sins, we can be forgiven when we sin and God will send our sins away from us because they have been taken by another!

It has to be said, this idea has not been without its many critics; a lot of folks feel it is a caricature of the true God. They believe it is unworthy of the God of the Bible to be seen to be involved in such an exercise. They reckon, in their not so blissful ignorance, it reduces him to the level of a pagan deity who has to be bribed to be gracious.

I have to say, such prejudiced 'off the beaten track' comments reflect a terribly misguided understanding of Scripture. The proponents of such erroneous views have failed to grasp the salient fact that under the umbrella of the attributes of God is sheltering the twin concept of wrath and justice. The Old Testament is full of it and the New Testament has a fair bit to say about it as well!

That means, as Christians, we should be jumping over the moon because, in his mercy and grace, God has provided the means by which sinful people like us can be welcomed into his near presence. We have nothing to fear, we are accepted by him because of what Jesus did for us at Calvary. God no longer has anything against us! The old account was settled long ago!

He paid a debt he did not owe!

In paying the bill to the full, in clearing the account in its entirety, in wiping the slate clean, Jesus both upheld the righteousness of God and, at the same time, he met the deepest need of man's heart. God's justice and mercy are equally satisfied. Such is the intrinsic wonder and miracle of Calvary!

So often when we see what is happening all around us on planet earth, we cry out for justice to be done and for justice to be seen to be done. We must never forget that what we desperately need ourselves is mercy. Only that can keep us from being consumed by the fire of God's holiness. We find that truth promoted in Lamentations 3:22 and again in Hebrews 12:29. Someone has said, 'His wrath is neither an emotion nor a petulant fit of temper, but the settled conviction of righteousness in action to destroy both sin and the sinner.'

Where wrath and mercy meet

To me, the consummate glory of the gospel is that we have someone to plead for mercy on our behalf, on the ground of his own righteous action when he died the death that we deserved to die. The banner headline is, once the account is cleared, payment can never be extracted a second time. When all is said and done, that is the gospel of redeeming love, plain and simple!

The cross of Jesus Christ is not the Father punishing an innocent third party for your sins and mine. It is God taking to himself in the person of his only Son all the punishment that his wrath and justice demands. He takes it all in place of you and me and, in so doing, he satisfied its penalty, he atoned for our sins, and the sword of divine justice is now back in its sheath! Thank God, Calvary covers it all! Your sin is under the precious blood of Jesus; my sin has been washed away in his cleansing tide.

He died for the sins of the world

But that is not all for John says the Lord Jesus died not only for our sins *'but also for the sins of the whole world'*. Tremendous words, but let me hasten to point out that John is definitely not signing up to the doctrine of universalism. Not by any stretch of the imagination is John supportive of the view that the entire world is saved. That is a flawed exegesis of the biblical text.

Having extinguished that particular fire, the question still needs to be asked, if he does not mean that, what then does John mean when he talks about the whole world?

It seems to me that John draws a line in the sand when he homes in on two very different groups of people: he distinguishes between us as the people of God and the *'world'* which is a reference to those who are outside the global family of God. It applies to those who are unbelievers, it labels those who are still living in rebellion against God, it pigeonholes all those who continue to reject the claims of Christ on their lives. This is the world for which the Saviour died at Calvary. And we must never forget, we were once an integral part of it.

Knowing you ... there is no greater thing

The glorious truth emanating from this phrase is that Jesus' death is efficient for us to know him as Lord and Saviour, and his sacrifice is sufficient for all those who as yet do not know him in a personal way. To me, this tallies beautifully with John the Baptist's great statement on the Lamb of God in John 1:29.

That is why we tell the world about Jesus; that is why we engage in missionary endeavour; that is why we reach out into our community; that is why we share the gospel with our friends and family; that is why we travel to the ends of the earth and into the regions beyond; that is the reason why ... because we believe no-one need be excluded from the vast company assembled before the throne of the Lamb. This uncountable number have gathered there in heaven from 'every tribe and language and people and nation'. To a man, they owe their salvation to the Lamb with 'whose blood men were purchased for God'.

I think it all comes together when we ponder the huge significance and ripple effect of the momentous event in the temple recorded for us in Matthew 27:51. When Jesus died for our sin and when he shouted in that glorious oratorio of triumph, 'It is finished!', an incredible, unrepeatable and supernatural incident took place. The thick veil which separated the worshipper from the holy of holies was torn in two from top to bottom. *It kept him out!*

This unbelievable feat took place when the hand of God moved in a special way and, in a split second, a way was opened up for man to freely appear in the presence of God. *It let him in!*

It was, as though God was saying to the whole world of sinners, 'Look folks, the door is wide open, you may come in now!'

It harks back to what I said earlier: an authentic Christian is someone who knows who Christ is and he is someone who trusts what Christ did. Charles Wesley picked up on this wonderful theme when he wrote:

> *Arise, my soul arise,*
> *Shake off thy guilty fears;*
> *The bleeding sacrifice in my behalf appears:*
> *Before the throne my surety stands,*
> *My name is written on his hands.*

2:3-5

A Christian does what Christ commands

The opening two words in verse 3 pop up with amazing frequency in John's epistle. He says, *'we know'* or, as the RSV translates it, 'this is how we know'. You see, it is all about assurance, it is all about having our confidence rooted in the person and work of Jesus Christ.

The story is told of the beloved Scottish pastor, Robert Murray McCheyne, that from his pulpit in Dundee he used to advise his people if they began to have troublesome doubts about their relationship with God, *'For every look at self, take ten looks at Christ!'* Sound advice, indeed. It is always the best place to start!

This section of John's letter stretches from verse 3 down to verse 11 and in it John proposes two tests for the professing Christian. They are two vitally important criteria for they give us a foolproof and failsafe assessment of our standing before God. The reassuring fact is, if we pass this examination, if we get over these two hurdles, we have nothing much to fear about the reality and dynamics of our present relationship with God.

Both of these x-rays probe into the latent depths of our spiritual experience, they get to the heart of the matter, they peel away all the extraneous layers and enable us to see what is left when the packaging has been removed. That may shock us and, if it does, it should give us the incentive we need to sort ourselves out before the Lord. If we come out of it well, our assurance will be stronger, our faith will be intact, and our commitment to walking with him will be given a whole new lease of life.

The test of obedience

When we put the spotlight on the first test, we cannot get away from the fact that Jesus often said to his disciples, 'If you love me, you will obey what I command' (John 14:15). Such clear-cut statements may not be the most popular directives for many people to take on board in the third millennium; they are not in vogue, they have gone out of fashion. It is no longer chic to do what someone else tells us to do; apparently, it seriously affects our street cred and it is supposed

to radically impair our ability to portray ourselves as role models.
The rising tendency among ordinary people who struggle with their
identity in Christ is that we all want to do our own thing and we
want to do it our own way!

That may be the attitude of many who have allowed themselves
to be squeezed into the world's mould, but that does not remove the
solemn obligation we all face to obey his commands. It is the height
of spiritual folly to contravene the bylaws of Scripture. This has
absolutely nothing to do with hard-hatted pedantic legalism; that
mindset is symptomatic of a false dichotomy between law and love.
The bottom line is, we obey him because we love him.

What happens is this: the grace of God does not abolish or
eradicate God's law, it simply repositions it in our thinking when it
internalises it by writing it on our hearts.

According to John, it is when we do what the Lord Jesus tells us
to do that we experience a deepening conviction that we really do
belong to Christ. In other words, if we do what he wants us to do,
we will be what he wants us to be!

The apostle informs us in verse 3: *'We know that we have come
to know him if we obey his commands.'* The word *'keep'* or *'obey'* is
an interesting word that means 'to guard carefully' as if a person
were guarding a treasure. When that is our humble attitude before
the Lord, it seems to me that a growing sense of obedience will
automatically lead to a growing perception of assurance.

Don't follow his example ... he blew it, big time!

The classic example of a man who lost his assurance because of a
rash moment of madness is King David. After he committed adultery
with Bathsheba in a fateful one-night stand of no-holds-barred lustful
passion, he tried to cover his tracks; he arranged for the murder of
her husband Uriah. Alright, I know he did not pull the trigger, but
he might as well have done; just because it was done by proxy does
not lessen the charge levelled against him! Sure, he was forgiven!
Thank God he was, when he confessed his sin to Nathan the prophet.

There is no question about that, we read all about it in 2 Samuel 12:13.

The undeniable fact is, David did not have much peace in his heart for an extended period of time; he was slipping, he was drifting from his moorings, he was losing his grip on spiritual realities.

That explains why he prayed the way he did in his solemn penitential prayer of Psalm 51. The calm waters of assurance flowed back into his heart and mind only when he sorted out his life before God. It was only when he got back on the right track that he started to value and appreciate the wonder of his relationship with God. You see, that underlines the point that when we disobey the Lord, it robs us of the thrill of knowing that we know the Lord. The sense of assurance that we previously enjoyed evaporates before our eyes; we blink, and it has gone!

It will return only when we manifest the green shoots of spiritual recovery and when we come to the point of total commitment in our lives, such as Martin Luther came to. He is reputed to have told the reformer, Zwingli, in 1529, that 'if Scripture commanded me to eat dung, I would do so!' Say what you will, but when we have a 'never say die' spirit like that, assurance will not be such a big problem!

We can talk the talk ... do we walk the walk?

John is crystal clear on this issue for he says in verse 4, *'The man who says, "I know him," but does not do what he commands is a liar, and the truth is not in him.'* Strong language, indeed! It is straight-from-the-shoulder stuff! It is tough talking!

It is relatively easy to see what is running through John's mind. In this verse he reinforces the logic of the preceding verse by denying its opposite. He pulls no punches when he tells us the disobedient person who professes to be a Christian is a liar because such claims are blatantly contradicted by his behaviour. John is a fairly shrewd operator; we see that when he poses the rhetorical question: how can the truth of God be in such a person?

We are all familiar with the old saying, 'actions speak louder than words'. What we mean is this, they are a closer indication of the real person, they are a better window into the soul of a man. It is easy to talk. Words are comparatively cheap. We can say one thing one minute and we can change our minds the next!

A man can talk from now until there is a blue moon in the sky, he can make all the claims he wants until he is blue in the face, but that does not alter the fact that the individual who disobeys God does not know God *as* God.

If he did, he would bow before him in humble submission to his perfect plan and purpose. He would recognise that God's way is the best way; it is the royal route to blessing.

A loving obedience

The path of obedience may be fraught with many life-size dangers, it may have many larger-than-life challenges; having said that, it remains to this day the path of unparalleled blessing. As the gospel song says, 'to know him is to love him, and to love him is to obey him.' This is the link with verse 5 where John says, *'But if anyone obeys his word, God's love is truly made complete in him. This is how we know we are in him.'*

The pendulum swings back again in this verse but John, being John, adds a little more to what he is saying. David Jackman has written in his excellent commentary, 'The more we obey God's word, the more we open the door for his love to accomplish his purpose in our lives. The test of living in the light is growing in love for God. And the ultimate proof of that is not in the heightened emotion of exciting worship, but in the daily, detailed, disciplined obedience by which our characters are being transformed into the image of the God we love.'

On to maturity

It is as we obey him, in the everyday things of life, in the humdrum, in the daily grind, that we are being changed more and more into the image of Jesus. It is in the run-of-the-mill ordinary experiences of life that we can know increasingly what it is to become more like

Jesus and, at the same time, we can feel the tidal wave of his love flooding our hearts and minds. The *'complete'* love of which John speaks is simply meant to underline that obedience is the way to growth and maturity.

When we obey him and when we show our genuine love to him, ours will be a well-rounded experience of divine love. His bounteous love will overflow in our lives as we receive it in all its fulness!

- *It will transform our understanding,*
- *it will change our outlook,*
- *it will strengthen our resolve,*
- *it will confirm our faith.*

It will enable us to say with concrete conviction and total assurance that he is ours and we are his.

2:6

A Christian walks as Christ walked

We are developing the theme of blessed assurance in this fascinating section of John's epistle and here he grasps the opportunity to flesh out precisely what he means. He says, *'Whoever claims to live in him must walk as Jesus did.'* (It is worth noting that, on occasion, John could be a little ambiguous in his use of pronouns. When he refers to *'he'* or *'him'* he can often mean God the Father *or* God the Son; in verse 6, he is obviously referring to the Lord Jesus Christ.)

John longs for the people of his day and for the people of our generation to imitate the Lord Jesus. His aspiration is that we might see Christ as a role model and that we would walk in his footsteps. His passion is that we might emulate the Saviour and that our lives might radiate something of his beauty and charm. John's desire is that our lifestyle will be consistent with our claims to be a follower of the Lamb. We are meant to copy the Lord Jesus, we are supposed to be living replicas of the Lord in the twenty-first century. We are to walk as Jesus walked!

Martin Luther said it is not the walk of the Saviour walking on the water that is intended here (the chances of us doing that are fairly slim, if not impossible); but it is our daily walk as we progress through the routine events that clog up the 'things to do' page in our daily planner.

Think about the walk of his childhood, when he walked as a boy in submission to his parents. Think about the walk of his manhood, when he tramped up and down the dusty roads of Galilee. Think about his walk down the Calvary road, when he set his face like a flint to go to Jerusalem.

It seems to me, in the light of all of this, we are to mimic his goodness, his meekness, his self-sacrifice, his love and his submission to the Father. You see, the way of love is not to surrender to mystical promptings or spiritual hunches or sentimental feelings. The way of love is to study the word of God, it is to study the example of Jesus Christ, and then for us to model our lives on these guidelines.

When we traverse this particular path, we are taking the high road of walking hand in hand with Jesus. To walk in his steps enables us to pass with flying colours the test of obedience; it means our personal faith in God is accredited.

2:7,8

The test of love

The second test of the Christian's profession is love and that is precisely what John is discussing here. He says with refreshing candour: *'Dear friends, I am not writing you a new command but an old one, which you have had since the beginning. This old command is the message you have heard. Yet I am writing you a new command; its truth is seen in him and you, because the darkness is passing and the true light is already shining.'*

The emphasis in this duo of verses is one of the constantly recurring themes of John's epistle - a genuine love for one another. In the final analysis, it is all about extending to a brother or a sister in the Lord, the right hand of fellowship, not the right fist of fellowship.

A warm, loving embrace speaks volumes to a dear soul who has come in off the street with problems up to his armpits when compared with the frosty reception offered by someone with a furrowed brow and an artificial smile combined with an arctic handshake.

In today's speak, it is one thing for a person to chill out, it is quite a different matter for that person to be frozen out!

God's high command

Its focal point is compatibility as expressed in the context of the local church, it is getting along with each other in the wider all-embracing circle of the family of God. One word appears three times in this duo of verses: it is the word *'command'* and that leads us to think about the law of God.

In some ways, we need to grasp afresh that the law of God was no bad thing. It was not a couple of tablets handed down by an ogre of a tyrannical despot who wanted to make life difficult for his brow-beaten subjects; instead, it can be hailed as an expression of the love of God for man. It is an open, no-strings-attached revelation of the heart of God for those whom he has created. We need to remind ourselves that the law of God does not inhibit us by putting us into some kind of custom-made straitjacket. Rather, it enables us, it releases us, by freeing us to be the kind of people God wants us to be.

The western mind often views the law as something which is fiercely impersonal and rigidly inflexible; it does not melt the heart of man and it does not bend either way! The torah of the Old Testament is an entirely different ball game. It is not an abstract compartmentalised code of do's and don'ts; it is not a cold, clinical set of requirements that are set for time immemorial in conceptualised concrete!

A look at the law

If it isn't that, let me tell you what it is! The law is the personal, loving instruction of an omniscient heavenly Father telling his children how to live their lives for maximum fulfilment. It is God's way of showing us how we can find our potential realised in him. It is his way of saying that he loves us for he desperately wants the very best for us!

From the first minute on day one of God's revelation, the law of love was taught because the law was an expression of the character of the one who gave it and, as we have discovered already, he is love! A Mosaic illustration of this is where we are encouraged to 'love your neighbour as yourself' (Leviticus 19:18).

When the apostle John speaks of an old command *'which you have had since the beginning'*, he probably means this was the first piece of practical advice they were given when they trusted Jesus as Lord and Saviour. It does not matter how many years we have been on the road, we never outgrow this particular instruction.

Jesus himself taught that the 'Law and the Prophets' were all summed up in the law to love God and one's neighbour (Matthew 22:37-40); and, of course, that is the essence of his teaching in the Sermon on the Mount. Paul was on the same wavelength when he made exactly the same deduction in his letter to the Galatians in 5:14.

When we pick up all the pieces and put them together, we soon realise that when John arrives at the same conclusion, he knows that he is saying nothing new. There is nothing novel about this brand of love: it is basic, it is fundamental, it is the norm, it is par for the course. I think that helps to explain why John often refers to his readers, as he does in verse 7, with the phrase, *'dear friends'*. A literal translation would read, 'loved ones'.

Love ... old but ever new!

In all our interpersonal relationships, love is paramount. Having said that, Jesus did call it 'a new commandment' in John 13:34 and that, I think, is the inference from John's comment in verse 8a. There is a possibility that the newness is linked to the fact that *'its truth is seen in him'*. The only time in the history of the world that this command was exemplified was in the human life of Jesus Christ; there was a depth and reality to his love that no-one could possibly imagine.

Even though the command was almost as old as the hills, it was never out of date. It is as relevant today as it was in John's day and further back in the annals of time; with the coming of Christ, it was personified in the only way possible. Tremendous!

But the real surprise comes in the next couple of words where John says *'and you'*. That is quite staggering, to say the least, for he puts the ball back into our court! We have no difficulty coping with the fact that love was fulfilled in the Lord Jesus, we have no hangups with that assessment, but John says it is *in* us. That is the part which is extremely hard to comprehend!

When all is said and done, that is what authentic Christianity is all about. We have passed from the kingdom of darkness into his kingdom of marvellous light, and that is just great! That is what happened at the moment of our conversion. At the same time, there is a more gradual process taking place all around us.

One day in the unfolding drama of redemption, with the ripening of God's purposes, the darkness will be removed and perfect light will rule. Until that day dawns, John intends this truth to be a challenge to each of us to live as the children of light.

It is a stimulus to all God's children to walk in the light. It is a clarion call for us to spread the gospel to the far-flung corners of the earth so that the light might permeate more lives the closer we are to the advent of Jesus Christ. Perhaps we need to remember, the light always shines brightest when the darkness is at its deepest.

2:9-11

Wearing the badge of love

I am sure you will be familiar with the saying, 'He's going round in circles!' It seems to me from reading the first epistle of John that is where the old preacher excels! I hope that does not sound too unkind; it is not meant to be a sniping criticism from someone standing on the sidelines with his arms folded.

John has a fairly small number of themes up his sleeve and instead of dealing with them one after the other in some kind of logical sequence, he circles around them. I think the spiral staircase structure of his letter demonstrates the complex relationship that exists between various aspects of God's truth. It is a wee bit like the vision God gave to Ezekiel in chapter 1 of his prophecy where he saw wheels within wheels!

One such theme is love. John deals with it briefly in chapter 2, then he opens it out and expands on it in chapter 3, then he really goes to town on it and deals extensively with it in chapter 4! The fact that we have affection for our brothers and sisters in the global family of God is an indication of the reality of our relationship with God. Francis Schaeffer had every reason to refer to love as 'the mark of the Christian'.

We discover in verse 9 that John is no less blunt. He says, *'Anyone who claims to be in the light but hates his brother is still in the darkness.'* Bearing in mind the direction of the prevailing wind in the context of John's comments, it is worthwhile noting that the emphasis here is on love, not knowledge.

Any Tom, Dick or Harry can come along to your church and mine and claim to have had some kind of spiritual experience, they can claim to be in the light, they can claim to know God in one way or another.

The heart of the matter

What we need to realise is this, it is incredibly easy for us to mistake intellectual understanding for spiritual reality. In other words, they may have it all in their head, it is stored away as data on a microchip in their mind, it can be retrieved at any time. The sad fact is, it has never reached their heart. It is possible for them to know all about it and yet never to have experienced its transforming power in their lives.

The hallmark of true believers is that love will be evident in their lives. True spirituality must infallibly express itself in love. I suppose it is natural for us to squirm and recoil when we see John using such a strong verb as *'hates'* in this verse. We feel a little uncomfortable with it and I think that is perfectly understandable.

But John is not using it as a kind of tactical ploy just to get our backs up; it is not even a knee-jerk reaction by the apostle in a serious attempt to squeeze our comfort zone. He is facing reality head-on. John is telling it like it is! The apostle pulls no punches for he firmly believes that love is the defining expression of our walking in the light with God.

The two are intertwined: *where we have light, we have love,* and *where we have darkness, we have hate.* One is the corollary of the other.

The bottom line is, since we are the children of light, we have a duty and an obligation to treat one another with warm love and utmost respect. We need to pull out all the stops and determine to channel more of God's love into each others' lives; by such proactive love, the watching world will see for itself the radical nature of a biblical Christianity which is kosher.

Jesus was thinking along similar lines when he set love as the benchmark. He said, 'By this shall all men know that you are my disciples, if you have love one for another.' Love is the badge we should be wearing on the lapel of our lives!

Love does not look down on other people

That is the concept to which John is encouraging us in verse 10 where he says, *'Whoever loves his brother lives in the light, and there is nothing in him to make him stumble.'* The insight which John shares with us here is most helpful and illuminating. One of the less attractive things about the Gnostics was their open contempt for people who did not share their super-spiritual ideas. They saw themselves as a kind of elitist group within the fellowship of God's people; they were living in the orb of a holier-than-thou syndrome.

So far as the apostle John is concerned, this is something which he finds well nigh impossible to tolerate, it is a bitter pill he struggles to swallow, it does not tally with our supposedly high level of commitment to each other in the family of God. If anything, it is a flat contradiction of our bonding as believers.

These well-intentioned folks who make all sorts of wild claims about their personal spirituality and, at the same time, look down on their fellow believers from an elevated perch give away the fact that they are grossly maladjusted in their spiritual vision. Basically, their perception of God's grace is seriously flawed and, because of that, their testimony is critically eroded. To all intents and purposes, they are walking around in the dark, they are living in error.

Love is not the 'me, myself and I' mindset

John says as much in verse 11 where his critique of the status quo is quite incisive. He says, *'But whoever hates his brother is in the darkness and walks around in the darkness; he does not know where he is going, because the darkness has blinded him.'* Sometimes the pendulum can swing in the opposite direction and we meet folks who have taken on board a particular brand of Christian piety which imagines that security is to be found by being hermetically sealed off from other people, even from other Christians, in a recluse-like detachment. Generally speaking, these are well-meaning people who want to be alone and who want to be left to go it alone!

I know some folks who have this warped mentality and I imagine you probably do as well. They feel secure in their own little world, they feel pure in their own protective environment, they feel strong when they are wrapped in the cotton wool of their personal cocoon.

The harsh reality is, any mindset which adopts and advocates a policy of spiritual isolation does not contribute anything to the body of Christ. If anything, it deprives other people of receiving the benefit of our love and sharing in the blessing of our fellowship. From John's perspective, such an attitude is not one of walking in the light for we end up short-changing our fellow believers. The baseline is, we need one another in the family of God!

Twilight zone Christians

It appears to me, the more a Christian gets wrapped up in himself, the more a Christian gets immersed in pursuing his own personal agenda, the more a Christian concentrates on the cultivation of his own character or the preservation of his own virtue, the less clearly will he see the light.

The chances are, his focus is such that he has become self-centred and it is only a matter of time (days rather than weeks) before self-love and self-indulgence take over. Such a person has the blinkers on and when that happens the red lights will start flashing for the greatest enemy of real love is self-love. And that, it has to be said, is the root of all hatred.

The absence of a compassionate love which reaches out to others is a clear indication of a life that is lived in the twilight zone; it is a tell-tale sign of a life that is lived in the shadows. According to John, those who live and walk in the light, those who open their hearts and show and express a genuine love to and for their brothers and sisters in the family of God, these folks find no stumbling block hidden in their pathway.

The Greek word employed by John at the end of verse 10 is *skandalon* which meant originally a bait-stick or a trap. The idea is of a hidden danger, often lurking beneath the surface, which may ensnare and destroy the unwary and unsuspecting traveller, especially if he is commuting in the dark. In other words, the only remedy prescribed by John is to keep walking in the light! I have said it before and it is worth repeating, light and love are ideal companions. They go hand-in-hand.

- *If we have a heart for people, we take care to avoid sinning against them.*
- *If we have a concern for people, we will take every precaution to make sure we do not cause them to stumble.*
- *If we have a love for people, we will do everything in our power to encourage them and build them up.*

The pit pony syndrome

When we display a lack of love, it seriously distorts our outlook and gradually blinds our vision. Slowly but surely, we begin to feel at home in the dark. The tragedy is, we become used to groping our way through life, constantly stumbling and being ensnared by all kinds of problems. Such people are often blissfully unaware of how dark it really is and how short-sighted they have become. It is the pit pony syndrome: if we keep an animal underground for long enough, eventually it loses its sight. Sadly, that is what is happening here! As one commentator says, 'The light that is ignored soon ceases to strike us. The conscience that is habitually silenced soon ceases to speak.'

The abiding lesson from this short section of 1 John is, if we lack love, we are pretty much in the dark!

2:12-14

Non-generational love

It is equally true to say, such love embraces every age group and every people group. Bona fide biblical Christianity is marked out by a love for all God's people, whatever their party label, no matter where they hang their coat on a Sunday. I think that is probably the motivation which gripped the heart of John as he penned this rather strange interlude.

The repetition of *'dear children, fathers and young men'* in this paragraph borders on the poetic; if you happen to have access to the NIV, you will notice that is how it handles it. This is an ideal opportunity for people to catch their breath, to quietly reflect on all that John has been saying so far, and for them to seriously consider the practical outworking of his teaching in their daily lives.

The fact that John mentions three groups of people has raised the eyebrows of some and the inevitable question has been asked: what distinction, if any, is John drawing here? Is it based on age, on church office or on spiritual maturity?

Where ageism is not an issue

Of one thing we can be sure: when John addresses his comments to the *'dear children'* in verses 12 and 13, it would seem that he is referring to the entire congregation. In the Greek language, the word tends to mean 'born ones' and it comes from a verb meaning 'to birth' or 'to bring into existence'.

The reason why I think that is the case is because he frequently uses the same term elsewhere in his epistle; actually, it is John's favourite expression when writing to them. He is not patronising them, nor is he treating them like people who have never grown up; he is simply writing to them as an old man, and a revered old man, at that!

'Fathers' would then mean the older church members and it is probably a specific reference to those who were involved in the leadership of the assembly. *'Young men'* would signify the next generation of future leaders. It can be narrowed down to those who will take up the baton, that is, those being groomed for responsible positions within the local church.

Notice that each clause is prefaced with the words, *'I write to you'*. John leaves them in no doubt as to what is on his heart; he is quite specific in what he shares with them and to each group is given a clearly defined statement of fact. It all hinges on the word *'because'* and that is repeated no fewer than six times. These clauses highlight in bold typeface the various convictions John wants each group within the church to hold; he wants them to be sure of the foundation on which they are building their lives.

When we put all of these together, they are a selection of glorious truths which are the bedrock of our faith in Jesus Christ. When we assimilate each of these, our light will shine brighter and our love will know no bounds and, to top it all, we will have a strong growing conviction in our hearts alongside a firm assurance in our minds. We will be a people who know why we believe what we believe! If you like, these are important imperatives for the people of God.

• His first word of encouragement is found in verse 12 where John says, *'I write to you, dear children, because your sins have been forgiven on account of his name.'*

- His second word of encouragement is found in verse 13 where he says, *'I write to you, dear children, because you have known the Father.'*

Children ...

The emphasis here is centred on forgiveness and fellowship and both are indissolubly linked to the Father. This is a fait accompli so far as they are concerned. He could not speak of them in the manner in which he does if they had not first experienced the joy and thrill of sins forgiven. Such a happy experience is theirs on *'account of his name'* and that immediately puts the spotlight on his nature.

When John talks about the name of Jesus, he is talking about his nature revealed by that name as Saviour or Rescuer. Peter states quite categorically in Acts 4:12 that 'there is no other name under heaven given to men by which we must be saved.' We are debtors to him and, because we have been forgiven, we have been brought into a dynamic relationship with God; it means, we know him personally and he is our Father.

Fathers ...

The mark of maturity is seen as a deepening of that knowledge and that is why John now addresses those who are fathers. He says the same thing to them on the two occasions in which he singles them out for special mention. In verses 13 and 14 he says to them, *'I write to you, fathers, because you have known him who is from the beginning.'* I think you will probably recognise that the phrase which John uses here is similar to the one which is recorded in the first verse of his epistle.

It is a reference to the pre-existence and eternal deity of the Lord Jesus Christ. It is an affirmation that Jesus Christ is God. It is a firm rebuttal by John of the line of teaching put forward by the phoney preachers of his day. John is laying it on the line to them that Jesus Christ is nothing less than God.

Young men ...

John moves up a gear when he talks to the young men. He says to them in the middle sentence of verse 13, *'I write to you, young men, because you have overcome the evil one.'* He follows on by saying to them in verse 14, *'I write to you, young men, because you are strong, and the word of God lives in you, and you have overcome the evil one.'* The focus here is on victory over Satan. David Jackman writes in his commentary in *The Bible Speaks Today* series, 'To know that we have been rescued from the devil's grip, and that he has no more power over us, is part of the glorious assurance that God wants to give to even his newest children.'

It is incredibly fascinating for us to discover that the reason for their success in the hour of battle is not attributed to their inbuilt zeal and enthusiasm, nor is it put down to their youthful energy. The sole reason given for their victory in the place of conflict is because of the colossal impact and permeating influence the word of God has had on their lives.

There is power in the word

The underlying thought is this, when we begin to get a grip on God's word, God's word begins to get a grip on us. How true it is; we derive our strength to fight the enemy and conquer the world, the flesh and the devil, from the truth of God's revelation.

Jesus showed us the best way to do it when he counteracted the triple temptations of Satan by his skilful handling of the word of God.

The power of Scripture is something we should never under-estimate; its potential is truly phenomenal.

All of these descriptions when pulled together give a marvellous vignette of a Christian. For example, a Christian is someone who knows Christ personally and intimately; because he is 'in Christ', he is someone who has overcome the devil, he is a person who is strong in the abiding word of God.

It is good for us to realise and appreciate that many of the key verbs in verses 12-14 are in the perfect tense. This tense is used only when an action in the past has effects which continue on into the present. The ripples of yesterday are felt today and we will still be aware of them tomorrow.

This activity is staggering for it means we continue to know forgiveness for sin through the Lord Jesus Christ; we continue to grow in our knowledge of the one who is the eternal Father; we continue to triumph over Satan; we continue to enjoy the privilege of immersing ourselves in the truth of Scripture.

This section may have been an interlude; obviously I have no idea how you feel, but I feel much better after the break! It was welcome!

2:15-17

A proper world view

The name J B Phillips is one you may be familiar with. Among a host of other achievements, he was known for his highly commended translation of the New Testament. The amazing story of his life is told in the book which bears the title, 'Your God is too small!' Every time I read that title, I am challenged to stretch my faith and elasticise my trust a little more because this God is a God who is bigger than all our problems.

Phillips is also given credit for coining the phrase, 'Man's extremity is God's opportunity.' I am sure that is something most of us can easily identify with, having proven the reality of it at one time or another.

When we read his translation of Romans 12:2, we very quickly realise this man is on the same wavelength as the apostle John. Phillips writes, 'Don't let the world around you squeeze you into its own mould.' If we read what John says in 2:15, it is fairly obvious the two of them are singing from the same hymn sheet; he says, *'Do not love the world or anything in the world. If anyone loves the world, the love of the Father is not in him.'*

The bottom line is, if the world cannot stop us obeying, it will try to stop us loving; if it is unable to stop us loving, it will try to make us love the wrong thing.

That explains John's injunction in verse 15 and it elucidates the thinking behind his command which he refers to in verses 16 and 17. The punchline, so far as John is concerned, is that we cannot love God and love the world at the same time; the two are mutually exclusive as objects of our love. They do not lie easily alongside each other as bedfellows. They are, in fact, diametrically opposed.

What 'loving the world' does not mean...

* **It is not Pharisaism**

When we flick through the pages of the Gospel narrative we very quickly discover what made the Pharisees tick. Their attitude was governed by the fact that they desperately wanted to be non-worldly, they wanted to be different from the world. You see, they were surrounded by a pagan culture which threatened the purity of their religion and that is why they reacted in the manner in which they did.

Having said that, Jesus was less than impressed with their policy and manifesto. In fact, he roundly condemned it on more than one occasion. They had endless rules stipulating what they could and could not do on the sabbath. They discriminated about the company they kept and the places they could go to. They had all sorts of regulations about what they could eat and drink and how they did it.

It is ironic but these aspects of Pharisaism are in precisely the areas of lifestyle which many Christians think important. We do not do this, we cannot do that, we do not go here, we cannot go there. The problem comes when we start legislating for other people. The sad and depressing fact is that so many Christians identify worldliness with exactly the same sort of things as did the Pharisees.

We remember that Jesus got himself into big trouble with them on more than one occasion because he failed to toe their party line;

he found himself in deep hot water more than once because he refused to bend to their legalistic dictates.

- **It is not asceticism**

Back in the early days of the church, the idea gained acceptance that the more someone denied the flesh, the less worldly they were. Many of the early church fathers practised such ascetic disciplines as celibacy. The Syrian Church at one stage went so far as to state that a person could not become a church member if they were married. That really is pushing it to the extreme, isn't it, but that is the way it was back then!

I discovered recently when doing some research on early church history that fasting was advocated not just to give an opportunity for single-minded prayer, but with the idea that the more a person's body was emaciated, the more God was inclined to listen to them. These well-meaning folks renounced worldly goods and went around in rags; they never washed, they let their hair grow, and some of them even engaged in flagellation. The simple life is one thing, but these folks went beyond the pale.

Such a mindset has nothing whatsoever to do with worldliness as we read of it in the New Testament for it seriously undermines the doctrine of creation. The Bible informs us that God made the world and he made it good! There is no dichotomy in Scripture which says the material world is bad and only the spiritual things are good. Paul gives us a robust defence of God's attitude to the world with his erudite comments in 1 Timothy 4:4 where his parting shot is, '... nothing is to be rejected if it is received with thanksgiving.'

- **It is not monasticism**

John is not advocating a hermit lifestyle or what some would call, monasticism. There is no place in John's theology for those who want to withdraw from the world and form some kind of holy huddle.

I love the way John Stott puts it when he refers to such people as *'rabbit-hole Christians'*. He has in mind the Christian student who pops his head out of his burrow, which he shares with a Christian roommate, and runs along to the lecture theatre where he sits with his Christian friends. After the morning tutorials are over, he proceeds to lunch, where he frantically searches for the table where all his Christian cronies are eating. When evening comes, he goes along to his in-depth Bible study, attended just by committed Christians, where he prays fervently for all the non-believers at his college or university. Then he scurries back to his Christian colleague in their shared apartment, safe again.

What has he done? He has spent all day dashing furiously from one Christian burrow to another. That is what a rabbit-hole Christian is! We may chuckle and smile when we hear a story like that, but there is a fair bit of truth in it as well. In some situations, it is not that far off the mark and well we know it.

These three philosophies are far removed from what John means by not loving the world! He is not talking here about shutting ourselves off from the real world in which we live; he is not saying that we should batten down the hatches lest we become infected with the non-Christian environment all around us. Far from it! There is no mileage in that argument.

Nowhere does the Bible encourage us to take on board a ghetto mentality. In fact, we have a solemn responsibility to the world in which we live, not only to be stewards of what God has entrusted to us, but in the sense that we are called to evangelise it. We have an obligation to declare God's glory among the nations. We have a mandate to take the gospel of Christ to the ends of the earth.

A phenomenon called 'worldliness'

This world, which John says is dangerous for us to love, is the same world which God so loved that he gave his Son to die for it; this is the world God loves enough to send his Son to rescue (John 3:16).

There is another meaning associated with the *'world'* in the New Testament. Sometimes it is seen as an organised system of human civilisation and activity which is opposed to God and alienated from him. It depicts everything that hinders man from loving and obeying his Creator. This shade of meaning of the word *kosmos* has much the same content as John's use of the term *'darkness'* in chapter 1 of his epistle.

We can see the way John's mind is working for here we have another of his many contrasts. It is the stark choice between loving the Lord or loving the world. To do the first is to live in the light; to follow the second is to walk in pitch blackness.

I believe Billy Sunday, the evangelist, was correct when he said, *'It makes no more sense to talk about a worldly Christian than it does to talk about a heavenly devil.'*

That helps to explain why verse 15 is such a direct and forceful command. There is no beating about the bush with John, he is not shilly-shallying around. He lays it on the line and, with John, people are left in no doubt as to what is required of them! John was not ploughing a lonely furrow, I hasten to add, for James said something similar in his letter in 4:4, 'Friendship with the world is hatred towards God.'

I suppose, human nature being what it is, we tend to dilute this radical demand, we want to water it down a little bit. We think it is not as relevant in the third millennium as it was in the first, we try to rationalise our thinking, we seek to justify our current behaviour. At the end of the day, we can wriggle and squirm all that we want, but God's word is final! It says what it means and it means what it says!

Let me round it off with a definition of worldliness: *it is anything that keeps me from loving God as I ought to love him and from doing the will of God as I ought to do it!*

The 'A' word

The 'A' word is of mega importance in John's analysis and assessment of what makes this old world go round. It is the word, 'attitude!' Your attitude and mine, our attitude to the things we can taste and smell and handle and see. It is the attitude factor in how we allow ourselves to be sucked into the vacuum of the world. It is what makes me tick on the inside, it is what drives me on, it is what motivates me to pursue some particular course of action. It is the manner in which our built-in reactor responds to the pressures from the environment outside. Our attitude to the world is like a potential time bomb ticking away inside us. It needs to be defused and that can happen only when we allow the Holy Spirit to shape and sharpen our thinking.

I think the apostle spells out very clearly for us what is on his heart and mind when he says what he does in verse 16. John writes, *'For everything in the world - the cravings of sinful man, the lust of the eyes and the boasting of what he has and does - comes not from the Father but from the world.'* Strong words from John!

It seems to me, John is attempting to remind us that the world presents a major problem for the spiritual Christian. His threefold description of what this world consists of is most illuminating. He gets to the nub of the matter for he takes us right back to life in the ideal and perfect environment of the Garden of Eden.

It is a superb illustration of what can go wrong even when people are living in a paradise of idyllic ambience.

The familiar story of Adam and Eve, who really messed things up, is a running commentary on John's triple assertion. We read about it in considerable detail in Genesis 3. One day the devil came along with a long list of insinuating questions which he pummelled at a couple of folks who were starry eyed. The reality is, every question was an attack on the character of God.

- He said in verse 1, 'Did God really say "You must not eat from any tree in the garden"?'
  In other words, did God really mean it?
- The comment in verse 4 is, 'You will not surely die.'
  Do you really have to believe it?
- The throwaway aside in verse 5 is, 'For God knows that when you eat of it your eyes will be opened.'
  Why is he hiding this from you?

No matter which way you look at it, each of these questions contains an implicit suggestion that God is someone who cannot be trusted, he is someone who may change his mind, he just wants to stop us from having a good time; he is a spoil sport and a bit of a killjoy, we cannot depend on him, he only wants to frustrate us and inhibit us.

Get a life!

The original temptation which confronted the first couple on planet earth was to break out of the straitjacket they found themselves in and start living. Times have not changed and neither have the scare tactics of the enemy! The world has an enormous pull, it tugs away at your heart and mine. It has an alluring appeal and it does not have to do much to attract us. The fact is, it is a deceptive attraction for all that glitters is not gold!

We may imagine that our goldfish swimming around in its bowl is tired of the restrictive confines of its environment. We may even feel we should liberate it to the wider world of the lounge carpet. But that sort of freedom is freedom only to die.

In the same way, man estranged from God is dead to those spiritual realities without which he cannot be completely human, but the devil will not let us believe that. Instead, he uses our natural desires, which God has given to us, to get us round to his way of thinking. Satan is not content unless he has us under his thumb; he will not be happy until he has us wrapped around his little finger. It is a terribly sad tale but Eve succumbed in the hour of temptation and then she dragged Adam down with her (Genesis 3:6).

Three stages of capitulation

The comparison between the account in Genesis and what John has penned is found right here:

- *stage one:* the fruit satisfied her appetite for good food,
- *stage two:* she liked the look of it,
- *stage three:* she wanted it to boost her ego.

In exactly the same way, the devil operates today using the same tack in a subtle attempt to get us to fall.

• *'the cravings of sinful man'*

This means all that panders to our fleshly appetites. Even though John's phrase includes sensuality, it is much, much broader than that. He is probably talking about every desire that arises from our physical appetites: gluttony, greed, addiction, and so on. It is a worldliness which indulges the body.

• *'the lust of the eyes'*

This is the bridge which spans the gulf between the flesh and the outside world. The thought uppermost in John's thinking is a spirit of covetousness; it is something which arises from the desire for aesthetic rather than physical satisfaction.

It is vitally important for us to realise that lust is not the monopoly of the sex industry. It is true to say that some men will sell their souls to possess a woman's body, but it is also true to say that some men will sell their souls to possess a great painting or even a rare postage stamp. Either way, it is lust!

It is the syndrome which says, 'I see it, I want it, I'll have it.' It is consumerism gone crazy. It is a worldliness which indulges its whims and fancies in an extravagant manner.

• *'boasting of what he has and does'*

John is talking here of the person who cannot keep his mouth shut; he is always bragging about what he has and boasting about what he does. I think if John were alive today, he would probably talk about status symbols and the gold or platinum card mentality. It is the attitude that I must not only keep up with the Jones' but I must be one better than them! It is when we are so eager to impress that we put others down and exalt ourselves. It is a worldliness which indulges our pride.

A transient enjoyment

John leaves us in no doubt in verse 17 as to the transient nature of each of these attractions. They do not last, they are temporary. We have them today but before the sun sets they may be taken from us! He says, in a verse rich with contrast, that *'the world and its desires pass away, but the man who does the will of God lives for ever.'*

The things of time are fleeting, beauty fades with the passing of years, wealth is uncertain because the value of stocks and shares can rise and fall, fame is short-lived because we will not always be on the front page, popularity is precarious for we are only as good as the last goal we scored. There is so much about life that is brittle, there is so much that is fickle.

John argues, what is the point in investing your life in something which does not last? Surely it makes a lot more sense to do the will of God and find in him an eternal dimension to life.

It was Augustine who said, *'The good make use of this world in order to enjoy God, whereas the evil want to make use of God in order to enjoy the world.'*

The mark of a real Christian is someone who enjoys life to the full and, at the same time, they enjoy God in a way they never dreamed of.

2:18-23

Eyeball to eyeball with the enemy

G K Chesterton is credited with the statement, 'When people abandon the truth, they don't believe in nothing, they believe in anything.' When we see what is happening in today's world, we know he is absolutely right. He hits the nail on the head. His analysis and his insights are spot on.

It is incredible but so-called enlightened man, living in the hi-tech world of the third millennium, is renowned for his ability to take on board all the latest fads and fashions. One of the seriously alarming trends of the last hundred years or so is the growth of public gullibility. The stuff that people believe is, quite frankly, mind blowing.

I find it incomprehensible that twenty-first century man with even an ounce of sense can swallow so much of what life throws at him. It never ceases to amaze me the ideas that ordinary folks are willing to absorb. Some of these are so far-fetched and over the top that they push the bounds of credibility well beyond the limits.

There are literally thousands of cults and sects in our world today, many of them straining the credulity of Simple Simon with their bizarre and fantastic speculations.

When we sit down to take an objective look at the current scene, it hits us between the eyes for the statistics are disconcerting, to say the least. We very quickly realise the accuracy of Chesterton's assertion. Yes, he was right when he said men will believe in anything! I think one of the real dangers facing the church in our day and generation is not unbelief, but wrong belief. It is not irreligion, but heresy. It is not the doubter, but the deceiver.

Beware of antichrists

That is what John is referring to in this short section - the stirring and resounding challenge here is to beware of antichrists! The apostle tells us in verse 18, *'Dear children, this is the last hour; and as you have heard that the antichrist is coming, even now many antichrists have come.'*

John continues to address these beleaguered people in the early church with tender tones to his voice as he calls them *'dear children'*. It is not hard to see why they called him the apostle of love when he constantly uses such heart-warming and affectionate language towards them. At the same time, the old man is not afraid to pack a punch for there is such a thing as tough love. I think John's flashing red light warning in this verse is indicative of that.

He links all that is predicted to the time span he calls *'the last hour'*. That is a fascinating turn of phrase for it relates to the second advent of Jesus Christ. It matches a phrase which is frequently used in the New Testament, 'the last days'.

Generally speaking, that time period spans the niche between the first and second comings of Christ. If we wanted to be more accurate, it is the time slot between Pentecost and the return of Christ in clouds with great power and glory. It is what some have referred to as the 'gospel age' or the 'church age'. In other words, it is a reference to this present dispensation in which we live!

This is the hour when the Holy Spirit is actively moving in the hearts of men and women, drawing them to faith in Jesus Christ. This is the hour when the Lord Jesus is building his church. This is the hour when the gospel of sovereign grace is reaching out to the ends of the earth and he is gathering unto himself a people for his name, a people for his praise, and a people for his glory.

It is during these significant and momentous days that we need to be on guard, we need to maintain a state of constant readiness so that we can effectively foil every attack from the enemy. We need to be on red alert. We must remain vigilant at all times and in all places, lest we be caught unawares.

Of one thing we can be sure, where there is divine activity, there will always be an upsurge in demonic activity, hence John's timely warning to the church of the last days! Jesus himself warned on many occasions that false Christs and false prophets would appear. So far as he was concerned, this is a clear diagnostic sign of the end times. The Lord gave advance warning when he said in his highly acclaimed Olivet discourse in Matthew 24:5 that, 'Many will come in my name claiming "I am the Christ" and will deceive many.' This sombre expectation of traitors infiltrating the Christian community remained a fixed part of the teaching of the apostles right through the formative years of the church.

There would always be those who would worm and wriggle their way in from the outside. Paul preached it over and over again;

Peter wrote about it many times in his two letters; Jude spoke of it with considerable clarity in his short epistle; and John himself was not behind the door in warning the people of God of the obvious dangers surrounding them. It was a big problem then, it is a greater problem now. It was massive in their day, it is monstrous in our day!

An interesting fact emanating from this clutch of verses in 1 John is that he links together this anticipated apostasy in the church with the emergence of the figure of the Antichrist. I was intrigued to discover that John is the only biblical author to use this particular expression. He employs the same term in 2:22, 4:3 and across in verse 7 of his second epistle.

We saw earlier that Jesus used a word which speaks of pseudo-Christs as in Matthew 24:24 where he said, 'For false Christs and false prophets will appear and perform great signs and miracles to deceive even the elect.' These impostors are far from genuine, they are phoney, they are masqueraders of spiritual truth.

Paul goes a few steps further in 2 Thessalonians 2:3,4 when he refers to a single individual who will be energised and empowered by the devil. In a deft touch, he describes him as 'a man of lawlessness'.

This thumbnail sketch portrays him as a tyrannical individual who commands unconditional obedience from the swooning masses who are deceived by his supernatural charisma.

In all fairness, it has to be pointed out that different people have different ideas on the Antichrist and all that he stands for. I personally believe he is a real person who will arrive on the stage of global affairs after the Lord has taken his church home to glory.

In other words, if we believe the advent of Christ is imminent, if we are of the opinion that Jesus could come back at any moment, then the logic is, this man could be alive today and waiting in the wings. Up to this precise moment, he has not yet been revealed, but when the trumpet sounds and the saints are raptured, then his identity will be made known to a waiting and watching world.

It is equally true to say, down through the centuries there have been many who have been antichrist in their thinking and teaching and not a few who have promoted and fostered the spirit of antichrist. A cursory glance, a quick read, at church history only confirms what John is saying. The indisputable fact is, such evil forces have consistently manifested themselves in their implacable opposition to Jesus Christ and his church in every generation.

That implies John is very much on target when he refers to the Antichrist as tomorrow's man, a man for the future. In the next breath, John shows himself to be someone in touch with reality. He is a preacher who has his finger on the pulse when he declares that many antichrists have already made their presence felt as yesterday's men, and the recognition is also given that they remain on the ground today as well. It seems to me, the person who thinks otherwise is living in cloud cuckoo land.

Antichrist defined

It is worth noting that the word *'antichrist'* has at least two predominant ideas associated with it.

The prefix 'anti' in the Greek language can mean 'against' in which case the word 'antichrist' refers to someone who is an opponent of Christ or a rival to Christ; he is someone who claims to possess all the power and ability of Christ.

It can also mean 'in place of' so that the antichrist becomes a substitute for Christ or a counterfeit of Christ, someone who resolutely and deliberately stands over against Jesus and his righteousness and truth.

In this context, the latter is the preferred meaning for it is the one that fits better. This antichrist is someone who has no scruples about proclaiming a Christ who is not the Christ of the Bible.

- *He may be a Christ who is not quite God and never quite saves, as many of the cults and isms teach.*
- *He may be a Christ who offers health and wealth, as proclaimed by a number of high profile, big name televangelists.*

- *He may be a Christ who is repeatedly sacrificed in the mass, as is the norm in certain groupings within Christendom.*
- *He may be a Christ whom I invite into my life to make me feel good, as so much of modern evangelicalism teaches.*

These are the teachings of religious antichrists. When we narrow it down to an individual, as John also does, this person is a usurper. He has no quibbles or qualms about conducting all his operations under false pretences, he assumes a position to which he has no right, he sets himself up in hostile opposition to Jesus Christ.

Now we see why John responded in the manner he did. In the light of current religious affairs and because of what lies around the next bend on the road, it all makes sense. That is the reason why John repeated his opening statement at the end of verse 18 where we read, *'This is how we know it is the last hour.'*

Antichrist displayed

There is a ring of reality combined with a high level of pathos in John's opening sentence in verse 19 where he writes, *'They went out from us, but they did not really belong to us.'* The inference John makes is fairly obvious, he acknowledges there was a time when these folks were in the church, they sang the hymns, they listened to the preaching of the word, they partook of the bread and wine, they went through the waters of baptism, their voices were heard in the prayer meeting; to all intents and purposes, they looked the part but, in their hearts, they were miles away!

Such chameleonic individuals are extremely dangerous in any church fellowship, not just because of what they believe, or do not believe for that matter, but because they often take a long time to surface. They have a tendency to lie low for a time and then mount a strike when people are least expecting it. John makes it abundantly clear that their eventual apostasy proves they are not simply confused, untaught Christians; they are rank heretics! They vigorously oppose the truth of Scripture.

And so their departure from the church fellowship is no great loss to the local assembly; instead, it is what an old pastor friend of mine used to call, 'a blessed subtraction'. When the dust has settled, the hurting folks who are left will discover it has turned out to be a tremendous blessing in disguise.

This does *not* mean that everyone who leaves a church, for whatever reason, is antichrist; we have to know the full story and be familiar with all the facts and keep everything in its proper perspective.

But when a group separates itself into an elite, holier-than-thou huddle, claiming a deeper understanding or experience than the rest of us, we need to beware and exercise considerable caution. As one seasoned campaigner observes, 'It will not be long before unbalanced teaching begins to lead its adherents away into undisguised error. Once the central truths of the faith are denied, the appetite for Christian fellowship is lost.'

My personal conviction is, those who leave the true people of God to embrace another Christ were never genuine believers in the first place.

Antichrist denied

The next two verses of chapter 2 expose us to John's fightback. These are wonderful words of confirmation and assurance. Having told us what the defectors were like, John now paints a positive picture in verses 20 and 21 of true believers when he says, *'But you have an anointing from the Holy One, and all of you know the truth. I do not write to you because you do not know the truth, but because you do know it and because no lie comes from the truth.'*

Some Bible teachers think the anointing spoken of here is akin to the word of God. They feel it refers to the catechism, the elementary Christian teaching in the fundamentals of the faith which a baptismal candidate automatically received in the early church. The evidence in the text to support this theory is the correspondence between verses 24 and 27.

Other believers come along and they reckon it signifies the experience of baptism itself. That is a perfectly reasonable interpretation as we know from church documents that baptism became associated with a ceremony of anointing in some Christian circles very early on.

However, I think we can examine it from another angle. The word John deploys here is *chrisma* and we see immediately that it is linked to *Christos*, which means Christ. You see, Jesus Christ is the Anointed One; he is the one who has given the *chrisma* to every person who is trusting him as Lord and Saviour. This makes us all *christoi* - anointed ones! We are Christians! It is as simple as that!

Paul says as much in Ephesians 4:7,8 where he quotes freely from Psalm 68:18. The apostle goes on to develop this theme further in 2 Corinthians 1:21,22. From each of these references, we have established that the universal gift of the ascended Christ is the Holy Spirit. It is his great and unique ministry to lead and guide all of God's children into an understanding of God's truth through the apostolic testimony. We find that amplified in John 16:13.

The bottom line is, every Christian knows the truth because without it he could not be a follower of Christ. The fact that anyone knows it at all is attributable solely to the gift of God's grace in the person and work of the Holy Spirit. I would suggest, therefore, that the anointing of which John is speaking is a reference to the gift of the Holy Spirit in each of our lives.

John progresses his line of teaching further when he says in verses 22 and 23, *'Who is the liar? It is the man who denies that Jesus is the Christ. Such a man is the antichrist - he denies the Father and the Son. No-one who denies the Son has the Father; whoever acknowledges the Son has the Father also.'* The repetition of the word *'denies'* underlines the seriousness of the situation which John is confronting. To say it once is powerful enough; to say it three times is exceptionally strong language.

Antichrist in doctrine

If someone does not believe that Jesus was and is the Christ, God's own Son, sent from the Father, then he is against the Lord. The ramifications of such a position are considerable for it means this person cannot be in a right relationship with God. This is the acid test which must be rigorously applied to any teaching which people are trying to ram down our throat. It means, all those belief systems which blatantly deny the deity of Jesus Christ are antichrist in their doctrine.

The tragedy is, so many folks are enmeshed in false religions and ideologies which are nothing more than a tissue of lies, and these people desperately need to hear God's truth. That is why we preach the gospel in the third millennium, that is why we engage in global mission, that is why we teach the truth on the airwaves, that is why we reach out into the regions beyond - because there are those who are living in darkness and there are those who are walking in error. We have a solemn obligation to tell them of the one who is 'the way, the truth and the life'.

They may embrace some form of religion, they may go through the motions of a meaningless performance, they may be worshippers of one deity or another, but John pulls no punches when he says that a man cannot have God, he cannot know God, without first believing in Jesus. Without the Son, we cannot know the Father! Jesus is the one and only way to God.

2:24-29

Staying on track

We are moving into a vitally important section in 1 John. It is a paragraph where the apostle gives us some solid advice on staying on course as a Christian. It is one thing to start the race with lots of zeal and enthusiasm, it is wonderful to get off to a good start; it is quite a different matter to end the race and cross the finishing line in a blaze of glory.

It is the marathon in between which makes all the difference!

It is how we handle the challenges of this life. It is how we cope with the many crises we are called to face which impact our lives and ministry. It is how we survive and surmount the various hurdles which sometimes can seem too big for us. It is how we disentangle ourselves from the mess we sometimes land ourselves in. It is how we come through the other end of a long dark tunnel. It is how we wrestle with the many problems life throws at us.

In such moments of high drama in your life and mine, it is incredibly easy to lose our sense of direction, it is relatively easy to stall on our vision and purpose. It is the easiest thing in all the world to forfeit our dreams and hopes. What we need to realise is this:

- too many fall out on the last lap,
- there is no automatic pilot.

In the light of what John is saying, the key question is: how am I to make sure that I am not sidetracked by glib talkers or smooth operators, that I really do develop as Christ wants me to and that his purposes really are accomplished in my life? At the end of the day, that is what these verses are all about. John grasps the nettle when he challenges the believers to remain unwavering in their faith and commitment to the Lord. He says in verse 24, *'See that what you have heard from the beginning remains in you. If it does, you also will remain in the Son and in the Father.'*

There is a glaring contrast between this verse and the previous two verses. It is the little word *'you'* which makes all the difference. Actually, in the Greek, the word *'you'* is in an emphatic position in the sentence and that best underlines the gaping difference between them and the liars of verses 22 and 23 who deny that Jesus is the Christ.

It is apparent that one is in contradistinction to the other and that is all down to the grace of God in their lives. He is the one who brought them out of inky blackness into his white light through the experience of the new birth. John says this is something we have no hand in, we do not create it, we do not make it, we only have to enjoy it and preserve it!

The word ... secure in our lives

We notice that six times in these six verses, that is, from verse 24 through to verse 29, John uses the same verb. It is usually translated *'remain'* or *'continue'*, as in the NIV. In other versions, such as the AV, it is translated 'abide'. This is a beautiful word in the original language; it is one which is rich in meaning and highly expressive - it means, 'to take up a permanent address' or 'to make a settled home'. The thought behind it is this: if we want to keep going and keep growing as Christians, then the objective truth of God in Christ and in his written word has to be allowed to settle in our minds and hearts.

If we are going to find our potential realised in Christ, then we have to welcome his word into our lives to such an extent that it makes our hearts its abiding place. If we are hoping to impact our world for Jesus Christ then his truth must be allowed to permeate our lives, and that only happens when our hearts become his home. It needs to stay there, it needs to reside there, shaping us and moulding us into the kind of people God wants us to be.

It is not so much that we need to be learning new truth or jumping on the latest bandwagon or following the latest fad or spiritual fashion. There is no biblical warrant for pursuing novelties which are, more often than not, here today and gone tomorrow, they just do not last. Rather, says John, we need to be learning more deeply and practising more fully the great truths we have been aware of from the early days of our Christian experience.

That is what John implies when he talks about *'the beginning'*. You see, the truth of God does not need to be updated to make it relevant; all that needs to be done is that it be applied faithfully every day in your life and mine.

It is a case of saturating ourselves with it so that it flows naturally from our lives; it is a matter of sticking to the old paths, adhering to what we know to be the truth, and holding on to the apostolic teaching.

If we do not, we become sitting ducks for the enemy. We leave ourselves exposed, we set ourselves up as easy targets for the devil to take a pot shot at us and, you know as well as I do, he rarely misses! John is more or less saying that it is only as we make time to let God's word work deeply in our lives that we shall remain in him.

Leith Samuel, who is now with the Lord, often put it like this, 'The Spirit of God takes the word of God to make children of God.' What transpires is this: the word of God roots us into the Lord Jesus and that is precisely where we stay.

The future ... secure in the Lord

The benefits of such a position are phenomenal and can be summed up in John's significant comment in verse 25 where he informs us, *'And this is what he promised us - even eternal life.'* I tell you, that is a promise worth waiting for! It means our future is secure in Christ, it guarantees the prospect of a bright and better tomorrow for all the people of God. It focuses our eyes on the other side of death, it points us upward in the direction of his throne, it speaks of heaven and home! We know the best is yet to be, we know the full enjoyment of that life awaits us on the other shore. It is beyond time, it is out of this world.

By the same token, we also know Isaac Watts was right to suggest in his classic gospel song, 'The men of grace have found glory begun below.' That less familiar line is tucked away in the old hymn, 'Come ye that love the Lord and let your joys be known.'

Eternal life is not restricted to the there and then, it is something we can really enjoy in the here and now. It happens on day one when the Holy Spirit lives within us. It all comes together when he plants the life of God in our hearts at the moment of our conversion to faith in Jesus Christ. We are united to our God with the strongest possible ties both now and for ever! It is an unseen cord that can never be broken, it is a link that can never be severed, it is an indissoluble bond.

When we contemplate glory and all that lies before us, when we think about our present life in Christ, how glorious and awesome it is for us to realise, the future is now!

The way forward ... secure against phoney preachers

John is a Bible teacher who is up-front in what he says to the Christians to whom he is writing. He is completely open with them, he does not beat about the bush. I think that is abundantly clear from the frank and honest comment which he makes in verse 26. He says to the people of God, '*I am writing these things to you about those who are trying to lead you astray.*'

He is referring again to the Gnostic false teachers who wanted to lead them into bypath meadow. John's spiritual radar detected a deeply sinister dimension to the activities of these particular heretics.

They were not innocently deluded! They were not the representatives of a different Christian tradition whose theological insights can enrich our own. These are emissaries of the evil one who have imbibed the spirit of antichrist. It seems to me, their emergence is part of a devilish plot to destroy the church, not by lighting the fire and fanning the flame of persecution, but by sabotage. There was something insidious about them. Basically, they wanted to conscript the unsuspecting people of God into their own clique.

Two thousand years later we grapple with the same problems. That sort of empire building mindset still lies behind many of the divisions caused by false teaching today. The Greek word for '*lead ... astray*' which John employs in verse 26 is a word which means, 'to cause to wander'. It gives us our English word 'planet'.

The picture we have here is this: the Greeks contrasted the planets which they observed to 'wander' with the stars which remained fixed in a state of permanence. The planets were all over the place, they were constantly moving; the stars, on the other hand, stayed in the one same position. The implication is self-evident, for many of the flourishing sects and cults in our day have often gained impetus by pulling the wool over people's eyes with their wildly extravagant claims and clever theories.

The remedy ... secure in the truth

John states the obvious when he asserts that the remedy is not just recognising the truth as an absolute, as something out there; it is the inward experience of that truth, it is when we personalise it. That happens as a direct result of the anointing of God on our lives, as indicated by John in verse 27.

John spells it out for us when he says, *'As for you, the anointing you received from him remains in you, and you do not need anyone to teach you. But as his anointing teaches you about all things and as that anointing is real, not counterfeit - just as it has taught you, remain in him.'*

We have looked at the anointing before, but let me refresh your memory on it. The anointing that a king or a priest received in the Old Testament was symbolic of the grace of God being poured out on him to equip him for a specific task or ministry. The truth which runs in tandem with this is encapsulated here by the apostle John. He asserts that New Testament believers have similarly been equipped with that same grace to live in the truth by the Holy Spirit whom God has poured out on every one of his redeemed people.

The proof text which springs to mind is the one penned by Paul in 1 Corinthians 12:13. Just as we were dependent on the Holy Spirit for our initial understanding of the gospel and response to it, so he continues to apply God's truth increasingly in our lives. That gives a cutting edge to John's phrase which has often been quoted out of context, when he says, *'you do not need anyone to teach you'.*

The simple fact is, when we take the statement at face value, if John was convinced that they had no need of teaching, he would not have wasted his time writing them a letter! He has already told them in verse 21 that he is corresponding with people who know the truth, but they still need to be taught.

They know it, but they do not know it all!

This phrase needs to be seen against the backdrop of Gnostic teaching to which they were being subjected, where the focus lay on the impartation of secret knowledge. The emphasis was always on the acquisition of something 'extra' being required if there was to be a measure of growth in one's relationship with God.

However, what John argues here is that, because the Holy Spirit is the divine teacher given to each and every believer at the moment of salvation, and irrespective of how far we have progressed in attaining new levels of spiritual maturity, there is no additional secret information into which they need a Gnostic sect leader to initiate them.

If you like, the Holy Spirit is the author of the entire word of God, spanning the sixty-six books from Genesis to Revelation, which is his exclusive teaching tool. As someone has said, and I am more than happy to concur with it, 'If you have God's word in your hand and God's Spirit in your heart, you have everything you need to understand truth and grow in Christ.'

I think that is the gist of what John is saying: the Holy Spirit is the one who gives life and freshness and vitality to the truth of Scripture. He is the one who revives and restores our spiritual experience as he teaches us what we need to know; he is the one who brings a vibrancy into our lives as he enables us to respond positively in a faith that obeys. His supreme and central task is to make Jesus real and increasingly precious to us and, when he does that, he enables us to remain in him.

The rapture ... secure in our performance

That quip from John leads on quite naturally to his forward look in verse 28 where he says, *'And now, dear children, continue in him, so that when he appears we may be confident and unashamed before him at his coming.'* Again, the old apostle lapses into his loving ways by referring to them as *'dear children'*. The last time he did it was in verse 18 and a lot of hard talking has flowed from his quill in the intervening verses.

It seems like John is tying up the loose ends of his teaching on fellowship in this section of his letter; it is as if he is attempting to draw his argument to a close when he says, *'and now'*. It is a summary verse and, together with verse 29, it serves as a bridge between the two main themes of the book.

- *He encourages them to continue in Christ, to abide in him.*
- *He aspires for them to remain close to the Lord in their daily walk this side of heaven.*

The motivation for such an intimate relationship with the Lord is clearly elucidated by John for he puts the spotlight on the second coming of Jesus Christ. In fact, there is a fascinating play on words here. He says that God's children should have *parrhesia* or *'confidence'* at the *parousia* or *'appearing'* of Christ.

John does not want us to stand before the Lord and hang our heads in shame, he does not want us to appear before him with a long list of regrets, he does not want us to see him and blush with sheer embarrassment, he does not want us to view it as an event filled with dread and apprehension!

He longs that we might be able to come before him with our heads held high in humble gratitude, he wants us to relish and savour the moment when we stand before him, he wants us to anticipate his advent as a special moment to look forward to with growing excitement and bated breath, he wants us to sort out our lives between now and then, he wants us to get our act together so that we can appear before him without guilt.

- The thrilling truth is, *we are saved by the grace of God!*
- The resounding challenge is, *are we ready to meet the Lord?*

Our present attitude towards his coming gives us some idea of whether or not we are ready to meet him. Someone has counted that the return of Christ is mentioned 318 times in the 260 chapters of the New Testament, yet so often we live as if there was no tomorrow. Therein lies the enormous challenge which John sets before us.

The evidence ... a partnership in righteousness

That automatically leads us on to verse 29 where John highlights for us the present results, the spin-offs and benefits, of truly remaining in Christ. He writes, *'If you know that he is righteous, you know that everyone who does what is right has been born of him.'* In some ways, this is a faint allusion to the Lord's teaching on the vine and branches in John 15. If I am in Christ, as a branch is in the stem of the vine, then the life of Christ must be flowing through me producing its own fruit of Christ-likeness.

To be righteous is to be like Jesus!

It makes a lot of good sense when we recognise the inevitable outcome of my being in him and his being in me is that my life will be increasingly marked by my doing what is right. The bottom line is, the habit of righteousness is the proof of the reality of the relationship. We can look at it like this: there is a family likeness developing between Jesus and me. As David Jackman reminds us, 'So the knowing of the fact at the beginning of the verse leads to the recognition of the logical consequence in the second part of the verse.'

John's parting shot is to lift his line of reasoning to a higher plane when he reminds us that we are *'born of him'*. The question is, is he talking about the Father or is he referring to Christ? Nowhere else in the Bible are Christians spoken of as sons of Christ; we are brothers according to Hebrews 2:11, not sons.

The fact is, the pronoun can refer to none other than the Lord Jesus. In a strange kind of way, that is typical of dear John, for he never thinks of God in relation to sinful man without first thinking of Christ. And he never thinks of the human nature of Christ without thinking also of his deity. The two are inseparable, they are intertwined.

It has been said, 'The dynamic is all Christ's, but the availability is all ours, provided we draw on his limitless resources, day by day.' It means, we will stay on the right track because our confidence is in him!

3

Love ... the ultimate apologetic

3:1-3

Our position before God

A little boy was cruelly teased at school because he was adopted. Plucky soul that he was, he suffered the merciless taunts and sickening jibes of his classmates patiently; and then, when he could take it no longer, he blurted out in fierce self-defence, 'You can say what you like. All I know is that my parents *chose* me. Yours couldn't help having you!'

And he was absolutely right! When we understand it that way, adoption is not a disgrace but a privilege. It seems to me, if that is true of those adopted by human parents, how much more true it is of Christians who have been called the children of God.

We are called his children!

Verse 1 is breathtaking theology! Without fear of contradiction, it is out of this world. We are moving in the orbit of God's unfailing love as the atmosphere is one of astonishment and exclamation. This is tremendous stuff! John says, *'How great is the love the Father has lavished on us that we should be called children of God! And that is what we are! The reason the world does not know us is that it did not know him.'*

We need to remember that John is an old man, he is on the last lap, he is well into his sunset years, he is close to death, but what thrills me about him is this, he has not lost the sense of wonder of God's undeserved grace. He is bowled over every time he contemplates the providence of God in his life. When he ponders the unique relationship he enjoys with his heavenly Father, it leaves him gasping for air.

We see the drama unfolding with the prolific use of exclamation marks in the opening verse. They are there to emphasise John's overwhelming sense of stupendous awe at it all. Literally, John says, *'Behold! What an extraordinary love!'*

The word suggests something exotic and mysterious that comes from a distant country. Cinderella had the help of a fairy godmother to make her beautiful but our Prince saw us in our tattered rags and still he loved us. I sometimes ask myself the question, 'Do I really appreciate the sheer wonder of that?' I do not think it has really dawned on us how excitingly wonderful it is to be called the children of God.

'Think of it,' he says, 'that such a righteous God should stoop down to the likes of us, whose very nature is a fetid stench in his nostrils and he lovingly calls us his children! By right, he should have nothing to do with us!' Those are the bare facts in the cold light of a new day.

Thank God, he reached down to where we were in the gutter of sin and, with a fast-beating heart oozing with tenderness, he drew us to himself! In the words of the prophet Zechariah, he has 'plucked us as brands from the burning.' That is love! That is grace! That is mercy! That is God!

He has done it before!

He stooped down to save Abraham who out of fear twice passed off his wife as his sister; he pulled out all the stops when he came down to save David who was guilty of adultery, deception and murder by proxy; he showed unbiased love when he came down to save Zacchaeus who cheated people out of their livelihoods; he went the second mile to save Paul who blasphemed the Saviour for so long and had his people put to death; he bent over backwards to rescue John Newton, caught up in the degradation of the slave trade; he is the same one who has stooped down to all sinners down through the ages who have cried out in repentance for God's grace.

When this truth grips our hearts and takes a firm hold of our lives, we will wish in the words of Charles Wesley that we had 'a thousand tongues to sing, our great Redeemer's praise!' It does not matter which angle we approach the subject from, the result is always the same. There is a sense of profound and utter amazement that God should do what he has done for the likes of you and me!

We certainly do not deserve it and, oftentimes, we are prone to be ungrateful for it. We sometimes lose the sense of initial spellbound wonder that leaves the eyes popping out of our heads; we begin to cool off in our relationship with him as we become more sophisticated in our outlook, and when that happens we start to take God's grace for granted.

I cannot help but think of the words of John Newton when he wrote, *'If I ever reach heaven, I expect to find three wonders there: first, to meet some I had not thought to see there; second, to miss some I had thought to meet there; and third, the greatest wonder of all, to find myself there.'*

I think John and Paul are batting from the same crease when they talk about the love of God. We remember Paul's description of the love of God in Ephesians 3:18 when he speaks of its four dimensions:

- *It is so high, we can never get over it.*
- *It is so deep, we can never get to the bottom of it.*
- *It is so wide, we can never get around it.*
- *It is so long, we never come to the end of it.*

The well-known gospel song sums it up beautifully when it says,

Could we with ink the ocean fill,
and were the skies of parchment made,
Were every stalk on earth a quill,
and every man a scribe by trade,
To write the love of God above
would drain the ocean dry,
Nor could the scroll contain the whole,
though stretched from sky to sky.

The *'wow'* of God's love

The unsurpassed theme of this almost-too-good-to-be-true verse is a glorious reality in your life and mine for, as John says, his great love is *'lavished'* on us! John wants us to grasp how radically different from all other sorts of love God's *agape* love really is.

The AV translation begins the verse with the word 'behold' and that is an excellent place to start, it gets right to the heart of what John is saying. It gives more of a feel of what John actually wrote. It is an aorist imperative which conveys the idea of 'look!' or 'see!' The force is such that we need to take time to allow its reality to sink down into the depths of our being. The penny needs to drop. He says, 'Take a long lingering look until it really registers, until it clicks!'

It is the 'wow!' syndrome for we are truly startled and staggered when we try to comprehend it. Our response to such a mind-blowing discovery is to pose the question, 'What sort of love is this?'

It is interesting to note that the word John employs in the text is one which originally meant 'of what country?' Again this comes out very powerfully in the AV with the inclusion of the word 'manner' in the text. It is a word which conveys the idea of something we are not used to or something we did not expect to find. For example, the disciples used the word in Matthew 8:27 and Mark 4:41 when they were stunned with the ability of Jesus to still the tempestuous storm on the Sea of Galilee. They exclaimed, 'What manner of man is this? Even the wind and the waves obey him!'

In other words, the man who did this is in a different category from anyone we have come across before; and when we stop and think about it, that is equally true of the Father's love for us. It is virtually unheard-of! As the song says, 'Such love, springs from eternity.'

A love that leaves us lost for words

It seems to me, John cannot find words to echo the sentiments of his heart. All he can do is celebrate it, rejoice in it and experience it. He did not try to define it, he did not attempt to explain it; all he could reasonably do was thank God for it!

His love has reached out to us in the depths of our need; it found us where we were, in the pits of our human experience.

No matter how low we have sunk in the gutter of sin, no matter how far away we were from the Lord, his love is so wonderful that it has brought us in from the cold into the warmth of his global family. It needs to be said that he is the one who made all the running; he is the one who not only took the initiative, he also seized the moment of opportunity to draw us to himself.

John goes on to explain that this new identity within the family of God is no mere formal title. It is not just a computer generated certificate that we frame and hang on the wall of our lounge. It is more than that, much more, for there has been a real change in our practical experience too. We are called the children of God because that is, *de facto*, what we are.

We share his status!

Not only does he give us his name (for he calls us the children of

God), but he gives us his status as well. John hints at that in verse 2 when he says, *'Now we are children of God'*. This is not legal fiction, this is not wishful thinking, this is an eternal reality. It may be fantastic to bask in the sunshine of the truth that we are personally chosen by the Father; at the same time, we have to face the chilling reality of John's closing comment in verse 1 where he tells us that we are shunned by the world. The world did not know Jesus, the world did not recognise Jesus, they did not know who he was. The fact is, they should have known better for he was no mere man.

No ordinary man ever before had lived as Jesus lived on this earth; no ordinary man ever did what he was able to do; and because they did not know who he was, they mistreated him. All he wanted to do was love them and die for their sins, but they constantly reviled and ridiculed him. That is what happened to Jesus. John says, we cannot expect any different! We cannot hope for any better treatment! We cannot anticipate an easier lifestyle!

The bottom line is, the world will not appreciate who we are and it certainly will not acknowledge the one to whom we belong. It will call us cranks and fanatics! We will be seen as misfits in society. We will be viewed as some kind of oddball in the community. We will be subject to scorn and jibe. We will be held up to all kinds of verbal taunt. We will be the butt of many a joke.

Well, that is what we are promised, but we need to remember we are pilgrims passing through en route to a far better land. We do not really belong down here! You see, their attitude should not surprise us; if anything, we should expect it. Basically, the world is sceptical of our personal relationship with God. At the end of the day though, they cannot rob us of our intimacy with the Almighty!

Our potential in God

In verse 2 John highlights the nature of our potential. He says, *'Dear friends, now we are the children of God'*. That is the here and now, that is today! Then he goes on to say, *'... and what we will be has not yet been made known'.* That is the there and then, that is tomorrow!

We can look at it like this: if we know the Lord today, we can say, 'Thank God, I'm not what I used to be, and I may not be what I ought to be, but, praise him, I'm not yet what I'm going to be, by the grace of God.' You see, great potential lies ahead for all of God's dear children.

In some ways, we see it anticipated! We sense the expectancy in his words. They are throbbing with vigour, they are pulsating with life, they are fast flowing with energy. We feel the anticipation in what John says, *'and what we will be has not yet been made known'.*

John is really excited when he says, 'Why, we haven't seen yet what God has in store for those who really belong to him!' He has a thrilling destiny for us. There is coming a day when Jesus will return, when he will break through the clouds, and when he does, he wants to introduce his children to a watching world. According to Paul in 2 Thessalonians 1:10 that is the magic moment when he will be admired in us. He is going to show off his people with a sense of divine pride; they are his family and he is really chuffed and elated because of that!

We are also reminded in Colossians 3:4 that, 'When Christ who is your life appears, then you also will appear with him in glory.' A great day awaits the people of God! This is what makes a world of difference between the destiny of the lost person and the destiny of the person who knows Jesus as Lord and Saviour.

When someone grows old without Jesus, all he can do is look back; when someone advances in years and he knows the Lord, he can look forward into the future with the exhilarating prospect of a bright and better tomorrow. He can live, as it were, sitting on the edge of his seat, standing on his tiptoes, because of what is just around the corner!

It is something we see actualised for the key phrase is *'when he appears'.* That means, when Jesus comes, everything God intended for us when he saved us will become reality. It will all come together in the twinkling of an eye.

Basically, God saved us in order to make us like Jesus. We may not look much like him now, but he has not finished with us yet! The resemblance today may be slim, but then it will be perfect. He says, *'We shall be like him, for we shall see him as he is!'* What wonderful words they are!

We shall see him ...

We shall see him, but how? John says, *'as he is'*. That is just great for it is not 'as he was'. If it were, it would be as a man among men, despised and rejected; it would be as one hanging on a cross of shame; it would be as one buried in a borrowed tomb in a floral garden.

But it will be, *'as he is'*. One enthroned on high, one exalted far above all, one ruling and reigning - the Lord of glory, the all-victorious one, the Lamb upon the throne, the crowned sovereign!

Yes, in that wonderful day, we will see the King in all his beauty!

... and be like him!

The icing on the cake is that we will not only see him, we will be like him! When John says this, he is not suggesting that God intends to populate heaven with millions of clones of Jesus Christ. Someone has said, 'It is one of the most distinctive features of the Christian hope that individual personality is preserved in eternity.'

Take heart! We are not going to be dissolved into some impersonal soup or goulash of spiritual energy which is what some of the cults believe. Nor are we going to be moulded into the stereotyped uniformity of the classless society, as Karl Marx would have it. The diversity of the human race is not in question.

It is the moral likeness of Christ that John is primarily speaking of here. We will share the sinlessness of Jesus, we will know purity of heart and mind and character, we will be saved to sin no more! He will change our bodies into a glorified body just like his! Mortal will give way to immortality and that which is corruptible will become incorruptible.

The bonuses of this transformation are incredible. Blind people will see Jesus with opened eyes! Deaf people will hear the voice and words of Jesus! Lame people will walk hand-in-hand with him! There will be no deficiency, no disease, and no death.

I think it is fair to say, there will be satisfaction of heart for in the words of Psalm 17:15, 'And I - in righteousness I shall see your face; when I awake, I shall be satisfied with seeing your likeness.' Our souls will never thirst again for things eternal. We will be taken up with him, we will be taken in with him, and our hearts will be blissfully content!

That leads on to John's next thought which he shares with us in verse 3. He says, *'Everyone who has this hope in him purifies himself, just as he is pure.'* There are two points worth mulling over in our minds.

To be hopeful

The big question is, 'Where is our hope? On what does our hope rest?' A better rendering of the phrase is, *'every man that has his hope set on him'.* The emphasis is not on the hope that we have in our heart, but on that on which our hope is resting. That is why we sing the gospel hymn, 'My hope is built on nothing less, than Jesus' blood and righteousness.'

Our hope is *in* the Lord, our hope is *on* the Lord.

To be holy

In a challenging turn of phrase, John links our hope to our personal holiness. The coming of Jesus is an incentive to live a life that is pleasing to the Lord. Such a cherished belief should stimulate us and motivate us to a life of walking close with the Lord. We will want to be the kind of people God wants us to be.

As always, the supreme example is the Lord Jesus himself. He never purified himself: he did not need to, he did not have to, he is inherently pure; but he demonstrated that whiter-than-white character in this filthy dirty hostile world, this same world in which we are called to display it. Therein lies the enormous challenge facing each of us at this point in time. That is where the rubber hits the road!

Having said that, it is the least we can do when we think of the prodigious love which he has so generously lavished on us. How can we do anything else than seek to honour him in all our ways? By implication, we have something to live for today, we have so much to look forward to in the future, and best of all, we have Jesus with us each passing moment. We will be with him and we will be like him for the never-ending aeons of eternity. That spells L-O-V-E!

3:4-8

To sin or not to sin …

That is the hot potato John is handling in this section. John tells it like it is in verse 4. As always, he pulls no punches, he gives it to them straight from the shoulder. He says in the opening phrase, *'Everyone who sins breaks the law'*. John cannot possibly make it any clearer than that, nothing could be more plain or simple! If we sin, we break the law of God! If we go our own way, if we do our own thing, if we think we know better, we are flying in the face of God's statute! We are flouting the command of God!

The closing phrase in verse 4 gives one of the most concise definitions of sin recorded anywhere in Scripture. It says, *'Sin is lawlessness'*. It has to be said, there are some commentators who feel that John's understanding of sin in this verse is rather naïve and superficial. They suggest he puts sin on the same level as someone breaking a set of rules or someone not adopting a code of practice. And yet when we place John's definition under the spotlight and subject it to a closer examination, it could not be better, it certainly cannot be improved upon.

I am sure John would be horrified if he thought he was being misrepresented like that; I have not the slightest doubt that John did not think of sin in such a narrow way and I am equally convinced that the word *'lawlessness'* does not imply that he did. What John is saying here is that the root of all sin is rebellion against God's authority and God's standards. That goes against the grain, I realise that. It is not in vogue to label sin like that; it is not the kind of comment we dare make in the public arena. If we think like that, we will never rise in the popularity stakes!

'Don't blame me, blame my genes!'

We hear a lot these days about the reasons why people do what they do and why they act in a particular manner in a given situation. It is all put down to certain propensities we have within us or other outside factors which influence us. We tend to blame this, that and the other! We wash our hands and say, 'I can't help it!' And every time we do that, we refuse to accept personal responsibility for our behaviour.

Sad to say, this trendy mindset has infected so much of our modern 'politically correct' thinking. Someone has said it well in describing this syndrome in rather colourful language as 'humanistic claptrap'. I think the Bible makes it abundantly clear that:

- sin is not the product of genetic inheritance or adolescent hormones,
- sin is not excusable on grounds of a deprived upbringing or cultural conditioning,
- sin is not a relic of evolutionary origins or an artefact of social development,
- sin is an attitude of moral anarchy!

'Why should I?' is the question everybody asks!

- The sulky child weeps it when he is told to tidy his room and put his toys away.
- The petulant teenager demands it when told to switch off the telly and do his homework.
- The irate employee mutters it when he is told by management to be more punctual.

- Adam said it when he was told to leave the tree of knowledge alone in the Garden of Eden.
- From that day to this, every sinner has said it! You have said it, I have said it, we have all said it!

That is what sin is! It is a blunt refusal to accept the authority of God over our lives, it is the failure to conform to God's norms for our lives.

The story is told about little Judy who was riding in the car with her father when she decided to stand up on the front seat. Her father told her to sit down and put on the seat belt, but she declined. He told her a second time and, again, she defiantly refused. 'If you don't sit down immediately, I'll pull over to the side of the road and spank you!' her father said. Judy did what she was told. She obeyed him! But they had travelled only a short distance down the road when Judy turned and whispered to her father, *'Daddy, I may be sitting down, but I'm still standing up inside!'*

Good story! Maybe, but it illustrates what sin is all about and we can see why John defined it the way he did. He said, sin is lawlessness, sin is rebellion!

The sin remedy ... Jesus!

Thank God, John did not stop there. If he had, we would still be grovelling in the dirt. He goes on to tell us about the remedy for the sin problem and, in verse 5, the main beam is shining on Jesus Christ. The apostle writes, *'But you know that he appeared so that he might take away our sins. And in him is no sin.'* This is a classic verse for it highlights for us the wonderful nature of the person and work of Christ.

He is presented to us as one who is sinless, one who is perfect, one who is without fault, one in whom there is no flaw, one without blemish or spot. He is someone with no stain on his character, there is no dark blot on his personality.

We read elsewhere the unambiguous testimonies of Peter and Paul where they both declare, 'he committed no sin' and 'he had no sin'. This triple affirmation from a trio of ordinary men, Peter, Paul and John, men who were extremely conscious of their own shortcomings, says a lot about the one who turned their world upside down and transformed their lives inside out.

Jesus did what no-one else could do! He paid the price for our redemption, he gave himself on our behalf so that he might secure our eternal salvation, he died for you, he died for me! He alone was able to do it because he alone is sinless!

He did not need a Saviour for himself for, as John confirms, *'in him is no sin'*. You see, only someone who was sinless in himself could effectively atone for the sins of others. That explains why the cross is at the heart of the Christian gospel. It is God's sole answer to man's deepest need. We understand that best when we have come as sinners to Jesus and knelt by faith at Calvary, when forgiveness has become a wonderful reality in our hearts, when we have tasted and seen that the Lord is good, when we discover that sin is no longer the flavour of the day.

Watch this space ... see the difference!

It is found in John's bold statement in verse 6 where he says, *'No-one who lives in him keeps on sinning.'* (By the way, that is in the present continuous tense!) And John goes on to say, *'No-one who continues to sin* (and that is in the same tense) *has either seen him or known him.'*

John is not primarily interested in what we are doing day by day for the Lord, nor is he supremely concerned with all that is happening in our interpersonal relationships with other members of God's global family. What matters to him is this: what is our attitude to sin, how do we treat it, how do we view it.

The punchline is, do we keep on sinning? John puts all his cards on the table when he unequivocally declares that the person who continues to engage deliberately or habitually in sin has not yet *'seen'* or *'known'* Christ. In other words, such a person has never truly been born again; he has never felt the joy and thrill of divine forgiveness; he has never known the sweet reality of being reconciled to his God.

Oh I know, he may have raised his hand at the end of an evangelistic meeting, he may have signed a decision card, he may have been counselled by one of his peers, he may have done all sorts of things and made all sorts of commitments but, the harsh reality is, if the life has not changed, the hard question must be asked and it cannot be avoided: does such an individual know the Lord? If he does, sin will no longer be a way of life to him! He will be significantly different!

This does not mean to say we will not have our moments when we slip and fall, *for we will*; it does not mean we will not face any struggles with temptation, *for we will*; it does not mean we will not let the Lord down, *for we will*; it does not mean we will not fail the Lord, *for we will*; but when we do, we can be forgiven!

What we need to always remember is this, forgiveness is at the expense of the precious blood of the Son of God. It cost him his life! Grace is free, but it is not cheap.

The implication from John's incisive and sharp comment is this, the mark of genuine appreciation to God is that we do not keep on sinning! We are not sinless, we never will be this side of heaven, but as God's grace works in our hearts and lives, we sin less and less as time marches on! The pattern of our life is not to sin, the practice of our life is not to sin.

To be a son in the family and keep on sinning against the Father, according to John, is mutually contradictory, it is wholly incompatible. So far as the Christian is concerned, we can look at it like this: sin is the exception, not the rule!

Some obvious pitfalls

John begins verse 7 with his customary greeting when he calls them *'dear children'*. Having warmed their heart with such an affectionate introduction, he proceeds to caution them when he says, *'Do not let anyone lead you astray. He who does what is right is righteous, just as he is righteous.'*

He continues in verse 8a with a further remarkable insight into such unacceptable behaviour when he says, *'He who does what is sinful is of the devil, because the devil has been sinning from the beginning.'* The chances are you have probably noticed that in this section spanning 2:29 through to 3:10, John is giving us a series of identikit pictures of two staggeringly different groups of people.

There are those who do right as in 2:29, and those who keep on sinning as in 3:4,5; there are those who live in Christ and those who have neither seen him nor known him as in 3:6; there are those who do what is right as in 3:7, and those who do what is sinful as in 3:8; there are those who do not continue to sin as in 3:9, and those who do not do right and do not love the brothers as in 3:10.

When we focus on 3:8, the two groups can be easily recognised as two families of people with two heads. Group number one is the children of God and group number two is the children of the devil. The bottom line is, if a tree bears apples, we can tell it is an apple tree; if a branch bears grapes, we can tell it is a vine; the same criterion holds good in today's world for today's generation. Jesus said as much in Matthew 7:16 when he advised us that 'by their fruit you will recognise them.'

What you see isn't always what you get!

The dilemma John faced was this, it is relatively easy for a person who is mature in the faith to smell a rat and spot someone who is not all that they claim to be. An 'older' believer has much more experience and we cannot buy that on a supermarket shelf; he has insights into the teaching of Scripture, he may even have the rare gift of spiritual discernment.

So, on the whole, it is not those who have been on the road for quite a while that John is concerned about; it is those who are young in the faith, those who are just taking their first faltering steps. They are more vulnerable than most and are fairly soft targets for those who want to take them for a ride and exploit them. This is the real danger confronting a new generation of believers and that is why John faces the problem head on. The false teachers looked really good, their ministry sounded exceptionally rich and helpful. The fact is, it was far too good to be true!

Even the devil can stand in a pulpit and pontificate on the doctrines of grace and glory, but he is like a wolf dressed in a sheepskin jacket. Even the devil can sit around a table drinking tea or coffee and talking theology, but he does it as an angel of light!

John wants to underline the message that appearances are not everything. At the end of the day they count for very little. We cannot judge a book by its cover. We cannot judge a man by his mantle.

It is the lifestyle of the speaker that makes the difference. It is what he does when he is out of the glare of the public eye. It is what he is at home with his wife and kids. It is the things he does and the way he reacts when his guard is down.

It was certainly true in John's day and it is equally valid in the third millennium - actions speak louder than words! If people know the Lord, they will do the things that are right. If they continue to sin and divert our attention away from the Lord Jesus, we can tell they are not the friends of God, they are sons of the evil one.

The devil is no gentleman, he is a spiritual rapist. He awaits an opportunity, not an invitation, to assault us.

Anyone with an ounce of spiritual sense knows he is not a brilliant example to follow, he is not a particularly good example to emulate. From day one, he has been sinning; from the first day, he had his own agenda, he has been playing a game of one-upmanship ever since with the God of heaven! He is not content to play second fiddle, he wants to be number one in the pecking order.

His problem ... our problem

That is his problem, and that same mentality has filtered through to each of his children; it is a classic case of, like father, like son! The devil was the very first sinner, and sinners today without Christ are his posterity. We may not always appreciate the fact, but we live on a planet which is submerged in a state of cosmic civil war. Our personalities are now enemy occupied territory. That is our problem and that is the principal reason why Jesus came.

The divine masterplan

If we had been capable of pleasing the Lord through our own efforts, if we had been capable of getting to heaven under our own steam, there would have been no need for such an extraordinary stratagem on God's part. He could have managed without Jesus and we would have no need of a Saviour. But the fact is, we have no hope without one!

I like the way one commentator has expressed it. He says, 'Like a computer in a science fiction thriller, the universe is in the perverted grip of an evil hacker, and it needs somebody to come in from outside to emancipate us from that programme loop of wickedness in which we are so helplessly confined.'

That, says John, is why Jesus appeared, it was in order to take away sin. We read in verse 8b, *'The reason the Son of God appeared was to destroy the devil's work.'* The root meaning of the verb which John employs here means 'to untie and so to set free'. It is used of the donkey on which Jesus made his kingly entry into Jerusalem on that first Palm Sunday, as in Matthew 21:2. It is also used of Lazarus' grave clothes being unwound when Jesus raised him up, as in John 11:44. It also came to be used of breaking up something into its component parts, tearing down a building, for instance, and so destroying it.

This gives us John's precise meaning here in terms of doing away with the devil's works. It seems to me, the overriding purpose of the incarnation was to demolish and bring to an end the work of the devil. And thank God, Jesus succeeded! Christ came not only to set the captives free, he came to destroy the captor. The coming of Christ, the cross of Christ, spells total triumph over all the hostile forces which have tied us in knots and bound us in chains of sin which we cannot loose. But what we could never do and what others could never do for us, Jesus did! He achieved what was, humanly speaking, impossible!

- *If our greatest need had been information, God would have sent an educator.*
- *If our greatest need had been technology, God would have sent a scientist.*
- *If our greatest need had been money, God would have sent an economist.*
- *Since our greatest need was forgiveness, God sent a Saviour!*

It is of the utmost importance that we grasp this: Jesus did not come primarily as a teacher to improve our moral education; he came as a sacrifice to make atonement for our lawlessness. Jesus did not come primarily as an example to demonstrate the way of love; he came as a warrior to win a victory over spiritual hosts of wickedness and to liberate us from their power.

This is the ethos of what John is saying here in chapter 3, this is the heartbeat of John's message, the entire purpose of Jesus was to overcome the power of sin in our lives. Since that is the case, John asks how we can possibly continue to surrender to it (we find that alluded to in verse 6).

Someone has wisely written, 'Every sin a Christian commits he knows he adds directly to the burden Christ bore on the cross. Every failure to conform to God's standards denies the spiritual victory Jesus won there and grants the devil grounds for hope. Nobody who understands why Christ came can possibly live in anything but a state of unceasing war against sin.'

I like to think of it like this: the devil has done untold damage and seeks to complete his work of woe, but Christ has restored his people and will complete his work of grace.

John reached an all-time high with the powerful declaration of the Saviour's intention to trounce the enemy. What a wonderful affirmation that is of the ability of God to overthrow the foe; it is a firm guarantee that the Lord has triumphed over sin and death! The long-term impact of that victory on your life and mine is quite incredible for it introduces an eternal dimension to our salvation and, in the short term, it means we can live a life on planet earth which is on a level we never previously enjoyed.

A radical change!

Jesus not only brings us freedom from the penalty of sin, he gives us a measure of release from the power of sin. He brings us into a dynamic relationship with himself and when we abide in him we quickly discover that sin is no longer our master, it no longer rules over us! We are different from what we were before, we are not the same people. Things have radically changed in our lives.

3:9-15

The ultimate goal ... holiness

It seems to me that is what John is focusing on in the first part of verse 9 where he says, *'No-one who is born of God will continue to sin, because God's seed remains in him.'* The unbelievable difference in our lives is attributed to the presence of the Holy Spirit living within us. God is the difference! Our attitude to sin is not what it used to be in our previous life, in our pre-conversion days. Then we ran after it and fell headlong into it; now we aim and aspire to run a mile in the opposite direction! We run away from it!

The singular reference to *'seed'* in this verse is a fascinating one. It is probably a cryptic comment on John's part and I think the clue to understanding his meaning is to recognise that John is probably using the vocabulary of the false teachers and trying to steal their thunder. He wants to play them at their own game. There is plenty of evidence to suggest the Gnostics taught that by means of a mystical vision of God a human being could actually become divine. I know it sounds a bit far-fetched but they labelled this process 'being fertilised by the divine seed'.

When we think of it like that, what John is demonstrating here is that there is an element of truth in what the Gnostics were saying, for there is always a tissue of truth in every powerful lie, there has to be or nobody would ever give it credence. You see, as the people of God, we do become partakers of the divine nature. Peter tells us that in his first epistle. Someone has observed, 'Our experience of God is not just a contractual arrangement, it is also a spiritual transformation.'

God does not merely shake our hands and wish us all the best with the rest of our lives; no, he regenerates our hearts, his is a deep work of grace within us.

His seed is in us and, in a sense, that is what makes the analogy of adoption an inadequate one; in human terms, when parents adopt a child, though they may give their child the legal status of being a son or a daughter, they cannot actually work the miracle of making that child biologically their own. There is the difference. They cannot do it, but God can!

If you like, when God adopts us into his global family, he shares his genes with us. His seed abides in us. For you and for me, it entails our entering into a brand new relationship and it also means we receive a completely new nature, God's own nature! We are the children of God and John has emphasised that glorious truth elsewhere in this epistle.

Because of that, it means we grow up to bear the family likeness. So far as John is concerned, this is another powerful reason why we must be holy. Sin is fundamentally inconsistent with our new birth, the two do not mix, they are mutually incompatible. Hence the terse comment at the end of verse 9, *'He cannot go on sinning, because he has been born of God.'*

I think it needs to be emphasised here that the last thing on John's mind is the possibility of attaining sinless perfection in this life. Some well-meaning folks and certain denominations have gone down that road and have taken these verses as a foundation for that line of teaching. The fact is, when we compare this verse with John's comments elsewhere, especially those in 1:8-10, it is clear that John is not flying the flag for such an impossible and unrealistic experience this side of glory.

It is progressive

We will never be sinless on planet earth but we should be sinning less and less as we grow in grace and make maturity in Christ our ambition.

I think this is fairly apparent when we look at verse 9 in detail and examine carefully the Greek tenses that are involved. All the verbs in this verse are in the present tense and in Greek this implies continuity of action.

We can put it like this: John's view is that what the seed of God does in the experience of the Christian is to break the habit of sin. It changes the general tenor of our lives from drifting towards sin to one that is geared towards righteousness, with the result that the Christian does not go on sinning as he used to do. Oh yes, we will sin in thought, word and deed, and we do sin, but we do not make a habit of it. That is the point which John wants to drive home.

An old Methodist evangelist named Dr Morrison taught the doctrine of holiness and it was said that he came closer to practising it than most folks do. Someone said to the preacher one day, with tongue in cheek, 'Dr Morrison, have you reached a point in your life where you cannot sin?' Dr Morrison wisely replied, with a twinkle in his eye, *'No, my brother, I have not yet arrived at such a place, but I can tell you where I am right now; I have come to a place where I sin but cannot enjoy it.'* That is the secret, it really is! The key question is, is that where I am today in my relationship with the Lord? Have I come to such a place in my life, a place where I sin but cannot enjoy it?

The challenge facing each of us is this, how do we get victory over sin? Remember in 1 Corinthians 15:45 the apostle Paul is talking about the old Adam, the first Adam, and he implies that is our old nature. We know from the same portion of Scripture that the 'last Adam' is Jesus. We can look at it like this: when temptation comes knocking at the door of our life, we have two choices - we can send the 'old Adam' to the door and end up sinning; or we have the wiser alternative of sending the 'last Adam' to the door, and when Jesus goes to the door, we get victory over that sin.

It is a matter of letting Jesus take over every day and allowing him to answer the door when the tempter rings the bell. You see, for the Christian, holiness is not an optional extra, it is the norm.

Examine the evidence

John establishes a clear link between verses 9 and 10 when he says, *'This is how we know who the children of God are and who the children of the devil are: Anyone who does not do what is right is not a child of God; nor is anyone who does not love his brother.'* That is why it is so important that we grasp what John is teaching in verse 9 regarding the place of holiness in our lives, he tells us here in verse 10 that our assurance of salvation depends upon it.

This is a clear and decisive test that John has given to us, here is one of the ways in which we can tell the child of God from the child of the devil. It is the old saying, isn't it, the proof of the pudding is in the eating! If a person is a genuine believer in Christ, then his life will match it; if he does not know the Lord Jesus as Saviour, then the traits displayed in his character will indicate that he still belongs to the devil. It is as simple as that!

In verse 10 John draws a line in the sand with his sweeping statement regarding the distinguishing marks of the authentic believer in the family of God; his parting shot though is one which takes up our interest for a short while for it leads on quite naturally to his next topic, that of our love for one another in the family of God.

The message is an old one, it is timeless, it is changeless, we have heard it many times, it has been around from day one! And we have it right here in verse 11 where John says, *'This is the message you heard from the beginning: We should love one another.'* This is a theme which is very close to the heart of the old apostle; in fact, it is a word which he uses nearly fifty times in the compass of five brief chapters. Some of John's thoughts on the subject are among the most memorable and moving in the entire Bible.

Powerful and appealing as they are, I believe there is a serious danger that we can miss the wood for the trees, there is a chance that we could miss the boat if we read his words through the filter of our contemporary sex-mad culture. John is certainly not referring here to some kind of emotional erotic experience, it has nothing to do with romantic feelings which leave us on a high, there is nothing ecstatic or mystical about it either.

The love which John is propagating is *agape* love. It is ironic, but in classical Greek it was a rather vague and colourless word. When John employs it in his writings he takes it the way that it is and he paints a picture beside it which would forever define *agape* in the Christian vocabulary. He lifts it on to a higher plane and he gives it a superb spiritual dimension which leaves us gasping for breath at the sheer wonder and beauty of it all.

So the love which John is talking about here is a love which impacts our lives, it influences our interpersonal relationships, it shapes our thinking, it colours our lifestyle, it flows through our spiritual veins, for love is at the heart of our relationship with God.

By the same token, love is also the hallmark of our faith in God. It is an indispensable mark of a faith that is real, it is the badge worn on the lapel of a real Christian. Paul was beating the same drum when he wrote in Galatians 5:6 that, 'The only thing that counts is faith expressing itself through love.' For his part, John's major concern is to explore and expand on the idea of what brotherly love means in the nitty-gritty of life.

Sound advice

What does it mean in the rough and tumble of life in the third millennium? We discovered in verse 10 that John grouped mankind into two different families: there are those who are members of God's family and there are those who remain as children of the devil.

Each family has a different mission or purpose statement, each family has a different set of core values, each family has a different way of looking at events as they unfold in daily life, each family approaches love from a different angle or perspective.

That is what John is developing here in this closing section of chapter 3. He targets each family and he elaborates on the basic attitudes and actions of each. The family of the devil is represented by Cain and the family of God is ably depicted by Jesus Christ.

John makes an emphatic and bold statement of fact when he pigeonholes Cain in verse 12. He says quite dogmatically, *'Do not be like Cain, who belonged to the evil one and murdered his brother.'* He progresses his argument further with a rhetorical question when he asked, *'And why did he murder him?'* The simple answer is a summary of the condition of Cain's heart for John says, *'Because his own actions were evil and his brother's were righteous.'* We read all about this horrible incident in Genesis 4.

The end result

Bearing in mind what Cain did to Abel, we should not be in the least surprised if the man in the street shows a similar enmity to us as the people of God. That is why John says in verse 13, *'Do not be surprised, my brothers, if the world hates you.'* We cannot expect any better treatment from those who do not know Jesus as Lord and Saviour.

Cain's basic problem was one of heart rebellion, it was a clash of wills. He wanted to come to God his way and he wanted to bring to God what suited him best. God was not amused, God was not impressed. And the net result was that, in a fit of pique, in a moment of madness, Cain butchered his brother. It was senseless and brutal.

He refused to recognise the authority of God, he refused to accede to the demands of a holy God. His anger boiled over, he flipped, he lost it, and innocent Abel paid the supreme sacrifice. It is worth noting that the Bible says that the first baby ever born turned out to be a murderer and the second one was the victim of his big brother's malice. Cain was tragically consumed with hatred towards his brother.

What was true in his day is also evident in our day. Hatred is still the world's currency; no matter where we travel, we are sure to find it is a cosmic problem. And so today, many of our brothers and sisters in Christ are being persecuted, a number of them are imprisoned, and some of them are laying down their lives for the sake of the gospel. This is happening because men and their ideologies are implacably opposed to the gospel of God's dear Son.

It should not surprise us. We have to face up to it and some in God's global family have to live with it day after day. We should never forget that the world is no friend of the Christian! Look at how they treated the Lord Jesus. If that is what they did to him, in all honesty and with more than a hint of realism, we cannot expect any more favourable treatment. Jesus never promised us a bed of roses. All he encouraged us to do was take up a cross and follow after him!

Staring death in the face

John puts all his cards on the table when he says at the end of verse 14 and into verse 15 that, *'Anyone who does not love remains in death. Anyone who hates his brother is a murderer, and you know that no murderer has eternal life in him.'*

John does not mince his words. The inference from his comments is quite staggering for it leaves people in absolutely no doubt as to where they stand in relation to God. There are no shades of grey so far as the apostle is concerned, it is black and white, it is cut and dried.

In actual fact, this is not vintage John riding one of his hobby horses. It goes right back to the words of Jesus as recorded in the Sermon on the Mount in Matthew 5:21,22. He said, 'You have heard that it was said to the people long ago, "Do not murder, and anyone who murders will be subject to judgment." But I tell you that anyone who is angry with his brother will be subject to judgment.' That rings a bell, doesn't it!

It seems to me, John and Jesus see a connecting link between hate and homicide. There is a difference between throwing a dagger at our neighbour with our eyes and throwing it literally with our hands. That is true, but the root of the problem remains the same, for it stems from hatred in a sinful heart.

From God's vantage point in heaven, the attitude and the action are equally despicable: both indicate an affinity with Cain, both find their roots in hell, both can be traced back to the devil.

Is there an alternative?

I am just so grateful that John does not paint only one picture for us to look at! Thank God, there is an alternative and it is the way of love. He says as much in verse 14 where we read, *'We know that we have passed from death to life, because we love our brothers.'* That is the contrast! Whereas it is the nature of hate to take life, says John, it is the nature of love to surrender life.

Someone has said with remarkable insight, 'The Marxist revolution will never create a loving society because its commitment to violence puts it on the side of Cain, not of Abel.' When we read the gospel narrative, it is clear that Jesus demonstrated that the only way to build a community where *agape* prevails was by carrying a cross, not by wielding a machine gun; by giving our own life, not by taking the life of another. That is the glaring difference between love and hate. And it is seen best when we look at Calvary.

Calvary is all about a God who reaches down to where we are; it is a love which takes the initiative, it meets us at the point of our need, it lifts us by faith into heaven itself.

John says, when we have this love in our hearts and when we show it to those around us, we have the growing conviction within that we really do belong to Jesus Christ. It confirms our position in the family of God and it affirms our standing as the people of God.

3:16-20

Actions speak louder than words!

That is a familiar saying to most of us. It is one we have heard many times over the years and when we stop to think about it, it is true! We can talk from now until doomsday, but if our life does not match our words, we may as well forget it. What we do matters a lot more than what we say!

Jesus' response to a need

That is the point John is making when he gives us a brilliant definition of love in verse 16 where he says, *'This is how we know what love is: Jesus Christ laid down his life for us.'* We cannot improve on that, we cannot better that; this is the benchmark, it is the supreme example, it is the illustration *par excellence.*

The finest exhibition of love is seen when we focus our gaze on Calvary and contemplate the Saviour's work of redemption on our behalf. He died for us, he died in place of us, he took on himself what we all deserve, he bore our punishment, he was willing to subject himself to the torrents of anger and wrath emanating from a holy God as he paid the penalty for our sin.

He did not have to do it, he did not need to do it, he did it because he chose to do it, he did it because he wanted to do it. He did it for you, and thank God, he did it for me!

A hymn which impacted the Welsh revival in a past generation puts it like this,

> *Here is love vast as the ocean,*
> *loving kindness as the flood,*
> *When the Prince of Life, our ransom,*
> *shed for us his precious blood.*
> *Who his love will not remember?*
> *Who can cease to sing his praise?*
> *He can never be forgotten,*
> *throughout heaven's eternal days.*

On the mount of crucifixion,
fountains opened deep and wide;
Through the floodgates of God's mercy,
flowed a vast and gracious tide.
Grace and love, like mighty rivers,
poured incessant from above,
And heaven's peace and perfect justice,
kissed a guilty world in love.

When we reflect on authentic love, we need look no further than Calvary. The cross is all about a God who reaches down from heaven to us, not because he saw anything attractive in us, but because he wanted to save us and secure a bride for his Son. We were by nature his enemies, we were on the side of the opposition, we were guilty, hell-deserving and devil-embracing sinners, we were repulsive to his pure unsullied holiness. Yet this God of grace and mercy, in a sovereign act of free will, set his love upon us and drew us to himself. That is love! That is *agape* love! That is divine love! That is God's love!

As someone has said, 'It needs no aphrodisiac to turn it on. It is a love born out of a heart whose nature and purpose is love. It is a love which takes the initiative, and that not in self-seeking passion but in self-denying grace.'

John's brief statement in verse 16 tells us three vitally important truths about the death of the Lord Jesus:

- **his death was voluntary** for he laid down his life. This is the rich quality found in the character of the one who referred to himself as the 'good shepherd' in John 10 and,

- **his death was vicarious** for he died on behalf of others. He laid down his life for us! The preposition *'for'* is of mega importance in the phrase I have just quoted. It means 'in place of, instead of' and the implication is crystal clear. It suggests that the death of Jesus Christ was substitutionary and,

- **his death was victorious**. The tense of the verb which John employs here is crucial to our understanding of the text. The words *'laid down'* signify a once-for-all action. When Jesus died on the cross, he exclaimed in triumph, 'It is finished!' That means, his death was that of a champion having pulled off a massive coup against the old enemy.

So when we talk about love, the pre-eminent example is that of Jesus. He is the prototype!

Our response to a need

John does not stop there. He takes his argument to a logical conclusion when he says at the end of verse 16, *'And we ought to lay down our lives for our brothers.'* The test of our commitment and love to Jesus Christ will be seen in our attitude to our brothers and sisters in the worldwide family of God. If that is what Jesus did for us, the least we can do is to show a similar spirit on behalf of others in the household of faith.

Our relationship with others will be one of love; we will do for them and we will share with them without any thought of ourselves. We will freely give to them without counting the cost and with no thought of getting anything in return. This kind of love does not look to be reciprocated, it is happy to give, and it is happy to keep on giving even when it runs the high risk of being spurned or, perhaps, less than appreciated or maybe even misunderstood.

Investors in people

The thought which John advocates is a willingness to invest our lives in others so that they too might experience the enriching love of God. And if the crunch came, we should be willing to sacrifice our lives for their sake.

A senior student once told the graduating class of a California high school, *'Class, I want you always to remember, it's your attitude that will determine your altitude!'*

In the light of the apostle's comments in verse 16, I have a feeling he would be happy to go along with that. I think he would agree!

John brings it even closer to home when he poses a serious question in verse 17. This is how he expressed it: *'If anyone has material possessions and sees his brother in need but has no pity on him, how can the love of God be in him?'* What a challenge that is to all our hearts! This is John's theology earthed to reality, he scratches where people are itching.

The punchline is, there is the need, what are we going to do about it? We have plenty of food on our table, we have clothes on our back, we live in beautiful homes, we have all that we need and sometimes we have more than we need; says John, there is a brother with an obvious need, what are we going to do to help him in his hour of crisis? What are we going to do to help alleviate his situation? That is where our love is tested! That is where actions speak louder than words!

When the need is presented to us, what is our initial response? Is it to walk on by with our nose in the air, humming a worship song? Is it to stop, have a closer look and determine not to get involved? Or will we take on board the mindset of the good Samaritan in the parable Jesus told? That is the strategy John is promoting here in verses 16 and 17.

He draws the strands of the argument together when he says in verse 18 in a kind of rallying call to the troops, *'Dear children, let us not love with words or tongue but with actions and in truth.'* The exhortation is a powerful one. He exhorts us not to be loving with the empty evidence of words, but with the genuine evidence of actions. In other words, we need to put our money where our mouth is!

God is not fooled by our fervent prayers for the starving millions. He is much more concerned about how we respond to that particular case of need next door. We see that with John's use of the word *'brother'* in the singular, whereas in the preceding verse, it was in the plural case.

There is little we can do for those starving millions around the world except donate a few pounds or dollars to some worthy cause.

But there is no limit to the big-hearted generosity we might show to the individual down the street if we value him highly enough. It is a matter of keeping everything in perspective. The love John is speaking of is one which focuses primarily on individual personal needs. It is not something we target on a vague generalised beneficence to the human race. The two-liner sums it up well: *'To love the world, to me's no chore; my big trouble, is the man next door!'* Well, we smile at that, but there is a lot of truth in it!

That is what they practised in the early church. They had a genuine concern for the man next door; the early church was renowned not only for its doctrinal purity but also for its down-to-earth expressions of love. The emperor known as Julian the Apostate complained during his relatively short reign from AD 361 to 363 that, 'The impious Galileans support not only their own poor but ours as well.' That is the brand of love John has in mind; it is the kind of love which can successfully impact every community and result in lives being transformed to the glory of God. It is infectious. It is contagious.

We really need to get our act together on this issue and be seen to be proactive in our commitment to one another. There is no room in John's thinking for a cosy and cushioned armchair philanthropy where every thought counts; that kind of faith cuts no ice so far as John is concerned, it is as dead as a dodo. And that kind of love is a poor reflection of Calvary for it is not really love at all. The old preacher, Rabbi Duncan, used to say, 'If you are without love, then the church bell is as good a Christian as you!' Sounds a bit like Paul in 1 Corinthians 13, doesn't it!

The best assurance policy to have

Confidence is the name of the game! That is a key word in the Bible. It makes a world of difference in your life and mine if we know with assurance the one in whom we have believed, the one to whom we have entrusted our future. Assurance of salvation is a tremendous bonus for the believer, living as we do in the third millennium. The corresponding Greek word is the word *parrhesia* which has its roots in the world of politics. It signified the democratic right of free speech. Slowly but surely it came to mean the kind of candid openness that is not afraid to expose itself to public gaze. It is the 'no hidden agenda' syndrome, it is when we put all our cards on the table. It is a word which is frequently used in the book of Acts to describe the fearless way in which the apostles preached the gospel of Christ.

When we come across it in John's epistle it has much more to do with one's personal assurance than with worldwide evangelism. In verse 21 it is used this way where we read, *'Dear friends, if our hearts do not condemn us, we have confidence (parrhesia) before God.'* The same word is found in 4:17 where John informs us, *'Love is made complete among us so that we will have confidence on the day of judgment.'* It is the confidence factor which John is addressing now in his letter. It is all about assurance. In these studies we have looked at a number of tests which an individual can conduct to see if he really is a believer or not; there are certain procedures we can follow which will authenticate our Christian experience or otherwise.

John wants us to be sure, he wants to eliminate all nagging and niggling doubts from our hearts and minds. He longs to remove any trace of uncertainty regarding the reality of our faith in Jesus Christ. We do not always realise that the whole question of assurance or confidence is closely intertwined with the subject of love that we have just been thinking about. There is a connecting link between them; in fact, the more we read of John in the second half of his book, the more obvious it becomes that Christian love and Christian confidence are really two sides of the same coin.

Tantalising ambiguity

Let us see what John says in verses 19 and 20: *'This then is how we know that we belong to the truth, and how we set our hearts at rest in his presence whenever our hearts condemn us. For God is greater than our hearts, and he knows everything.'* Those are fascinating words, they really are! But like so much in the word of God, there is a lot more to it than meets the eye.

I read recently that 'this is a passage which commentators delight in, because it is so pregnant with tantalising ambiguity.' I suppose there are at least half a dozen ways these verses could be legitimately translated. I think the most important issue is the meaning of the phrase tucked away in the middle of verse 20 where John declares that *'God is greater than our hearts'*. If we get this right, then everything else will fall neatly into place!

• *Does this mean severity?* Does John mean that God is greater in the sense that he is likely to be more severe with our failures than we are ourselves?

When all is said and done, our hearts are only aware of a fraction of our sins, but God misses nothing, for the one who is omniscient sees all things.

The question is, is God's overwhelming greatness presented as a serious challenge to us? We can reason like this: if our own morally seared consciences give us no peace of heart and mind, what hope can we have of peace before a God whose holiness is untarnished? That is one way of unpacking the teaching of John in this duo of verses. You will be interested to know this is the way John Calvin and Augustine chose to interpret it. Dr Martyn Lloyd-Jones was singing from the same song sheet for he also believed that this verse is not meant to comfort us but to warn us.

• *Does it mean mercy?* Does John mean that God is greater in the sense that he is able to be more merciful with our failures than we would be ourselves?

Some of us know from personal experience, and we all know from observation, that a person with a sensitive conscience and a tender heart has a hard job forgiving himself. Such people tend to magnify failure and blow it up out of all proportion. When they find themselves in such a blur, they are inclined to obscure the positive and upbeat aspects of their lives. What we need to remember is this, God sees everything in perfect perspective. He sees the entire situation in sharp focus.

If that is the proper way to understand the text, and I think it is, then God's greatness is not seen as a threat to us, it is a source of enormous consolation and comfort. It means, our God is able to overrule all our anxious doubts. He knows us an awful lot better than we think we know ourselves! These words are, therefore, not an indictment against us, but a source of tremendous reassurance for us!

The edge of paradise

The old Puritan, Thomas Brooks, called assurance, 'the suburbs of paradise'. The problem John is wrestling with is that so many of these first century believers felt as though they were living out in the wilds of the bush! I have a hunch that many of us can easily identify with them! I would go further and say that it is par for the course for genuine believers to suffer feelings of spiritual uncertainty. It happens to all of us from time to time. We know the feelings which so easily ravage our minds and we end up on yet another guilt trip. This is what transpires when, as John says, *'our hearts condemn us'*.

It is true that some folks will suffer more than others because of their psychological makeup and because of their temperament, but none of us is immune because nobody is perfect! Any believer worth his salt wants to know whether his faith is real or not. He wants to know if he is anchored to the rock or if he is tied up to some shifting object embedded in quicksand.

The prayer of David in Psalm 139:23,24 for God to 'search him' is a reasonable one to pray in such circumstances. On the one hand, the unbeliever will find the experience too hot to handle; on the other hand, the Christian will be affirmed in his faith. He will be strengthened as a direct result of it.

So, when the going gets tough, we need to make a beeline to God. We need to zoom in on the character of God. We need to appreciate who God is and what our God is like. That seems to be the gist of verse 20. Paul was batting from a similar crease when he penned Romans 8:31,32 where he says, 'What shall we say to these things? If God is for us, who can be against us? He who did not spare his own Son but delivered him up for us all, how shall he not with him also freely give us all things?'

Yes, there are occasions in your life and mine when we need to be reminded of the awful holiness of God and there are plenty of other times when we need to be reminded of his abounding graciousness and his unfailing and undying love. Even when we feel as though our backs are to the wall and that we have been dragged through a thorn bush backwards, it is good to know that 'the Lord knows those who are his'.

There is another way to combat the problem. We need to get up out of our seats and get out there and gently minister to the needs of other people. That way we quickly forget about ourselves and gradually the confidence factor returns to our hearts and minds. Assurance will not be nurtured through wallowing in self-pity or ploughing a lonely furrow in the dark vale of depression. Moping is no substitute for active service!

Take heart, be glad your confidence is rooted in God, not in man!

3:21-24

Think big thoughts about God!

For the second time in this chapter, John refers to these Christians as *'dear friends'*. The first instance was further up the chapter in verse 2 and we have the same phrase repeated here in verse 21. He also addresses them as *'dear children'* in verses 7 and 18. This is John at his paternal best. He is a doting father figure to these first century believers and they respect and appreciate him for that.

In verses 21 and 22 the apostle highlights one of the spin-offs of a clear conscience before the Lord. He says, we reap massive benefits from that relationship while enjoying the added bonus of answered prayer! In this context, Robert Candlish is quite correct when he says, 'I cannot look my God in the face if I cannot look myself in the face.' It is the 'no-earth-born-cloud-arising' syndrome which can often intrude into our hearts and minds which serves only to eclipse the shining beauty of Jesus' lovely face.

These are immensely encouraging words which John shares with us, *'If our hearts do not condemn us, we have confidence before God and receive from him anything we ask, because we obey his commands and do what pleases him.'* Before we get into the nitty-gritty of obedience to his will for our lives, let us examine a little closer the matter of believing prayer and the net result of that.

The blessing of answered prayer

Confidence before God is fundamental to our prayer life. It is absolutely essential for us to have it if we are going to see anything achieved through our combined ministry of intercession and supplication. The Lord accepts us the way that we are, he never gives us the cold shoulder. There is always a warm welcome for his people at the throne of grace. We have nothing to fear when we approach him, we have nothing to dread as we anticipate an audience with the king.

We can touch the throne by simple childlike faith and trust, we can come boldly into his courts and meet our God face to face, we draw near to him as children coming to a loving heavenly Father, he is one to whom we can turn in every time of need, he is one to whom we can pour out our hearts, we can be open and honest with him regarding all our anxieties and burdens.

It seems to me, such confidence and assurance is vital if we are to pray effectively. It is so easy for us to become tight and tense about our failures, to be so hard on ourselves for not being better, and so miserable about the state of our soul that we lose the sunshine of God's love.

When the channels of communication are clear, there is nothing to hinder us from coming before him and making our requests known to him. He longs that we might ask great things from him for he can hardly wait to surprise us with the answers. In such sacred moments in the trysting place, we need to think big thoughts about God.

Here is a God who can do anything, but fail! Here is a God who never disappoints us! Here is a God who is able to do immeasurably more than all we ask or imagine! Here is a God whose resources are unfathomable! Here is a God whose reservoir is never in danger of drying up! Here is a God who desperately wants to help us! Here is a God who passionately longs to intervene on our behalf! Here is a God who loves to come alongside his people and show them the way forward! Here is a God who is oozing with kindness and whose generosity we cannot comprehend! Here is a God who finds endless delight, pleasure and satisfaction in answering the prayers of his children!

We need to let this truth sink in and when it does we need to revel in that superbly joyous relationship! Our prayers are hugely effective because God is more than keen and enthusiastic to play his part in seeing our dreams turn to reality. I was impressed when I read the insights of one Bible expositor when he said, 'God is not a mechanical blessing dispenser who coughs out the goodies every time we insert the appropriate prayer coin. He is a Father, and he answers our requests in a way analogous to that in which any parent listens to and responds to his children.'

Getting our prayers answered!

The baseline in all of John's ideas on prayer is that prayer is not a technique, nor is it some kind of magic formula. Prayer is not a divine and human concoction where ideas and resources are pooled. Prayer is a vibrant and pulsating relationship and, in any meaningful relationship, mutual confidence is terribly important. It is an essential ingredient. When we have it, we know it; when it is missing, our lives are sadly impoverished.

Elijah's prayer in 1 Kings 18 is a breathtaking example of a man whose confidence in God was running at an all-time high, his relationship with God was utterly secure. He knew the mind of God, he knew himself to be an instrument of God's purposes and all that mattered to him was the outworking of God's agenda. We find echoes of that inner assurance in verse 36.

Jesus emphasised the same point in his teaching on prayer in the Sermon on the Mount in Matthew 6. He told us how not to do it in verses 7 and 8; then he proceeds to show us how to do it in verses 9 and 10.

It is not a matter of knowing how to get my will done, it is a matter of knowing God well enough to get his will done!

It makes a lot of sense, doesn't it. It follows that confidence in prayer lies very much in the intimacy with which we know God and the degree to which our human wills are aligned to his. That is the secret! It is not what I want for my life, it is what he wants for my life. When our desires and aspirations are in sync with his, then our prayers will be answered and God will receive all the praise and glory.

A God shaped heart

According to John in verse 22, there is yet another connecting link regarding answers to prayer. He uses the word *'because'* to introduce this new concept. It is related to our obedience to his commands and our willingness to do what pleases him.

It is important for us to realise that these great promises about prayer do not give us *carte blanche* to get anything we want from God. That would make God indulgent, but hardly loving. At the end of the day, God knows what is best for each of us and the last thing he wants is for us to turn into a brat pack of spoiled children!

On a similar note, prayer is not a sort of *quid pro quo* by which God rewards or compensates us, answering our fervent prayers according to the time we have put in and how pleased he is with us.

I think if we grasp these two basic principles, then we are well on the way to understanding John's implicit encouragement of verse 22b. As we seek to live in a way that pleases the Lord, practising his truth and love, our aspirations and dreams become moulded to his. They take on a God shape. The more we enjoy and work at deepening that relationship, the more we will find ourselves on the receiving end of God's blessing through answered prayer.

Faith and love are like Siamese twins

In verse 23, John leaves us in no doubt as to what is on his heart. The overall package of commands enshrined in Scripture is narrowed down to two basic essentials; they are John's irreducible minimum for Christian faith and experience. John says, *'And this is his command: to believe in the name of his Son, Jesus Christ, and to love one another as he commanded us.'* David Jackman is right when he says, 'The verse provides both a summary of all John's teaching and a fulcrum for the whole letter.' These are cardinal truths, these are the central tenets of John's timely instruction.

... belief in Christ as Saviour

The Greek verb for *'to believe'* is in the aorist tense indicating a definite action at a specific point in time. It is something which has happened already. It is a one-off experience; when it is done, it is done! It cannot be repeated.

... commitment to one another in love

The verb *'to love'* is different for it appears in the present continuous tense and, therefore, it carries the idea of something which is ongoing. It will have had a starting point and that was the moment we believed in Christ; but it has no cut-off point, it just keeps on flowing from us to others around us. We become channels of God's love to those in life's wider community and we become a conduit for blessing others.

You see, from John's perspective, faith and love walk hand-in-hand together! Real faith will always manifest a love which ministers to others. Genuine spiritual love can always be traced back to a healthy and vibrant faith.

Belief and behaviour

This is the final thought John brings before us in chapter 3 when he says in verse 24, *'Those who obey his commands live in him, and he in them. And this is how we know that he lives in us: We know it by the Spirit he gave us.'* The prominent idea here is that of abiding in Christ. John harks back to the message couched in chapter 15 of his Gospel and repeated endless times in his epistle: it is a two-way relationship, not only do we live in him, he lives in us! That is a wonderful scenario, isn't it! But it is more than just fantasy or an imagination run riot; thank God, it is the ultimate reality!

This is our experience in the here and now and we know it because of the presence of the Holy Spirit who resides within us, he indwells us. It is his unique ministry to make Jesus real to us and to testify also to our hearts as to the reality of our trust in God. We find that hinted at in Romans 8:16.

> He is all we need,
>   he gives us all we need,
>   he meets our every need.

That is why our confidence is rooted in God for in him we have someone whose power is able to keep us and someone whose grace will lead us home!

4
Getting it right on the night

4:1-3

Spiritual radar

We need a God-given capacity to tell truth from error. God's people need discernment every bit as much in the third millennium as they did in the early years of the first. If they had big problems then, we have huge problems today. There have always been those who have plied their wares on unsuspecting saints; there is nothing new about pseudo pilgrims who try to sideline the people of God. The sad fact is, so many Christian people are gullible, they will believe anything that sounds remotely credible. The truth of God's revelation has always been counterfeited by false prophets and peddlers of error.

From day one, the world has never been without a plethora of cults and ism's. You name it, we have had it!

In some areas, they are pandemic, they are unchecked. They are so rampant and apparently successful that rent-a-sect has risen to the fore. The pernicious influence of such masqueraders of truth has caused enormous problems to the worshipping community of God's people; more often than not, we have been caught on the back foot and we have been a little unsure as to how to handle a worsening situation.

The litmus test of Scripture

It seems we have forgotten to read and take on board John's incisive comments in the opening verses of chapter 4 of his epistle. If we had listened to John, we could have saved ourselves a lot of heartache and, in the process, we could have spared others from major headaches! People make all sorts of wild claims today; they can do this, they can do that, they can do the other. In the light of such claims, the challenge facing the thinking Christian is a simple one: are they real, are they from the Lord?

We need to carefully assess all their claims and subject them to the litmus test of Scripture. We need to examine their teaching with meticulous care so as to determine whether they are genuine or bogus. Naïveté is not a spiritual virtue when it comes to such matters. Too many have slipped through the net, too many have fallen by the way. That is why extreme caution is a prudent option in such potentially dangerous situations.

The man is a wise man who follows John's suggestion in verse 1 where he says, *'Dear friends, do not believe every spirit, but test the spirits to see whether they are from God, because many false prophets have gone out into the world.'* The implication is, we should not swallow willy-nilly everything that is thrown at us within the four walls of a church. Just because it happens within the hallowed walls of the sanctuary does not mean to say it is right!

Don't throw caution to the wind!

By the same token, John is not saying that we have to be cynical about all that is happening in the name of Christ. He is plainly urging us to exercise spiritual restraint. There are times when we need to stop in our tracks and ask the question, 'Is this of the Lord or is it not?' The wise apostle is imploring us not to throw caution to the wind.

Human nature being what it is, we have an inbuilt tendency to enjoy and appreciate those things which are novel and new; we have a soft spot in our hearts for that which is unusual and out of the ordinary. The temptation is to ascribe all such phenomena to the power of God. That is where John exhorts us to apply the brakes and get our brains in gear. He specifically warns us not to believe all that we are told. We need to discover and discern its origin. We need to pay attention to the signals coming to us from our spiritual antenna.

John's concern is real for he has seen the terrible devastation the false prophets have caused. He has seen the untold damage they have done. He has seen the lives they have wrecked and the fellowships they have split down the middle. The apostle faces reality head on. He is quick off the mark to acknowledge that this is a perennial problem and we have to be on red alert to guard against the spurious. It comes in all shapes and sizes. Some of it sounds extremely plausible, some of it is hyperbole and the product of an overactive imagination which has been well oiled by the great deceiver himself.

It does not matter who says it, it does not matter who does it, such signs and wonders have to be tested in the light of biblical truth. This is especially true of spoken prophecy which purports to be a word from the Lord.

This is the burden weighing heavily on John's heart. It was no new problem for God's people. Back in Deuteronomy 18:21,22 through his servant Moses, God addresses precisely the same issue. Five chapters earlier in Deuteronomy 13:1-5, it is the content of the message that is the all-important factor. In other words, it is not so much who says it, it is what they say! When we read between the lines, it is clear that what the prophet says matters far more than how he says it or whatever apparently supernatural signs he can produce to support it. It is a question of content! The test is not whether it feels right or whether it sounds right, but whether it is true!

Don't bury your head in the sand!

The thought behind the word *'test'* is to 'prove'. In Bible days, the word was used with reference to putting metals to the test to see if they were genuine. There is a tremendous need today for us to vet those who stand in our pulpits. It is most imperative that we examine the teaching of many throughout our nation. We need to be vigilant lest the enemy creeps in unawares.

No matter how articulate a brother or a sister may be, no matter how plausible they may appear, no matter how sincere they are, no matter how convincing they sound, no matter what their academic abilities are and irrespective of whom they are accredited with, the acid test is, are they genuine, is there a ring of authenticity to them?

And here the plumbline of God's revealed truth in the Bible must be rigorously applied. You see, God's word is truth, it is eternal truth, it is timeless truth, it is truth unchanged and truth unchanging. From Genesis to Revelation, it is all truth and God will not contradict himself by saying something today which is contrary to what he said yesterday in Scripture.

No second edition

God's revelation in the biblical canon is complete. Nothing more needs to be added to it, nothing can be removed from it. There is no second edition of the Bible, there are no amendments required from the original. From beginning to end, it is the living word of the living God. Every Christian, not just those in positions of assembly leadership, has that solemn responsibility delegated to him.

In the final analysis, we have to determine whether the message is from God. It does not mean we see reds under every bed! It does mean we keep our wits about us when listening to others!

For a mechanic to know what is wrong with your car, he needs to know something about engines; for a doctor to diagnose your illness, he needs to know something about how the human body functions; for a Christian to distinguish truth from error, he needs to know his Bible from cover to cover. We may not understand it all, we may not be able to unravel its mysteries, but we must be able to test the spirits by the word of God.

Recognise the truth

John moves on in verses 2 and 3 to clearly advise us as to how we can recognise that which is real and how we can discern that which is spurious. The apostle writes in his usual lucid style, *'This is how you can recognise the Spirit of God: Every spirit that acknowledges that Jesus Christ has come in the flesh is from God, but every spirit that does not acknowledge Jesus is not from God. This is the spirit of the antichrist, which you have heard is coming and even now is already in the world.'*

The best way to handle the prevailing problem which John is confronting is to have a firm grasp of the great doctrines of the faith as outlined in the word of God. There is no substitute for knowing the truth of Scripture. The application of God's word to the situation in hand is essential. That is what John advocates in verse 2.

The ministry of the Holy Spirit in the situation is equally important for he is the one who shines the main beam on Jesus, and that is when many of the false teachers are left squirming in discomfort. They do not like to see Jesus take centre stage; they fail to appreciate who he really is; they have not recognised that the Lord of all glory is God manifest in flesh! They are busy proclaiming 'a' Christ, even a Christ with a small 'c' instead of 'the true' Christ.

Basically, according to John's frank analysis, they are antichrist in their sentiments. Let us remember, the antichrist is not necessarily an insidious bureaucrat working for the United Nations. The Greek word 'anti' means 'instead of'.

You see, to believe in the wrong Christ, one who is less than the God-man of history and the Bible, is to sell your soul to antichrist. To believe in the wrong Christ is to ultimately perish. At the end of the day, we cannot hedge our bets, we cannot sit on the fence, for the person of Christ becomes the touchstone of truth or error.

Truth … a touchstone or a tombstone?

The question, 'What do I think of Christ?' is as relevant in this context as it was in the days when it was first uttered in Pilate's hearing. A man's understanding of 'who Jesus is' makes a vast difference to his outlook on life and to his eternal destiny.

It is interesting to note that Paul is on the same wavelength as John when he adopted a similar strategy for detecting error in the early church when he wrote in 1 Corinthians 12:3, 'No-one who is speaking by the Spirit of God says, "Jesus be cursed," and no-one can say, "Jesus is Lord," except by the Holy Spirit.'

The influence of the Holy Spirit in the heart and life of a real believer should not be underestimated. His presence is paramount for he is the one who has ultimate responsibility to lead us into a fuller and deeper understanding of truth.

There are many well-meaning individuals who will ring our doorbell and talk openly and freely about Jesus and a host of other things. There are many groups operating around the world in a vast array of challenging situations who pay lip service to the teaching of Jesus and to the brilliant example he set, but their charm offensive cuts no ice with the apostle John. He is not overly impressed! He is not that gullible! He is not fooled! He is looking for truth, the whole truth and nothing but the truth.

If we are to be biblically positive about Christ, we have no option, we have no alternative, but to be negative about error. This is not an incentive to indulge in theological witch hunts, but to plainly recognise where the Scriptures draw the line between truth and error and to draw it there ourselves.

It is amazing and yet it should not really surprise us that two millennia have come and gone and times have not changed that much; the battles gallantly fought in the first century continue to be fought in the twenty-first! It seems to me, the person and work of Jesus Christ is not only the central question of all our outreach and evangelism; it is, by virtue of that fact, the central test of Christian orthodoxy.

4:4-6

Examine how people live!

Let us recap! John's emphasis in verses 1-3 is primarily focused on the message of these pseudo preachers: we are to check on the content of what they say or, in some cases, what they leave unsaid! We have discovered already in John's epistle that what a man believes generally influences the kind of life that he lives; his personal values impact his behaviour. That explains why John expands his thinking in the manner he does in verses 4-6.

I find it fascinating that each of these verses begins with a different pronoun, for example: in verse 4, he writes, *'you'* - in verse 5, he says, *'they'* - in verse 6, he commences with *'we'*.

Why the difference? Because he is addressing different groups of people!

* The *'you'* in verse 4 refers to all those who make up the global family of God, an exclusively Christian company.
* The *'they'* in verse 5 is appropriate to the non-Christian false prophets who seek to lead astray the people of God.
* The *'we'* in verse 6 is relevant to the apostles and true teachers who labour in the word and doctrine.

You!

John progresses his argument with some incisive and illuminating snapshots of these individuals. He says in verse 4, *'You, dear children, are from God and have overcome them, because the one who is in you is greater than the one who is in the world.'* Isn't it lovely the way John speaks to these battered and bewildered saints. This man has a tender touch even when writing on tough subjects. He is at pains to point out that they belong to the Lord Jesus for they find their roots in him; they have, by his grace, been born and brought into the worldwide family of God. He commends them for their victorious life in that they have not fallen foul of the tactics of the enemy, nice as he may have been!

They have not caved in even though they have been placed under enormous pressure. They have not capitulated, they have remained loyal and faithful to the word of God. They were not over-awed nor were they intimidated with the super-spiritual jibes from these men in pin-stripe suits. Theirs has been a demanding path. It has been incredibly difficult for them and John is quick to acknowledge that. At the same time, he is the first to congratulate them for their overcoming spirit.

Pastor John is profoundly thankful to God for two main reasons: number one, their faith was not destroyed, and number two, their Saviour was not denied. It did not matter one iota how astute and powerful the enemy was, it did not even matter for a single minute how innovative and creative the adversary was, these good folks outwitted him every time because the Lord was on their side. They were on the winning team!

Losing is out of the question!

The truth is, when the Lord is with us and the Holy Spirit is in us, losing is never on God's agenda. The enemy has nothing to depend on; the enemy has no-one to whom he can turn. We have! We have Jesus! On top of that, we have all the resources of heaven placed at our disposal. We have the power of God, we have the inner dynamic of the Holy Spirit, we have the assurance of his presence in a dog-eat-dog world where the puppies do not survive and, by childlike faith and trust, we can draw upon his limitless resources at any time and in every place.

Paul hit the nail on the head in Romans 8:37 when he said that, 'We are more than conquerors through him who loved us.' I think this is a truth which is so fantastically great, it is sublime, it is absolutely and deliriously thrilling. Oh yes, let us shout it from the rooftops! It is headline news! The Lord is greater, sure he is!

He is the one who successfully routed the enemy at Calvary; he is the one who roundly defeated Satan at the cross. He is the one who landed a double whammy on sin for he dealt with it effectively and efficiently. He is the one who rose triumphant from the dead and today is alive for evermore! Jesus is enthroned on high! He is exalted far above all!

We join hands with the redeemed down through the ages and we declare unequivocally that the Lord is greater than the devil - there is no question about that! Period. End of argument, and John moves on to talk about something else!

They!

There is a marked contrast between the true people of God in verse 4 and the false teachers who are propagating all kinds of falsehood in verse 5. John describes them thus: *'They are from the world and therefore speak from the viewpoint of the world, and the world listens to them.'* Well, we do not have to be New Testament scholars to make sense of that verse, do we!

There is one word which appears no fewer than three times and that word is the master key which opens the door to a clear understanding of the kind of men we are confronting here. That word is the word *'world'*. It highlights their origin for it tells us where they have come from. They are earthly individuals, they are earth bound and earth oriented. Their roots go down a long way in the soil of planet earth.

The text exposes a definite slant and bias to their teaching by informing us that it is governed by the latest fad to hit the high street. They spend their time delivering lectures and homilies on current affairs and they present themselves as God's answer to the big questions engulfing humanity.

The fact is, they are so immersed in the things of time, they have nothing worthwhile to say about the issues of eternity. Inevitably, if you are bold enough to stand on a soapbox on any street corner and shout at the top of your voice, believe me, you will always gather a crowd. You are guaranteed a hearing and probably a fair bit of heckling as well and that is what has happened to them. You know it as well as I do: the empty can makes the most noise!

It all sounds very appealing, it is all so enticing and cajoling. There are many allurements. There is something attractive about the show that is presently in town. Whenever these impostors are around, there is an air of congeniality which permeates the atmosphere. There is a nice feel to it, it has a certain ambience associated with it.

That is why so many well-meaning people are sucked into it, most of them unwittingly and unintentionally. With the best will in the world, they did not plan to get involved; it just happened for it seemed the proper thing to do at the time. The pressure was applied ever so subtly and before they knew it, and before they could back off, they were enmeshed in the web.

In other words, the popular preacher is not always right. The popular preacher is not always proclaiming the truth of Scripture. The popular preacher may have a crowd gathered around him but that does not mean very much for he is only as good as his last sermon. A crowd can be very fickle and before he knows it they could be gone. It is equally true to say that popular preachers do not often stick around too long, and before the crowd know it he could be gone!

I reckon John knows what he is talking about. He has been around for a very long time, he has seen it all before. There is nothing new under the sun! Surely that puts him in the ideal position to warn us lest history repeats itself in the third millennium.

We!

John then switches gear in verse 6 when he puts the spotlight on faithful preachers of the word of God. He says, *'We are from God, and whoever knows God listens to us; but whoever is not from God does not listen to us. This is how we recognise the Spirit of truth and the spirit of falsehood.'* The contrast between the men of the world in verse 5 and the men of the word in verse 6 is mind-blowing. It is quite incredible.

The glaringly obvious difference is in our origin for we are said to be from God! We have the Lord living within us, we have heaven in our hearts, we have eternity graven on our minds, we have a hope beyond death etched into our thinking. Our life in the here and now is different, our life in the there and then is significantly different!

Genuine servants of God will place themselves under the authority of Scripture and they are happy to do that. Those members who comprise the body of Christ are most blessed when they sit under the anointed preaching of the crucified Christ. The gospel of sovereign grace has warmed their hearts, it has touched their lives, it has transformed their outlook; to all such, an ear for the word of God is the most natural thing in all the world.

There is an affinity of heart between the true believer in Christ and the true servant of the cross. They may not know one another by name, they may never have met before, but there is an immediate bond because they have something in common. There is an instant link-up between them for they share the joys of God's full salvation. They discovered the undiluted wonder of sins forgiven when they knelt before the cross of Jesus and now, in him and because of him, they are brothers. That is an extra-special relationship which is staggeringly unique to the people of God. It does not happen anywhere else, it does not happen to any other group.

On the other hand, John pulls no punches when he advises us that the non-believers have little or no interest in the things of God. They do not have a heart to absorb the teaching of truth as it is in the Bible; they do not have a mind that is stirred with the solid preaching of God's word. They do not have an ear that is tuned to listen attentively to the ministry of Scripture. The chances are, they may be sitting in the congregation on a Sunday morning, they may go through the worship rigmarole week after week, they may put their money in the collection basket, they may exchange all the usual pleasantries that we normally associate with a centre of evangelical witness. They may even open the pew Bibles and follow the Scripture reading.

But when it comes to the proclamation of the truth of God's word, it goes in one ear and straight out the other. That is immensely sad! In fact, it is so unthinkably sad, it causes many of us enormous concern. It is a serious and urgent matter for prayer. At the end of the day though, John is spot on when he says what he does for only God can open blind eyes, only God can unstop deaf ears!

A classic case of us and them!

The parting shot in this opening paragraph is found in the final sentence where John more or less formulates his conclusion. To him, it is as clear as crystal; there are no ifs or maybes or any other shades of grey. There are two groups of people.

The man with an open heart for the Lord is someone in whom the Holy Spirit of truth is actively working, and the man who shows no real interest in the doctrines of grace and glory is an individual in a sad and sorry state for he has operating in him the spirit of error.

So far as John is concerned, it is as simple as that. He does not beat about the bush. We are either one or the other, we cannot be both! It is clear cut!

If we are on the side of truth, and I sincerely hope that we are, that is great, that is tremendous, that is wonderful - John warmly offers to us the right hand of fellowship and he says, 'Welcome to the global family of God.'

If we are not on that side, the side of truth, then we are still on the side of falsehood and that is tragic for it will drag us down and down and down, until one day, when it is too late, we will come to a point where we end up spending eternity banished from the presence of God. When that day comes and our eyes open on the other side of death, in hell itself, we will wish we had followed Jesus, 'the way, the truth, and the life'.

4:7-12

The divine philanthropist

When we think of this grubby tennis ball of a planet, set in the vast infinity of time, and our individuality among countless millions, can we really talk meaningfully about God loving us? And when we look at the world with all its rampant evil and indescribable suffering, so many damaged and broken lives, how can there be a God who really loves? Two vitally important questions which have to be asked and which deserve an answer.

John insists in remarkably clear and unequivocal language, this is the very nature of God. God is love! He is love personified. It comes naturally for him to love, he does it because he *is* it. It does not matter how dark the night may be, how bleak the future looks, how devastating the experience is, how catastrophic the situation may appear to be - these vacillating influences in your life and mine do not impinge or encroach even for a moment on the unchangeable truth that God is love.

God's love for us

It is incredibly important for us to realise that such an infinite yet personal Creator God is not too great or preoccupied to be bothered with each of us individually. I am just so grateful to the Lord that he does not treat us like bricks on an assembly line of some impersonal multinational corporation; instead he sees us as living stones which need to be chiselled by the Master's hand.

He is a God who specialises in the personal touch for he patiently shapes us into the kind of people he wants us to be.

Whatever that may entail for any one of us, it will always bear the imprint of his love upon it.

Over these last few pages we have covered a lot of ground in terms of our developing relationship with the Lord. We have seen the sheer splendour of our God's magnificent provision for us in that his grace enables us to handle all that life throws at us. We have been bowled over as we have contemplated his detailed love and care for each one of us.

Here is one who accepts us the way we are, here is one who has not given up on any of his children, here is one who plants the seed of confidence in our hearts and then quietly works in our lives to see it flower and blossom.

Sure, there have been times when we have been gasping for air, it has all been too much for us to assimilate and take on board. His incredible love and boundless grace have left us speechless! But right here in verses 7 and 8, the doors swing wide open and we discover the identity of the one who has done all of this, and more besides: it is none other than the God who is love!

One Bible commentator puts it like this, 'Everything else in the splendour of these verses circles around this one supreme reality: God is love.' It is small wonder that Augustine said of John in this first epistle, 'He has spoken many words, and nearly all are about love.'

We read elsewhere in John's tiny epistle that God is light; we find in the Gospel of John that God is spirit; but nowhere do we read that God is wrath! It says that God is love, for wrath, as Martin Luther expressed it, 'is God's strange work'. Wrath is something which is foreign to his essential nature; it is, in a very real sense, a temporary indignation. But when we think about God's love, that is an eternal energy.

Though the Bible tells us, there was a time when there was no sin in this world to make God angry, there never was a time when there was no Son in God's heart to make him love!

That is what makes the difference! John is not identifying a quality which God possesses; he is making a concise statement about the essence of God's being. It is not simply that God loves, but that he is love.

Where there is ... let me bring your love

It seems to me, if we can grasp that particular truth, it will enable us to understand more clearly what John means when he challenges us in verses 7 and 8 by saying, *'Dear friends, let us love one another, for love comes from God. Everyone who loves has been born of God and knows God. Whoever does not love does not know God, because God is love.'*

You see, love flows from him like water flows from a spring. It is dynamic, it is refreshing, it is the norm; realistically, he cannot do anything else but love! God is the source of love, he is the origin of love. It has accurately been said that 'love does not define God, but God defines love.'

When we love one another in the extended family of God, we are reflecting the Father's love to us and for us. Actually, it is not our love which is reaching out to others, it is his love flowing through us to them. The basic fact that we love one another is irrefutable evidence that we belong to Jesus Christ. Love for our fellow believers is a clear token that we have experienced the new birth for love is the badge that we wear on the lapel of our lives.

The same is true in reverse. Should there be a distinct lack of love in our hearts, then our relationship with God can be brought into serious question and the man on the street would have every right to wonder concerning the reality and sincerity of our claim to be followers of Jesus Christ.

John says, if we do not show love to one another, then we do not love the Lord! It is as straightforward as that!

Biblical love is never divorced from biblical faith.

The cross ... a window on God's heart

Verses 9 and 10 afford us a brilliant opportunity to see what God did, for God's love is best seen in the cross of our Lord Jesus Christ. John says, *'This is how God showed his love among us: He sent his one and only Son into the world that we might live through him. This is love: not that we loved God, but that he loved us and sent his Son as an atoning sacrifice for our sins.'* When we read such amazing verses like these, we feel as if we are standing on holy ground. We are out of our depth for they are packed full with meaning.

John is drawing aside the curtain for he wants us to get to the bottom of love. The fact that God is love is seen in what he did on our behalf. He gave his one and only Son for us at the place called Calvary.

Love communicates, love gives; true love is never static, it is never inactive, it cannot sit around all day twiddling its thumbs and doing nothing. Real love, authentic love, manifests itself in what it voluntarily does for others, even to the point of self sacrifice.

I think if we are to appreciate this brand of quality love, we have to understand the heart of God himself, we need to feel his heartbeat. The opening words in verse 9 intimate to us the meaning of love from God's viewpoint. We see Calvary from the heavenly Father's perspective. We see the greatest exhibition of love this world has ever known from the divine angle.

To all intents and purposes, the death of Jesus, God's Son, is seen here as the public appearance of God's love for his people. That is the thought behind John's use of the Greek verb *phaneroo*. The same word is used at the start of the letter in 1:2 where John focuses on the coming of Christ into the world. This is God proving beyond a shadow of a doubt that his love for us is genuine.

It is interesting to note that this is the only place in the epistle where Jesus is called God's 'only begotten Son' (AV translation). We have it a few times in his Gospel (the one reference we are probably most familiar with is John 3:16), but nowhere else in his letter does it appear. The phrase means, 'unique, one of a kind, the only one of its kind'.

It was amazing that God should send a Son, but to send his *only* Son is a measure of the magnitude of his love. The same word is used of Isaac in Hebrews 11:17 to illustrate the greatness of Abraham's faith and obedience when God tested him with the ultimate trial at Mount Moriah. Father Abraham was prepared to sacrifice his one and only son, the son who had been promised to him and Sarah for many long years; he was willing to go along with it if that was what the Lord commanded.

The picture we have emerging is of a Son who is extremely precious and greatly loved because he is the only one. That makes him supremely special!

God had only one Son and he was sent into a hostile and unforgiving environment, into a rebel world, on a rescue mission to redeem us and reconcile us to God.

I think the fact that God *'sent'* his Son into a pagan world is one remarkable strand of evidence surrounding the deity of Jesus Christ. Babies are not sent into the world from some other place; they are born into the world. But, as the eternal Son, Jesus was sent into the world. This is love for this is God!

And that is why the name of God is repeated over and over again in this brief paragraph in chapter 4. It underlines the truth that God should bother with human beings like you and me!

The great consequence of his coming is that we might receive eternal life in the place of certain death. We could never know it any other way. It can be experienced only through a personal relationship with Jesus Christ and that is what John proposes at the end of verse 9. We not only live in him, we live through him. He is the source and the channel of spiritual and eternal life. It is something of a paradox that Christ had to die so that we might live!

The glorious truth is, not only are the rebels pardoned, they are made sons and welcomed into the ranks of the family of God. Again, says John, this is love at its finest and best!

A twofold question remains to be asked and only we can answer it: where would we be without Jesus? And what could we do without him?

We could not do for ourselves

John takes the wind out of our sails by tactfully reminding us that we had nothing to do with God's gracious and generous offer of salvation! The clause at the beginning of verse 10 is of mega importance when it says, *'not that we loved God'*. The plain fact is, it has nothing to do with us, it has everything to do with him.

He is the one who came,
he is the one who stepped into our dire situation,
he is the one who intervened when there was no hope for us,

> he is the one who exercised mercy and showed fathomless grace,
> he is the one who seized the initiative and made all the running,
> he came toward us; it was definitely not the other way round!

There is no reciprocation by God meeting a person halfway because he has shown an inkling of interest in his eternal destiny. Someone has written and I wholeheartedly concur with his view, 'God decides to manifest his love to those who do not love him and who do not want to love him, to enemies and rebels armed to the teeth against him, to a world of lost sinners.' We need this truth to sink into the depths of our hearts and minds!

If it were not for God taking the first step and making the initial move, we would have no hope in this world and no future in the world to come. The fact that we have something to live for today and so much to look forward to in all our tomorrows pays an eloquent tribute to the love of God.

Justice was satisfied

We have established that we are the recipients of God's love, we are the beneficiaries of his undying love, but John does not stop there. He proceeds to remind us of a truth that we first came across in 2:2 where he talks about him *'as an atoning sacrifice for our sins'*.

The Greek word which John employs in this phrase is the word *hilasmos* and it is one which is highly suggestive. It reminds us that love finds the means by which just and righteous wrath can be satisfied and so turned away in order that forgiveness may be offered and reconciliation achieved. The bottom line is, there was absolutely nothing that we could do to appease God or placate his anger.

Propitiation is something God does to make it possible for men to be forgiven.

- *'God is light'* and, therefore, he must uphold his holy law.
- *'God is love'* and, therefore, he wants to save sinners.

The question is, *how can God forgive sinners and still be consistent with his holy nature?*

The answer: the cross! The only way that could ever happen was at infinite cost to the one who loves. It was there Jesus bore the total punishment for sin and met the just demands of a holy God. He pulled out all the stops in order to purchase our eternal salvation; he went to considerable lengths to redeem us to himself; he left no stone unturned as he sought to release us from the bondage of Satan and sin; he went well beyond the second mile as he successfully opened up a way for us to be reconciled to God. There is only one way this can be fully understood and explained. It is with the welcome inclusion into the equation of the four letter word, *l-o-v-e*.

Love makes a world of difference for love makes all the difference in the world! You see, as the old gospel song says, 'there was no other way a God of love could find, to redeem a lost mankind, but Calvary.' It was the precious blood of Jesus that flowed for our forgiveness. There was no alternative route afforded to him, there was no other option made available to him.

Warren Wiersbe is right when he says, *'The death of Jesus was not an accident, it was an appointment; he did not die as a weak martyr, but as a mighty conqueror.'*

The least we can do is … love

John then issues a rallying call in verse 11 when he pleads with the believers to love each other. We read, *'Dear friends, since God so loved us, we also ought to love one another.'* In the light of all that God has done for us, how can we not love one another? John raises the stakes when he includes the two letter adverb *'so'* in the phrase pertaining to God's love.

The problem is we are so often wrapped up in ourselves, we have our own ideas about things, we become immersed in what we are involved in that we cannot see any further than our nose. We become so petty about things that do not really matter that much and we get so uptight about a wide range of trivial pursuits that love flies out the open window of our hearts. It is quite often the last thing on our minds!

The challenge is, take a long look at Calvary and do to others what the Lord has done to you! Because we have received his love so freely, we should dispense it to those around us with similar enthusiasm and zeal. According to John, God's love supplies both the reason for doing it and the resources to implement it. It seems to me, we owe it to our God to share his love with others and, at the same time, we have an obligation to them anyway.

The people of God, the church of the twenty-first century, should be a community of love unlike any other human society. It is true that the church exists for those who are not yet members, but it is also true that love among her members should be one of her most powerful magnets. Dr Francis Schaeffer rightly described such love as *'the ultimate apologetic'*. Love is the hallmark, it is the trademark, it is the benchmark, of the family of God.

When people look at us and reflect on our interpersonal relationships, they should see an unparalleled display of love between us. This focuses on the wonderful nature of God for, although he cannot be seen with the naked eye, there is no better medium for modern man to be made aware of him than for him to see love among the people of God.

That is why John says what he does in verse 12, *'No-one has ever seen God; but if we love one another, God lives in us and his love is made complete in us.'* You see, Jesus is no longer physically with us in this world but if people want to see Jesus, they should be able to meet him where and when God's people are gathered together.

In our lives, that means 'not just mystical visions, or wonderful warming words, but practical down-to-earth actions, the modern equivalent of washing one another's feet.'

The Church is his audio visual presentation to a dying culture and people are looking and people are listening. People should be able to walk into a Christian fellowship and see the God of love within the lives and activities of his people.

The challenge is, if we know that God really loves us and we cannot argue with that, are we prepared to allow that *agape* love to flow into our lives and then overflow from our hearts as we bless others?

It's who you know!

Over and over again, John uses the word *'know'* in his first epistle. The reason why is fairly obvious, he wants the sinner to know Christ personally as his Lord and Saviour. That is what it means to be born again. He also wants the believer to *'know'* that he knows Christ. That is what is meant by the term 'assurance'.

John insists that God wants us to really know that we are his and that our Christian experience is real. He does not want to see us floundering in the quicksand of uncertainty. A fundamental truth has been woven into the fabric of this section in chapter 4 which stretches from verse 7 down to verse 16.

God is love! This sublime truth is revealed to us copiously in the sacred writings of Scripture; it was also manifest on the cross where Christ gave his life as a ransom for many.

In other words, God has said something *to* us and God has done something *for* us! All of this is tremendous preparation for yet another stupendous fact: God has done something *in* us!

Warren Wiersbe is spot on when he says, 'We are not merely students reading a book, or spectators watching a deeply moving event. We are participants in the great drama of God's love.'

I came across a fascinating story which illustrates what John is attempting to do in this section of his first epistle. In order to save money, a college drama class purchased only a few scripts of a play and cut them up into separate parts. The director gave each player his individual part in order and then started to rehearse the production. But nothing went right! It was a flop, it was a failure! After an hour of missed cues and mangled sequences, the entire cast gave up. They had had enough. At that point, the director sat the disheartened actors on the stage and said, 'Look, I'm going to read the entire play to you, so don't any of you say a word.' That is what he did and when he was finished one of the actors said to him, *'So that's what it was all about!'*

When they understood the storyline they were able to fit all their parts together and have a successful rehearsal. It all made terrific sense! In some ways, that is what verses 12-16 are all about. We read them through and we feel like saying, 'Ah! Now I see it, so that's what it's all about!'

In these few verses we discover what God had in mind when he devised this great plan of salvation. And when we see it all coming together beautifully like pieces in a jigsaw puzzle that, in itself, will reinforce our trust and belief in a great God. It will firm up our assurance; it will strengthen our resolve to walk closely with the Lord this side of heaven. Right at the heart of our assurance lies the conviction with which the previous section ended and which John repeats here in verses 13, 15 and 16 that we live in God and he lives in us.

That is a concept which is difficult to grasp especially for those of us living as we do in the hi-tech age of the third millennium. We are used to a culture where everything can be tested and tried by our senses but this is something totally different. We cannot see this God with our own two eyes (we find that in verse 12); the reason why is because he is spirit (we find that back in John 4:24). How true it is that 'God is not a collection of sensory data to be discovered and analysed, but an infinite, eternal person.'

The simple fact is, God is someone who is there to be trusted; he is there to be believed. I think that is where faith enters into the frame!

4:13-21

The questions we ask ourselves are these: How can we be sure our lives are built on a solid and reliable foundation? What are the grounds of assurance which the Christian can embrace in the best of times as well as in the worst of times?

We have the Holy Spirit

John writes in verse 13, *'We know that we live in him and he in us, because he has given us of his Spirit.'* According to John, the gift of the Holy Spirit is an inevitable corollary of our union with Jesus Christ. That means, every child of God has the Spirit of God living within him. We know the presence of the indwelling Holy Spirit day after day.

The unbeliever knows nothing of his abiding within; the sinner is destitute of any life in Christ, his life is empty like a vacuum (we find that teaching amplified by Paul in Romans 8:9). I like to think of it like this:

God lives in me ... that is what John says here in verse 13,
Christ lives in me ... that is what Paul says in Galatians 2:20,
and they both do it in the person of the Holy Spirit.

It is as simple and yet as profound as that! Perhaps the greatest gift of the ascended Christ to his church on planet earth is the Holy Spirit. He is the one who equips us for every role we are asked to fulfil; he is the one who enables us to live for the Lord; he is the one who energises us and empowers us for the task at hand.

The thrilling fact is, when we expose our hearts to his operational fulness, then we know his dynamic influence permeating every area of our lives and this results in the fruit of the Spirit being reproduced in us and through us to others in the church and in the community at large.

It is true to say, where the life of God is at work, it sweetens bitterness, it melts hardness, and it multiplies love. All of this affirms the reality of our relationship with Jesus Christ and it is concrete evidence that *'we live in him and he in us'*.

They said it ... I believe it!

John says in verse 14, *'And we have seen and testify that the Father has sent his Son to be the Saviour of the world.'* Inextricably linked to the witness of the Holy Spirit is the witness of the apostles. They can be compared to two links which latch on to each other in the chain of our conviction. The one empowered the other yet both were essential for the mission to be completed!

Our Lord introduced this concept when conversing with his disciples in the upper room, as recorded in John 15:26,27. Jesus said, 'When the Counsellor comes, whom I will send to you from the Father, the Spirit of truth who goes out from the Father, he will testify about me. And you also must testify, for you have been with me from the beginning.'

When John speaks about *'we'* in verse 14, it is a clear reference to the apostolic company as it did at the start of his first epistle. It was their unique privilege and responsibility to witness to what they saw and heard; that was their prime role in a ministry which took them into the regions beyond. Yes, they saw what he did, they heard what he said, and because of that, our assurance finds root in the soil of their testimony.

It is worth noting in passing that John here refers to Jesus as the Saviour of the world. The mandate of the church is to take this message of a full and free salvation to the uttermost ends of the earth, that is our mission.

We should take a moment and thank our heavenly Father that the gospel of Christ is not a segregated gospel. There are no apartheid overtones to the great commission. We have a glorious gospel for all people, regardless of face, place or race!

Nailing our colours to the mast

Verse 15 is a relatively easy verse to understand for John spells it out as simply as he can. He says, *'If anyone acknowledges that Jesus is the Son of God, God lives in him and he in God.'* It is probably helpful to read this verse alongside John's comments in verse 12 for when we do that we recognise John's blend of truth and love.

The focus of John's teaching this time is on the outward confession of the inner conviction. It is when we go public over what has happened in the confines of our heart. It is when we come out into the open and unashamedly nail our colours to the mast. It is standing up and being counted for the sake of the gospel of

Jesus Christ. This is a clear-cut testimony to our personal belief in the Lord of history, the Lord of the incarnation, the Lord of our salvation!

The term *'acknowledge'* means more than mental assent to what Jesus has done in the past; it means more than an intellectual acceptance of a series of facts etched on the granite of history; it is more than signing a decision card at the end of an evangelistic meeting; it is more than raising a hand when an impassioned appeal is made for people to follow Jesus!

Our saving faith depends on a doctrinal confession concerning the person and work of Jesus Christ! We may not fully appreciate the implications of that step when we take it but the whole of our experience of God actually depends on it. The proof that we have the real thing is when our lives reflect his glory and when our attitudes and actions correspond to his word.

I was intrigued to discover that there are three different witnesses mentioned in these verses. In some ways, this is not unlike a threefold cord which cannot be broken:

- in verse 13, we have the witness *in* the believer by the Holy Spirit;
- in verse 15, we have the witness *of* the believer that Jesus is the Son of God;
- and the witness *through* the believer that God is love and that he sent his Son to die for the world.

The world will not believe that God loves sinners until they see his love at work in the lives of the people of God.

The moving story is told of the Salvation Army worker who found a derelict woman squatting alone on the street. She invited her to come into the chapel for help, but the woman refused to move. The worker assured her, 'We love you and want to help you. God loves you. Jesus died for you.' But the woman did not budge; she stayed where she was. As if on divine impulse, the Salvationist leaned over and kissed the bedraggled woman on the cheek, taking her into her arms. The woman began to sob and, like a little child, was led into the chapel where she eventually trusted Christ as her Saviour. Later on she confided in the lady officer, *'You told me that God loved me but it wasn't until you showed me that God loved me that I wanted to be saved.'*

Therein lies the secret of missionary endeavour and every form of evangelistic outreach. Our lives speak so loud, the man on the street should be pleading with us to turn the volume down!

Living in the orbit of God's love

We read in verse 16, *'And so we know and rely on the love God has for us. God is love. Whoever lives in love lives in God, and God in him.'* The basic thought encapsulated in this verse is that we are constantly enveloped in the love of God. We live our lives in the orbit of God's unfailing love and, so long as we stay close to his heart and remain sensitive to the promptings of the Holy Spirit, we will always feel the warmth of its vibes reaching out to us. It is a pulsating, vibrant, heart-stopping relationship of intimacy with the Almighty.

Again we can see what John is trying to do. He is at pains to underline the twin towers of security which we have as the children of God: we are in him and he is in us. I think that is where Pauline theology as so often outlined in his upbeat letter to the Ephesians and Johannine theology as we have it expounded here complement one another beautifully.

The wonderful fact is that his love is such that we can depend upon it fully; we need have no quibbles about his love. It is a changeless love and that means we should have no niggling qualms about relying on it. We can stake our lives on it for it is a love that never fails. And when all is said and done, it can be no other way for God himself is love.

The best of times, the worst of times

That surely means, in the good times, when everything in the garden is rosy, we know his love filling our hearts; it also means, in the bad times, when our dreams are shattered and our castles have tumbled and our faith is stretched to the limit, we still can experience his love flooding our lives.

Sometimes in his providence he leads us through deep waters and into dark valleys so that we might learn to rely on his love more completely or to trust him more fully. He uses every changing season of our lives to mould us into the kind of people he wants us to be, a people moving in the sphere of his love.

The future is bright, the future is ...

Verse 17 says, *'In this way, love is made complete among us so that we will have confidence on the day of judgment, because in this world we are like him.'* John looks forward into the not-too-distant future; he is anticipating tomorrow in the ripening purposes of God. He is thinking of the day when we will stand before the Lord at the judgment seat of Christ. Such a locale is often referred to as the *Bema*, as outlined by Paul in 2 Corinthians 5:10 and 1 Corinthians 3:5-15. It is also mentioned in Romans 14:12 where Paul sees it as a day of accountability for the people of God.

John's aspiration is that when we stand before the Lord, we can do so with a high level of confidence. He does not want us to be overwhelmed with regret because of the lifestyle we have chosen to live; he does not want us to be red faced with embarrassment because of our neglect to serve him this side of heaven. He does not want us to stand there with our head buried in our hands and the words of the gospel song ringing in our ears, 'I'll wish I had given him more!' I can assure you, that is the last thing John wants for us!

The secret to our passing the examination on that final day is for us to be like him down here on planet earth and the more we are like Jesus the greater our confidence will be. Basically, we want to hear him say to each of us, 'My child, well done!' He will only say that if we have done well!

The fear factor

In verse 18, John introduces a new dimension to his thinking when he talks about fear and what he says is most interesting. We read,

'There is no fear in love. But perfect love drives out fear, because fear has to do with punishment. The one who fears is not made perfect in love.' I think you will agree with me when I say that fear and love are mutually exclusive. If we are scared stiff that God is going to punish us, we cannot yet be aware of the fulness of his love in our hearts.

There are so many of God's people today who are enmeshed in a web of fear, they live their lives on a treadmill for one reason or another. It is fear that drives them on and, sadly for some, it drives them over the edge.

John implies that when we have God's love in control of our lives, we have absolutely nothing to fear, we have nothing to worry about. God is not waiting for us at the end of the road with a big stick in his hand ready to beat us up! Far from it! He longs that we might have total trust in his Son, the Lord Jesus, who came to deal with fear in our hearts and minds; he came to eradicate it, he came to expel it, once and for all!

Punishment is not on the agenda for the believer. That was effectively dealt with on the cross of Calvary. It will never be handed down a second time! That is passed, it is consigned to the annals of history.

We face the future with our hand in his, we face tomorrow with our confidence grounded in the character of God. We look ahead and keenly anticipate all that God has for us and we can do that with a measure of hope because we know he is for us and he is with us. The simple truth is, his is a love that will never let us go! In that sense, John and Jeremiah (29:10,11) are on the same wavelength.

The reason why

The final thought is found in verse 19 where John says, *'We love because he first loved us.'* The main reason why we show compassion to others is because we have known the Lord's incredible compassion in our hearts. The reason why we minister with a tender touch to others in their need is because we have known a similar touch from the Lord. The reason why we love others as they are is because we continue to enjoy and experience his love on a daily basis! That, it has to be said, is where genuine love wins the day!

I don't like him, but I love him!

One of the major themes of this entire section has been love and our attitude towards one another. John has taken us to many mountain peaks in the course of his argument as he has widened our vista concerning God's love for us, a love which he consistently revealed to us even when we were like sheep on the wrong side of his fold. That did not put him off! That did not deter him! Not for a single moment!

So says John, in verses 20 and 21, in the light of what the Lord continues to do on our behalf, how can we show anything else but love to those around us? We may not particularly like the individuals concerned, they may not be our first choice for friends, but we can still love them for the sake of Jesus. To say anything else flies in the face of the character of a God who is love personified; to respond in any other way is a contradiction of what we say we are.

The bottom line is, we cannot say we love the Lord one minute and turn around and snub our brother the next! The two do not tally, they do not make sense!

John takes it to a higher level when he reminds us that our love for our heavenly Father is an act of simple faith because our eyes have never seen him. The man sitting next to us in church on Sunday, well, we can see him, we know he is there and, theoretically, that should make love a more natural proposition. Sometimes it is easier said than done, it is so much easier to verbalise it than it is to practise it but that in no way exonerates us for not exercising genuine and sincere love to him.

I reckon this is probably one of the greatest shortcomings of the church today. *We can talk about love all around the clock, we can sing about it in our times of worship, but how come we do not show it within five minutes of the benediction being pronounced? Why are we so critical of other believers? Why are we so quick to jump to negative conclusions about other people? Why are we so slow and reticent to bear the burdens of those who are facing massive problems and considerable pressure? Why are we so unwilling to step into their shoes?* Those are questions that need to be asked, they also need to be answered!

At the end of the day, we have no option but to love him, we have no alternative Plan B to fall back on. Basically, we have no excuse for it is a command enshrined in Scripture which must be obeyed at all costs. The good news is, when we do not feel up to it and when we do not feel as if we can go through with it, our God is there to help us, he will enable us and he will equip us for the task in hand.

A spin-off from such caring practical love is that it can be a wonderful ground of assurance. That has to be seen as a real bonus for it confirms our faith in God and it affirms our relationship with him.

It is the seventeenth century Pascal who is credited with the saying, *'We must know men in order to love them, but we must love God in order to know him.'*

What he says is absolutely true but John would insist that we add another proviso: *'Whoever loves God'* must also *'love his brother'*. That makes love a vital component, an essential ingredient, of down-to-earth Christian living. John is looking for reality in our lives. He has no time for play acting; he has no sympathy for those who are living a lie; he gives no leg room to those who are pretenders. His is an impassioned appeal for an authentic Christian lifestyle and that is best seen when we love one another.

Perhaps the last word on chapter 4 should belong to poetry rather than prose. I was hugely impressed with the insights of Horatius Bonar when he wrote,

> *Beloved, let us love: love is of God;*
> *In God alone hath love its true abode.*
> *Beloved, let us love: for they who love,*
> *They only, are his sons, born from above.*

Beloved, let us love: for only thus
Shall we behold that God who loveth us.

The old-world language of Bonar may be quaint, sure it is, I am happy to concede that, but the challenge and the sentiments are no less potent and real for that.

As the American evangelist D L Moody said on one memorable occasion, *'Every Bible should be bound in shoe leather!'*

5

Winners ... every time!

5:1a

The birthmarks of a believer

The opening paragraph in this section is a fascinating one for we are introduced to a term which John has not spoken of previously. In actual fact, the noun is found nowhere else in this epistle and, strange as it may seem, it is also conspicuous by its absence in his Gospel narrative too. Having said that, there is no need for us to get up on our high horses and panic for the verb form is mentioned on a number of occasions with his deployment of the word *'believe'*.

The new word in John's vocabulary is the word *'faith'* which is the Greek word *pistes*. I suppose when we sit down and analyse the thrust behind these verses, it is fairly obvious what John is driving at. He concentrates on the true nature of Christian faith and its evidences in the life of the one who believes in Christ as Lord and Saviour. At the same time, his closing comments in chapter 5 automatically link it to assurance and love; if you like, there is an umbilical cord between them!

Faith matters

The two great constituents of New Testament Christianity, faith and love, are joined together in verse 1. No sooner has John defined the core belief that Jesus is the Christ than he immediately jumps to the impact that should have on our lives. It must of necessity result in a love for God and a love for the children of God. So far as John is concerned, these two elements of biblical Christianity are as inseparable as two sides of the same coin.

'Faith that does not lead to love is meaningless, and love that is not based on faith is powerless.'

In one sense, there is nothing new in what John is promoting and encouraging in the church. Paul was singing from the same song sheet a few years before. For example, in Ephesians 1:15,16 Paul warmly commended the church when he said, 'Ever since I heard about your faith in the Lord Jesus and your love for all the saints, I have not stopped giving thanks for you, remembering you in my prayers.' With the Colossian believers, he goes down a similarly well-travelled route of congratulatory praise when he writes, 'We always thank God, the Father of our Lord Jesus Christ, when we pray for you, because we have heard of your faith in Christ Jesus and of the love you have for all the saints' (1:3,4).

There is another instance which springs to mind. It is when he gave the infant church in Thessalonica a well-earned pat on the back for their exemplary Christianity when he said, 'We continually remember before our God and Father your work produced by faith, your labour prompted by love, and your endurance inspired by hope in our Lord Jesus Christ' (1:3).

It was good enough for John, it was certainly good enough for Paul; but Peter, not one to be left behind, also jumped on the bandwagon when he writes in 1 Peter 1:8, 'Though you have not seen Christ, you love him; and even though you do not see him now, you believe in him and are filled with an inexpressible and glorious joy.'

You see, for a New Testament believer, neither faith nor love was an optional extra; combined, they are the twin pillars on which all true Christian experience rests. This was the sure foundation on which they were building their spiritual lives and it was the immovable rocklike formation on which they were staking their future in God.

No middle ground

It seems to me, the emphasis in John's opening phrase is on the nature of faith. The apostle states, *'Everyone who believes that Jesus is the Christ is born of God.'* The first few words have been used by John on numerous occasions in his letter. It is a turn of phrase that draws a line in the sand, it makes a distinction with a difference. It refers to those who are 'in' and it highlights the need of those who are 'out'.

* It is *inclusive* when it includes all those who satisfy the condition John lays down;
* it is *exclusive* for it excludes all those who fail to toe the party line!

All those on the inside have their faith and confidence rooted in the Lord as their shepherd; they could rightly be called the 'sheep of his pasture'. It necessarily follows that those who are left outside, those who find themselves on the wrong side of the sheep pen, are those who have still not experienced a personal, living relationship with Jesus Christ and, in that sense, they could be described as 'lost sheep'.

Faith is ...

John is at pains in this phrase to underline that which is of maximum import. The stress is laid on the object of faith not the subjective experience of believing. He is basing his entire argument on historical data; he is focusing his thinking and his theology on facts which cannot be disputed. Personal feelings do not enter into the frame at all. All that John can see in his lens is the object of faith and that just happens to be Jesus Christ.

It has nothing to do with any esoteric experience I may have had or may not have had and how I personally feel on the issue as I bask in the afterglow. It has everything to do with evidence which remains fixed and constant, no matter how I feel on a given day! And that testimony is compiled of actual realities and irrefutable evidence.

Faith from a New Testament perspective is not an abstract idea or a theoretical concept; faith is not even an intellectual exercise limited to the highly intelligent! Faith has a distinctive and irreducible content. We will discover this in a moment when we get down to verse 4. In the meantime, however, when we join together the first part of verse 1 and the last part of verse 5 we see what it is.

From this angle, a Christian is a person who believes *'that Jesus is the Christ, the Son of God'*. That is not just a standalone article of faith, it is the faith! It is this alone that makes a person a child of God.

The bottom line is, if an individual does not believe that Jesus is the Son of God, he or she has never been born of God and, consequently, cannot be called a Christian. Such folks are not numbered among those who are members of the household of faith! John touched briefly on this subject in a slightly different context (4:2,3) but the principle remains the same; it holds true for both situations. A firm commitment to the deity of Christ is the deciding factor; it is the kingpin and that is what ultimately clinches the argument for John.

Forty shades of grey

It is worth noting that the tenses used by John in verse 1 are of the utmost importance. That is certainly the case as we face the challenge head-on from a generation of people who live in a society where history is either downgraded or rewritten. We live in a society for whom everything is relative. Without question, this is definitely not an age of absolutes, it is the 'as you see it' mindset; and yet John's message has never been more relevant than it is today as we present our case to a community with an existentialist mindset, people who have relegated truth to an incredibly low level, individuals who have dumbed it down to the point where it is only what they perceive it to be!

Nevertheless, our mandate is still the same. It has not been rescinded nor has it been amended! It has not even been put on the back burner! We are commissioned to proclaim an historical Jesus, the Christ of faith, to a rapidly changing world. The nagging question is, is that really possible today? Sure it is!

John tells us in verse 1 that the person who *'believes'* (present tense) is someone who has been *'born of God'* (perfect past tense). I am no Greek scholar but I am reliably informed by those who are 'in the know' that the perfect tense is used when something which occurred in the past has an abiding influence into the future. So John, in a deft stroke coupled with his expert use of grammar, is employing this tense to indicate something that is a present and continuing reality to the Christian. He is also stating that when a person believes that Jesus is the Christ, he or she has been born again.

The divine ice-breaker

When we read between the lines of what John is teaching, it is clear that it is God who takes the initiative in the new birth, it is God who makes the first move in this great work of salvation; it is God who in grace takes a step in our direction.

Faith is both the gift of God and the first tell-tale sign of new life in him as the brand new Christian confesses that Jesus is the Christ. This truth is not always the easiest one to grasp but it is one which pays eloquent tribute to the love of God in reaching down to sinful man.

John's teaching tallies with Paul's understanding of this sovereign event when he affirms that 'God ... made us alive with Christ even when we were dead in transgressions ... it is by grace you have been saved, through faith - and this is not from yourselves, it is the gift of God' (Ephesians 2:4,5,8). When we combine the teaching from the pen of both apostles, it is crystal clear that salvation is unmistakably a work of God from the very beginning.

The comeback kid scenario

When we present the gospel of new life in Christ to dead men in our day and generation, we know from personal experience there is nothing in them which can clean up the mess they find themselves in, it is only the living God who can give to them abundant life in Jesus.

To me, a brilliant illustration of this truth is found in the moving story of the raising of Lazarus from the dead (John 11). The Lord Jesus spoke and, before we blink an eyelid, it happened! You see,

- there is 'a blow your mind' power in his word, it is limitless;
- there is 'the stuff that dreams are made of' life in his word, it is legendary;
- there is the phenomenal potential of re-creation in his word.

Unfazed?
Not impressed?
What's the big deal?
Where's the catch?

Well, if that is your cynical response, could I suggest you need to ask Lazarus: he could do nothing before it, he could do nothing about it, it was only when the Lord spoke directly into his situation that he knew anything about it! Right up to the point of divine intervention, Lazarus was as dead as dead can be. It was only after Jesus spoke to him personally that he emerged as large as life, ready to tell the tale of what the Lord did for him!

That is why the Bible convincingly declares that the word of truth in the gospel message is the agent of new life in Jesus Christ. Romans 10:17 says as much: 'Faith comes from hearing the message, and the message is heard through the word of Christ.' Someone has rightly said, 'It is as the message that Jesus is the Son of God is faithfully presented that God regenerates and grants the gift of saving faith.'

The old Methodist revivalist, Charles Wesley, was spot on when he penned the lyrics of his classic hymn, 'O for a thousand tongues to sing'. This is what he wrote:

He speaks and, listening to his voice,
new life the dead receive;
The mournful, broken hearts rejoice,
the humble poor believe.

Business as usual

This is tremendous news for the Christian who wants to give away his faith. It means, we do not need to fear for the gospel. It is out of our hands! We can hold our heads high as we share our faith with others. It does not matter what direction the prevailing wind may blow; it does not matter one micro bit that we just happen to live in a post-modern, post-Christian era.

The unassailable fact is that the Lord by his Spirit will continue to do his sovereign work in the hearts of ordinary men and women, young and old alike. Take heart! He has been actively doing it from day one and he is not going to stop now! He has not pulled the shutters down, he has not shut up shop; for him, it is pretty much 'as you were', it is business as usual, and that business is the salvation of perishing souls!

Remember, when it comes to faith, it is not what I feel, it is not how I think! Faith is what I know! More often than not, faith is believing in advance what will only make sense in reverse!

5:1b-5

Three main effects of faith

Faith is like calories - we cannot see them, but we can always see the results! John wholeheartedly agrees.

There is love ... we appreciate God's children

When we speak about love, we are left in absolutely no doubt as to what John is thinking for he says at the end of verse 1, *'Everyone who loves the father loves his child as well.'* When we are born into the ever-increasing family of God we are given a total new identity. In an instant, we become children of our heavenly Father; and because of that, it is the most natural thing in all the world to show and express our appreciation to him for his transforming grace in our lives.

We are not ashamed to say that we love him, we are not embarrassed to openly confess our heart's admiration for him. We are happy to share with others our sincere affection for the one who brought us into an intimate and dynamic relationship with himself. The conscious reality is, we have so much to thank him for, we have so much for which we can legitimately praise him. We owe everything to him and, for the ages of time and the aeons of eternity, we will always remain deeply indebted to him.

That is all part and parcel of the spiritual mindset which says, 'to know him is to love him'. You see, our upfront love for the Lord flows from a heart filled to overflowing with gratitude and appreciation.

A family affair

Such love reaches out to his children as well for he is in the business of gathering to himself a people for his name and a people for his praise and glory. Sure, they may be his children, but that does not diminish the fact that they are our brothers and sisters and, on top of that, they have come into his big happy family from the four corners of the earth.

A natural extension of our love for the Father is for that same love to be applied and shown to those who are in the family alongside us. That means, we are totally committed to each other and the high level of our commitment is reflected in the quality and depth of love that we share with one another.

John has covered an incredible amount of ground on this vitally important subject of interpersonal relationships that I do not want to go into it again; suffice to say, our love for our fellow believers is a tell-tale sign of the reality of our faith in Jesus Christ.

Our aspiration for intimacy with the Almighty, our desire for a deeper relationship with the Lord, a passion to see his kingdom extended, a healthy love for the one who is our Saviour, these are all wonderful spin-offs from our being linked to him in faith.

As we work with one another in the harvest fields of the world, as we pray for one another, as we bear one another's burdens - all of these, and many more, are indicative of a growing awareness of who we are in Christ. But they are also born out of a heart filled with fervent love and devotion to Christ and his people.

The 'show' time religion

It is the old, old story: the proof of the pudding is in the eating. That is what John implies in verse 2 when he says, *'This is how we know that we love the children of God: by loving God and carrying out his commands.'* We know the radical and far-reaching implications behind this verse, don't we! The hidden message is that we have no viable alternative but to go God's way and actively pursue a course of loving our brothers and sisters. If we say it, we need to show it!

This is a command which we are under an obligation to obey; it is a responsibility placed on our shoulders and the man is a fool who thinks he can shirk it or shelve it. The plain fact is, we cannot!

You see, the real assurance of our salvation, in a strange kind of way, is interwoven with our positive response to the word of God. The internal affirmation that we belong to the Lord is best seen in our love for others in the worldwide church of God.

If we are the kind of people he wants us to be, if we are doing what he wants us to do, then we need not fear, there is no need for us to press the panic button in relation to the reality of our faith in God. We are in, we are there; to all intents and purposes, we are home and dry! It is fairly obvious that if we are walking closely with the Lord and fulfilling his unique plan for our lives, then we are already numbered among those who are privileged to be called his children on planet earth.

There is obedience … we apply God's commands

John takes a significant stride forward in his thinking when he writes in verse 3a: *'This is love for God: to obey his commands.'* He makes it clear and plain that not only is obedience to God's commands related to love as an evidence of faith; it is actually the predetermined way in which we love God. That adds a new dimension to it, doesn't it! We tend not to think of it like that but that is what John says and there is no way that we can avoid the issue! We cannot circumnavigate the sentence and pretend it does not exist. It seems to me, this is what gives love its moral fibre.

There is a lot more to biblical love than meets the eye! It is more, so much more, than expressing a nice, lovey-dovey, fulsome sentiment to someone we particularly admire or genuinely appreciate.

Love is not merely a tingling emotion with mega moments of feeling associated with it; true love is an act of the will, it is a fitting response from a captivated heart. To me, it is a thinking man's devotion to Christ.

When we turn back to 4:9,10 we discover the heartbeat of God's love for us is sacrifice and there is no other sort of love with which we can suitably respond to his initiative. To profess our love for the Lord Jesus and to fail to obey his commands is a contradiction in terms. It is a nonsense! It makes a mockery of the whole thing. In fact, it does more, it blows the connection apart! Obedience to the teaching of Scripture is not only important for the child of God, it is imperative! According to John, this is what genuine love is all about and where we have real faith, we have real love.

Too hot to handle

John puts a fascinating slant on all that he has been saying when he says at the end of verse 3, *'And his commands are not burdensome.'* If our attitude to his word is not what it should be, if we have serious hangups about what he says we should do, it means we are effectively undermining his truth in our lives for we perceive that his commands are one big long bore, a bit of a chore, and nothing less than a heavy load for us to handle. Basically, if that is our outlook, we see them as a burden too big for us to carry!

'His commands are no more burdensome than wings are to a bird. They are the means by which we live in freedom and fulfilment, as God intended us to do.' (David Jackman)

If we do what God wants us to do, we are lifted on to a higher plane. In every sense, the rewards are out of this world! We take off and begin to soar with him in a brand new world of spiritual reality! We become high-fliers in the unfolding purpose of God.

When we look at the less than user-friendly legalistic regime of the Pharisees which constantly dogged people down and kept them under the thumb of legislation, we have so much to be thankful for that the law of the Lord sets us free rather than bringing us into bondage! The many rules and regulations of the Pharisees were intended to keep the people in line; the law of God will only keep us in line with his great masterplan for our lives. It will also enable us to live a life which is characterised by love. Love is never a burden. It is a real blessing!

The long and the short of it

You probably realise that the longest chapter in the Bible is Psalm 119 with a grand total of 176 verses; what you may not realise is that its theme is the word of God. In virtually every verse it mentions the word of God in one form or another. I think the only exceptions are verses 122 and 132. The interesting thing about it is this, the Psalmist loves the word of God and he enjoys telling us about it!

He says, for example, in verse 97, 'Oh how I love your law!' Here is a man who rejoices in the word of God, a man who delights in Scripture; he even tells us that it is like honey to his taste, there is a sweetness to the truth of God. I was struck when I read verse 54 where he says, 'Your decrees are the theme of my song wherever I lodge.' That means, he has turned the law of God into a song.

Can you imagine, turning statutes into songs!

Warren Wiersbe writes with more than a hint of humour, 'Suppose the local symphony orchestra presented an evening of the traffic code set to music!' I reckon it is a fair comment to say that most of us do not consider laws a source of joyful song but that is how the Psalmist viewed them. The bottom line is, because he loved the Lord, he loved his law. The commandments of God were not grievous and burdensome to him, they were a sheer, unmitigated delight and pleasure.

The helpful comparison can be made: just as a loving son or daughter happily obeys their father's command, so a Christian with maturing love joyfully obeys God's command. We need to remember that God's law is not some kind of imposition for us to grudgingly embrace and slavishly follow with our hands tied behind our back; rather, it is best seen as an emancipating and liberating force in our lives.

It opens up a whole new vista in our relationship with himself. You will recall I said earlier, 'to know him is to love him' - I believe we can take that noble sentiment a step further now by saying, 'to know him is to love him and to love him is to obey him.'

There is victory ... we appropriate God's conquest

I imagine the name *Nike* is one that you will be familiar with. It is the name of a well-known brand of sportswear; perhaps not so well known is that it is the name of a US aerial missile and it is also the name of the Greek goddess of victory. Victory ... that is what John is talking about here in verses 4 and 5. He is referring to a life of victory, a life of overcoming. The gospel song informs us, 'There's victory in Jesus!' This is the third evidence of true faith in the life of a Christian.

He starts the ball rolling by reminding us in verse 4 that *'everyone born of God overcomes the world. This is the victory that has overcome the world, even our faith.'* It is a bold move on John's part when he makes such a comprehensively sweeping statement in his assertion that every Christian overcomes the world.

There is always an inherent danger in generalisation but John moves swiftly to allay our fears and defuse our concerns when he earths his comments to reality. He goes on to remind us that a believer is someone who has been born of God and, because of that dynamic relationship, he can be triumphant in the rough and tumble of everyday life.

Victory over sin and every alluring temptation is foreign to the unbeliever. He knows little or nothing about it, he falls for it nine times out of ten. For the Christian though, it is a different ball game. We experience a measure of victory for we have the seeds of new life planted in our hearts. We have the presence of the Holy Spirit within us; he makes all the difference in the world, he makes a world of difference!

The Holy Spirit is the one who enables us to appropriate the risen life of Christ; he is the one who facilitates us as we apply the triumph of the cross to our daily battles with the enemy. In every skirmish we have with the adversary, the Holy Spirit is the one who comes to our aid and, thank God, we are not on the losing side. We are on the winning team, every time!

We shall overcome ... *not*, **some day ... today!**

Furthermore, the aorist tense in verse 4b indicates a victory which has been achieved, once and for all! That is the thought behind the words *'has overcome'*. We rewind the tape and focus our attention on that first Good Friday and Easter Sunday; as we step back in time, we think of the unrepeatable, one-off events of the crucifixion and resurrection of Jesus.

Two millennia later through the eye of faith, we rejoice in an empty cross as it stands on a lonely hill outside the walls of the city of gold, and we marvel as we look into an empty tomb in the beautiful setting of a floral garden; it is apropos that both have been vacated and have given way to an occupied throne in heaven itself!

Lest I forget ... lead me to Calvary

That is where the victory was attained; that is where the triumph was achieved; that is where the battle was fought and won in a magnificent display of sovereign power. Jesus did it! Jesus did it all! All that he set out to do he skilfully accomplished when he crushed the opposing forces of darkness. His was an overwhelming knockout of the enemy; he pulverised them, he dealt them a lethal blow and the devil has not recovered since! That is what spells victory for the child of God. That is what puts a smile on the face of every Christian!

This is the sole object of our faith. It is the Lord Jesus Christ. It is the Son of God. The focus is exclusive for it zooms right in on his eternal work of redemption and it is in this faith alone that we can and do conquer. The great news is, the victory is already ours in Christ. All that he accomplished for his people at the place called Calvary is the substance of our faith; it is the core, the crux, the nub, the quintessence of our faith.

The hard part comes when we seek to live in the good of it day after day. We need to personalise it and appropriate it in our daily experience and that only happens in your life and mine when we exercise a high level of faith in a great big wonderful God.

The story is told of an American Civil War veteran who used to wander from place to place begging a bed for the night and a bite to eat. No matter where his travels took him, he always talked about his friend, Mr Lincoln. Because of his serious injuries, he was unable to hold down a steady job, but as long as he could keep going, he would chat about his beloved president. 'You say you knew Mr Lincoln,' a sceptical bystander retorted one day. 'I'm not so sure you did. Prove it!' Well, the old soldier had his wits about him, and he replied, 'Why sure, I can prove it. In fact, I have a piece of paper here that Mr Lincoln himself signed and gave to me.' From his old tattered wallet, the beggar took out a much-folded piece of paper and showed it to the inquisitive man. 'I'm not that good at reading,' the old man apologised, 'but I know that's Mr Lincoln's signature.'

'Man, do you know what you have here?' one of the spectators asked. 'You have a generous federal pension authorised by President Lincoln. You don't have to walk around like a poor tramp living on scraps on the streets. Mr Lincoln has made you rich!'

When we hear a story like that and then turn around and read what John wrote, we can paraphrase it like this, 'You Christians don't have to walk around defeated because Jesus Christ has made you victors! He has roundly trounced every enemy and you share in his victory. Now, by faith, claim his victory!' That is what being a child of God is all about, it is living and walking in victory. The key to it all is summed up in a single word: faith!

I came across a saying the other day which summarises succinctly what John wishes to convey: *Faith is not simply saying that what God says is true; true faith is acting on what God says because it is true.*

It is equally true to say that faith is not so much believing in spite of evidence, but obeying in spite of consequence. When we live our lives in the orbit of God's perfect will then we are able to face the world and all that it throws at us with a conquering faith; we can overcome instead of being overcome! That has to be exceptionally good news for the people of God!

Switched on or turned off!

John does not stop there, he does not leave us in the lurch, he continues in verse 5 by posing a rhetorical question and then providing the answer. We read, *'Who is it that overcomes the world? Only he who believes that Jesus is the Son of God.'* That is the secret! The only secret!

Victory is available to us and, thank God, it can be actualised in our lives when we tap into it by faith. The limitless resources are there, we simply have to take advantage of them. As it were, the Lord has given us a blank cheque, we only have to cash it!

You can see what is happening, can't you. One more time John goes back to basics, he harks back to the fundamental truth of the gospel. If we are going to live a life of victory in the here and now, if we are going to live on top of things today, then we have no option but to affirm our belief in the deity of Jesus. He is the Son of God and he is God the Son!

When we tie all the loose ends together, we discover that we are called principally to a life of faith, a life of dependence upon God. That will be demonstrated by our love for him and for one another. It will be seen in our implicit obedience to his commands and by our victory over the world.

When we fall flat on our face and end up with a bruised ego or a tarnished reputation, the problem is not the Lord's; when we make a mess of things and end up with an omelette on our face, the problem is not his! There is no mileage gained in blaming our heavenly Father. We do not like to face up to it but the problem has been largely one of our own making, it is solely our responsibility for it was coming to us and we did not jump out of the way. The chances are it has come about through a failure in the realm of faith. To add insult to injury and a pinch of salt to the wound, it could all have been so different for it need not have happened!

What faith does is connect my situation to God's resources, rather like plugging my electrical gadgets into the power circuit. Only then will the light of God's truth dispel the darkness, only then will the warmth of God's love expel the coldness of this world's ethos.

The potential is there, the supply is there, the dynamic is there; it is not just a matter of being plugged in, we have to flick on the switch!

When we do that, we are guaranteed to experience victory in Jesus! We will fight in the trenches, we will be out there on the front line, we will operate in enemy territory, we will advance with our eyes fixed on the commander in chief, and we will do it with the words of Paul ringing in our ears, 'But thanks be to God! He gives us the victory through our Lord Jesus Christ.' By any stretch of the imagination, that is real faith!

5:6-10

Faith in the dock!

There is one thing I like about John, he is not someone to dodge the vital issues; he is not prepared to skip over something which he feels is of major importance, no matter how tough and difficult it may be to handle. That is certainly the case when we reflect on the portion in chapter 5 which we are studying together now. A fitting caption for these verses would be the opening words of the old hymn, 'Begone Unbelief!'

What we have here is a valiant attempt by John to press home the issue of faith and unbelief. He does that by stating a number of related facts and by inviting a number of key witnesses into the witness stand. I was interested to note that the Greek word for *'testify'* or *'bear witness'* is used no fewer than ten times in verses 6-11 which gives us some idea as to John's line of argument.

Basically, John is keen to show us that the testimony to Jesus Christ is so incredibly strong that we have no viable reason for rejecting it. The case for Jesus Christ can be substantiated with little or no difficulty. If the truth be told, it is watertight!

It probably needs to be said at the outset that the manuscript support for verse 7 and the first part of verse 8 is extremely weak. You may have a footnote to that effect in your personal copy of the Bible; if you do not have it, do not worry, do not lose any sleep over it, as it all depends on the translation you are using. For example, it is mentioned in the NIV but there is no reference to it in the AV.

Apparently the words came from a fifth century Old Latin version and were incorporated into the Vulgate about AD 800 where they remained. When Erasmus came along, he included the extra text in his third edition of 1522. Luther translated this into German and Tyndale into English. Other printed editions of the Greek New

Testament also included it and by this route it was incorporated into the Textus Receptus and the Authorised Version of 1611.

Three in one, one in three

Having said that, the teaching contained in these few lines is solidly biblical. The Lord our God is a triune God, he is three persons in one; such a truth is echoed in the words of the baptismal formula of Matthew 28:19 as well as the Pauline benediction found in 2 Corinthians 13:14.

However, this passage about the three heavenly witnesses is only found in a few late Greek manuscripts. It was almost certainly added with the best will in the world by some enthusiastic and keen Trinitarians, rather than removed by a handful of mischief-making Arians (the group which vehemently denied the doctrine of the Trinity.)

What the text does say is that there is a trio of witnesses, the water, the blood and the Holy Spirit, and these three witnesses unanimously agree in testifying to the truth of Jesus Christ. We recall it was 'by the mouth of two or three witnesses that the matter shall be established' (Deuteronomy 19:15). So we can understand why there are three witnesses. We do not have a problem in that area, but what does John mean when he talks about the water, the blood, and the Holy Spirit? That is the one I will try to answer.

Water and blood

'This is the one who came by water and blood - Jesus Christ. He did not come by water only, but by water and blood. And it is the Spirit who testifies, because the Spirit is the truth. For there are three that testify: the Spirit, the water and the blood; and the three are in agreement.'

The preposition *'by'* in the middle of verse 6 is an important inclusion on the part of the penman. It can be taken literally to read, 'by means of' or 'through'. What it suggests is this: it reminds us that *'water and blood'* are to be seen as the means by which Jesus

Christ came into the world to accomplish his mission of salvation. We need to keep that to the front of our minds as we unpack these verses.

If you have read any commentary on these verses, you will realise that reams of paper and gallons of ink have been used to promote a wide range of possible explanations for the phrase, *'water and blood'*.

What it isn't

The reformer Martin Luther claimed the water was a reference to baptism and the blood was indicative of the Lord's Supper. In his mind, he felt it was a foreshadowing by the apostle of the two great sacraments of the church.

As far back as Augustine there has been a long line of worthies who have applied these few words to the unique events surrounding the cross of Calvary; to a man they see it as a distinct reference to the blood and water which flowed profusely from the Saviour's side when it was pierced by the Roman soldier's spear (John 19:34,35).

Over the years other folks have come along and they are inclined to see more than a sprinkling of Leviticus permeating the concept, for they portray the water as a cleansing agent, while the blood retains its atoning capability.

I think most of you will agree with my assessment that some of these ideas are quite reasonable, others are a bit more fanciful and some are not a little far-fetched.

What it is

From my perspective, I feel the best way to understand this phrase and the only one which offers a clear and concise interpretation of the text is to see the water as a reference to the baptism of Jesus in the River Jordan and the blood as a reference to the death of Jesus. We read all about his baptism in Matthew 3:13-17 and Mark 1:9-11.

This event was feted as the beginning of the public ministry of Jesus. This was a hugely significant day in his earthly life for it marked the occasion when his identity was revealed to all and sundry; this was the hour when the heavens opened and the Father paid a fulsome tribute to his only Son. It was then, in a moment of high drama, that the Spirit of God descended upon him like a dove.

If you like, it was a *'coming by water'* to take up the unique work which the Father had entrusted to him. That was a task and a role which would eventually lead him to Calvary; it was there he would die as our substitute and as our representative on a cruel cross. Hence the reference to the *'blood'* in John's inclusive phrase.

A complete Jesus

This powerful statement succeeds in pulling the rug from under the feet of the false teachers! At the end of the day, they do not have a leg to stand on. John means that the one who came into the world two thousand years ago, the one whose first coming the prophets of the old covenant anticipated, the one whom all true believers recognise and confess to be the Son of God, this one was as fully and thoroughly the eternal Son, the Christ, at his death as he was at his baptism or his birth. The reality of the passion points to the reality of the incarnation for the whole spectrum of the public ministry of Jesus from his baptism through to his crucifixion shows quite clearly that Christ had come in the flesh.

This was the pivotal point which Cerinthus and his fellow heretics in the Gnostic movement denied. But we affirm that the Jesus who died on the cross was not just a man from whom the divine Spirit had been withdrawn, as the heretics would say, but that when he paid the supreme sacrifice, he was nothing less than God! That is the underlying thought behind the tiny phrase, he *'came by blood'*. Ultimately the entire earthly ministry of Jesus testifies to the veracity and authenticity of his person and work.

The primary purpose of the Lord's advent from heaven to earth as enunciated at his water baptism in the presence of John the Baptist was fulfilled only in his sacrificial death.

As someone has said, 'The same Son of God became the atoning sacrifice for our sins, and it is faith in him alone and in his completed work that brings eternal life, love for God and for his children, and victory over the world.'

I like to think of it this way: your faith and mine which is a personal faith, a real faith, a genuine faith, an authentic faith, is a faith that lays hold of a complete Jesus.

It embraces one whose life's mission started in the Jordan River with the descent of the Holy Spirit but whose mission was not culminated until Calvary. The preacher-cum-poet, William Cowper, was on the right track when he wrote the well-known hymn:

There is a fountain filled with blood,
drawn from Immanuel's veins;
And sinners plunged beneath that flood,
lose all their guilty stains.

E'er since by faith I saw the stream,
thy flowing wounds supply,
Redeeming love has been my theme
and shall be till I die.

That is the focus of a true faith: a Jesus who comes not *'by water only, but by water and blood'*.

It is a robust faith centred in a Jesus who not only lives the life of God, but a Jesus who shed the blood of God.

The Spirit

The source of that faith to which John draws attention in verse 6 is the Holy Spirit. He is witness number three. The previous two, the water and the blood, have been external witnesses; this one is an internal witness for it is the principal role of the Holy Spirit to testify of those things which pertain to Jesus Christ. We find that alluded to and expanded upon in John 15:26.

The old apostle leaves us in no doubt whatsoever as to the integrity and utter reliability of the Spirit of God. He says it a few times in his Gospel narrative when he shares with us the insights of Jesus' teaching in the upper room and he virtually repeats it here: the Holy Spirit is none other than the Spirit of truth. Because he is who he is, the Holy Spirit is the ultimate authority and undergirding of what John and his fellow apostles teach to the church.

If we continue to pursue John's excellent metaphor of a witness in a court of law, it means when the Holy Spirit is called to testify, he does not need to declare, 'I swear by almighty God that I will tell the truth, the whole truth and nothing but the truth'. The reason for this is that he is God! He is truth personified! He bears witness to the truth because he is the truth.

One noted Bible teacher makes a most helpful contribution to the discussion when he says, 'There is no truth apart from God, for truth is grounded in God's character alone.' You see, truth is not the majority view ascertained from a random selection of the public in an opinion poll; truth is not feeling good about something or someone; truth is not an emotional encounter gleaned from a roller-coaster experience. It is none of these. All truth is God's truth because only he is the ultimate reality.

We take heart from the fact that the Holy Spirit continues in his ministry even to this day. He bears witness through the Scriptures, the word of God, the word of truth.

Thank God, the Spirit of God still takes the word of God and produces children of God in the likeness of the Son of God!

Great ... they all agree!

It is exciting to realise when the three witnesses are assembled they are found to be in complete agreement. We find that in verses 7 and 8 where John says, *'For there are three that testify: the Spirit, the water and the blood; and the three are in agreement.'* There is total harmony and unanimity between each of them.

The NIV does not make it quite as clear as it should be due to an unfortunate omission in the text. In the original manuscript, the verse actually begins with the word *'because'*. It is because there is a trio of dependable witnesses - the Spirit, the water and the blood -

so united, that we can have certainty and confidence in our convictions surrounding the Lord Jesus Christ.

In any court of law this would provide the strongest evidence of truth and, beyond any question, the case is carried! Here the three witnesses all agree that Jesus is the Son of God, just as John testified at his baptism (John 1:34) and the Roman centurion testified at his death (Matthew 27:54.) The implication is, whenever that same Spirit brings the truth to light in our lives today, we are brought to confess Jesus as Saviour, Lord and God. Many of us can identify with that because that too has been our personal experience.

He is as good as his word

This leads on very nicely to verse 9 where John states, *'We accept man's testimony, but God's testimony is greater because it is the testimony of God, which he has given about his Son.'* This verse is a robust attempt by John to keep everything in perspective in relation to the whole gamut of truth, trust and testimony. A useful starting point is for John to declare that God is infinitely greater than feeble mortal man; God is greater in every sense but that is especially true when the main beam shines on his nature.

John is at pains to point out both the greater trustworthiness of God's testimony because of its origin and also its greater importance and value because of its content.

The chances are the focus of that testimony is the water baptism of Jesus. It was on that memorable occasion in the Jordan River when the voice of the Father and the descent of the Spirit united the trinity in a powerful combined witness that Jesus is the Son of God. That is the gospel in a nutshell! That is the content of the Christian message! It is stated and authenticated by God himself and confirmed by his three witnesses.

John argues, if we have no serious hangups or qualms accepting human testimony under such circumstances, how can we in all honesty refuse to accept the divine? That is the straightforward logic behind John's line of reasoning and, I have to say, it makes a lot of sense.

I was there when it happened, so I ought to know!

There is a fairly natural and easy progression from verse 9 to verse 10 where John makes the initial comment, *'Anyone who believes in the Son of God has this testimony in his heart.'* This is the outcome of saving faith in Jesus Christ: the sinner is not only aware of his personal sinfulness, he is strangely aware of the eternal deity and perfect holiness of Jesus Christ.

He may not fully understand it, he may not be able to adequately explain it, but he has an inner conviction in his heart, an internal awareness brought about by the influence of the Holy Spirit that Jesus is who he says he is. He realises that Jesus is Lord, that Jesus is the Saviour of the world and that Jesus is the Son of God.

This is borne out by John's use of the Greek present participle which indicates a permanent and continuous action on the part of the one who believes. That is immediately followed by the preposition *'in'* which shows that John means much more than simply believing what Christ says. To believe *'in'* Christ or *'on'* Christ is to commit yourself to him as fully as you know in faithful reliance upon him. It is only as we abandon ourselves in total surrender to him that these great truths hit us between the eyes. That is when the conviction deepens, that is when the realisation of who Jesus is grows on us.

An idiot's guide to knowing Jesus

The negative side of the coin is best seen in the closing half of verse 10 where John declares, *'Anyone who does not believe God, has made him out to be a liar because he has not believed the testimony God has given about his Son.'* John does not beat about the bush, he does not mince his words, he goes straight for the jugular! When man rejects the testimony of God out of hand and gives it an ice cold reception, when he relegates Jesus Christ to the outer fringes of his life, that man is, first and foremost, guilty of calling God a liar! That person is a complete idiot, he is a fool!

To cite John Stott, *'Unbelief is not a misfortune to be pitied, it is a sin to be deplored.'*

The voice of the Father is heard from the highest heights of heaven declaring, 'This is my Son, he is true, listen to him!' But the headstrong sinner digs in his heels and says, 'So what! What's the big deal? Other things are more important in my life!' It has to be said that is an attitude of crass stupidity but, sad to say, that is the mindset of tens of millions of ordinary people all around the world.

Such an appalling response to the claims of Christ in the gospel reveal a heart of rebellion and a heart unmoved by the Spirit of God. It is not that he cannot believe but rather that he will not. Every person who chooses to go down that road is digging a bigger hole for himself and, sooner or later, he will fall into it!

Biblical theology was turned into prayer as Charles Wesley grasped this great reality and put it into words.

'Tis thine the blood to apply,
And give us eyes to see;
Who did for every sinner die,
Hath surely died for me.

Inspire the living faith,
Which whosoe'er receives,
The witness in himself he hath,
And consciously believes.

That faith that conquers all,
And doth the mountain move,
And saves whoe'er on Jesus call,
And perfects them in love.

5:11-13

A matter of life and death

The next couple of verses rank among the greatest in the entire word of God! They are heart stopping! They are staggering! They elasticise our faith well beyond the bounds of easy believism. They are magnificent for they elevate us to life on a higher plane and, at the same time, they give us a marvellous vista of eternity.

Its source

We read in verse 11, *'And this is the testimony: God has given us eternal life, and this life is in his Son.'* In some ways what John says here complements what he has just been referring to in the previous short section of his letter. It is all about the credibility of the witnesses and when those witnesses make up the Godhead, there is not a problem on that particular front! John has also challenged the non-Christian by stating the sobering consequences of a failure to believe. He did that in verse 10 and he touches on it again at the end of verse 12.

Make no mistake! According to John, unbelief is a sin for it is a serious defamation of God's person; it is a slander against his veracity and the net result of that action is a life bereft of God in time and eternity. The contrast is therefore patently obvious when John writes in the manner he does in verse 11.

The Christian is someone who has received the gift of new life in Christ; it is a benefit which is of eternal value and it is one which finds its focus exclusively in Christ. It is not something we have arranged with him to pass on to us at a time which is mutually convenient; there was no bargaining conducted around an open table in an ante-room of some church or chapel. Not a penny changed hands.

The salvation we received has come our way as a direct result of the goodness of God's big heart. It has nothing to do with me or you or anyone else. It is a gift! A free gift! It is a superb present from a wonderfully generous benefactor. Some gifts we receive from family and friends do not last very long, some gifts are better than others in terms of quality and usability, but this gift is decidedly unique for it outlasts the years of time and it stretches forward into the infinity of eternity. It is eternal life! It is life eternal!

The underlying thought bound up in that phrase is, 'the life of the world to come'. Oh yes, we look forward to enjoying it to the full in the there and then but, thank God, we also experience it in the here and now! It is not some futuristic dream, far from it! It is for this precise moment! It is the present possession of every believer in the family of God.

Eternal life is a personal encounter knowledge of God leading to a lifetime of fellowship with him which cannot be counterfeited. It will be climaxed, however, in glory!

Its lack

John continues in a similar vein when he writes in verse 12: *'He who has the Son has life; he who does not have the Son of God does not have life.'* We can see that this verse divides neatly into two halves.

- The first half is a glorious affirmation of the present experience of the Christian: he has life!
- The second half is a tragic reminder of the heart condition of every non-believer: he does not have life!

To all intents and purposes, the sinner is nothing more than a dead man walking. It is the live-body-in-a-morgue syndrome. It is modern man in a mobile coffin. John, in his careful choice of words, makes it glaringly obvious that there is no intermediate stage whereby someone can be flitting from one side to another side. There is no halfway house kind of arrangement when it comes to the gift of eternal life. The bottom line is, we either have it or we do not have it. It is as simple as that, it is as final as that!

I was preaching somewhere recently and I happened to notice the following message emblazoned on a church notice board as a kind of wayside pulpit:

> *KNOW* Christ, *KNOW* life;
> *NO* Christ, *NO* life.

That is the message John is keen to convey and it is as relevant today in the twenty-first century as it was to John's audience in the first.

Its certainty

It seems to me, when we turn to verse 13, that John is attempting to reinforce all that he has been saying. It is one thing to have salvation, it is one thing to have received the gift of eternal life ... it is quite another matter to know it and be sure of it. This was one of the prime reasons for John to put quill to parchment: it was to give those of us who have believed a measure of assurance regarding our personal relationship with Jesus Christ.

When Sir James Simpson, the discoverer of chloroform, was on his deathbed, a friend who ought to have known better asked him, 'Sir, what are your speculations?' Simpson replied, *'Speculations! I have none! "For I know whom I have believed and am persuaded that he is able to keep that which I have committed unto him against that day."'*

In a wonderful way, that is the gist of what John says here: *'I write these things to you who believe in the name of the Son of God so that you may know that you have eternal life.'*

Simpson was absolutely right for the Christian lives his life not on explanations or speculations; he lives his life with a calm assurance grounded in the promises of God in Scripture. Christianity is not a hope-so, it-might-be-alright-on-the-night kind of religion; rather, it is one that guarantees the future and allied to that it promises a bright hope to all who embrace Jesus Christ in an act of simple faith.

There is no air of uncertainty hovering over the gospel of Christ. No dark ominous clouds can threaten our long-term future for in the words of David Livingstone, 'Our future is as bright as the promises of God.'

Our faith in God is based on timeless truth and changeless facts. We stand four square on a rock solid foundation! Even when our weary steps may falter and we fall on the rock, thank God, we will never fall off the rock! We are secure in Christ, we are eternally secure in Christ, and day after day we are held in the firm grip of his grace. Ours is a 'so great salvation' and, I am thrilled to say, I believe it and I know it!

This is where evangelical Christianity is so radically different from many of the cults and other world religions which come knocking on our doorstep. They offer no assurance, they leave people with no confidence in where they will be five minutes after they die! So much of what they offer depends on fate and how everything turns out in the end. A lot of it is performance related and it is down to the whim of a last-minute divine appraisal. They tell us we cannot be sure of anything in this life, so how can we possibly expect to face the future with a high level of confidence in our heart and mind? We are advised that if we have it today, the chances are we might lose it tomorrow because life offers no cast-iron guarantees. I am glad to say, they are all wrong, they are all barking up the wrong tree.

We *can* be sure!
We *can* be certain!
We *can* be saved!
And, thank God, we *can* know it!

- *The worst thing the church can do for non-Christians is to convince them that they are Christians.*
- *The best thing it can do for true Christians is to assure them of God's electing and everlasting love.*

5:14,15

Highly effective prayer

I agree with Peter Barnes who writes in the Welwyn Series of commentaries, *'Presumption and doubt put the sinner to sleep; faith and assurance animate the believer to greater godliness.'*

That is the thought which John carries with him into the final section of his timely epistle. Each of the themes he covers in verses 14-21 he has touched on before to a greater or lesser degree. In that sense we are going over old ground.

Having said that, there is a big plus here for John highlights for us four ways in which these God given certainties can be deepened as we work out our faith in practice. It is the ripple effect. It is what happens when we throw a pebble into a pond, the impact is far reaching and that is what John is keen to encourage; that is what he wants each of us to actively pursue.

Lord, teach us ...

Verses 14 and 15 go hand in hand for they are all about the fundamentals of intercession and how we can see answers to our prayers. John provides us with some outstanding insights on the dynamics and power of prayer and he leaves us in no doubt that prayer is immensely worthwhile.

For most of us, prayer can be a tough assignment at the best of times. It is something many of us struggle with. There always seems to be so many other pressures encroaching on our time so that prayer is something we often do on the hoof, and even when we do get down to it, we are never quite sure how to go about it!

I imagine the early disciples felt much the same as we often do. It never ceases to amaze me that they did not come to Jesus and ask him, 'Lord, teach us to preach', *or* 'Lord, teach us how to witness to our family and friends', *or* 'Lord, teach us to work miracles'. They did not do any of these. They came with something much more basic than that; their request was, 'Lord, teach us to pray'.

Well, that is what John is seeking to do in these two verses, where he writes, *'This is the confidence we have in approaching God: that if we ask anything according to his will, he hears us. And if we know that he hears us, whatever we ask, we know that we have what we asked of him.'*

We can do it!

John is batting here on the front foot. Did you notice how he opens up the subject? He introduces his teaching on prayer with a reference to the confidence factor in our lives. The fact that we have eternal life should be an enormous boost to our spiritual lives and it should send the adrenaline flowing through our veins. That should be evident when we seek to touch the throne of God in prayer. It means, we can draw dear to him with a high level of confidence in our hearts, we can come close to him and approach him with boldness, for that is the real thought behind the Greek word *parrhesia.*

When we think of boldness, we are not thinking of arrogance or someone flaunting himself before the Lord. We are not thinking of someone being downright cheeky and brazen before the Lord. The idea here is of freedom of speech. It suggests our conversation with God will be something which is uninhibited, it will be open and relaxed. The words will flow from our hearts via our lips in quite a natural manner and we will do it with an attitude of reverence and submission.

The art of communication

Prayer should be a mirror of our relationship with God.

He is, after all, our loving heavenly Father. This is a term John has used on three other occasions in his epistle (2:28, 3:21, 4:17). By and large the emphasis there has been on confident living and confident dying. John draws our earnest attention to the coming again of Jesus and he speaks of the great need to be able to stand before him on that final day without any regrets. He shows us that our confidence is linked to his deeper work of grace in our hearts for his sanctifying touch is making us increasingly more like Jesus. So when John uses the word here in the context of communication with heaven, it is obvious he wants to give us some vital information on confident praying!

Spending quality time with God

I love and appreciate the apostle's excellent choice of words when he specifically refers to prayer as *'approaching God'*. That is exactly what it is. It is a definite act on our part, it is something intentional, but it also shows that we recognise the need to turn away from everything else which is occupying our interest to seek his face alone. I know we can talk to him anywhere and we can do it at any time, but I am sure he appreciates it so much more when we set aside quality time each day just to chat and converse with him.

We approach him not out of curiosity, but with confidence; we come to him not with a spirit of dread or apprehension, but we come with a full heart, an open heart, an honest heart. And in the words of the evangelical cliché, we rapidly discover that God hears and answers prayer!

'Lord, it's not what I want ... it's what you want'

The prime secret according to John to getting answers to prayer is to pray in the will of God. The old saying is true, 'Prayer is a mighty instrument, not for getting man's will done in heaven, but for getting God's will done on earth.'

George Mueller could rightly be described as a man of prayer. His biography records many instances when God abundantly answered his prayers, especially in relation to his ministry to the thousands of orphans who came across his path. Mueller is on record as saying, *'Prayer is not overcoming God's reluctance; it is laying hold of God's willingness.'*

Prayer is not an attempt to get God to see things my way and to extract from him what I have decided I need or I want. Prayer is putting all my cards on the table and leaving the final decision to him. Prayer is submitting my will to his perfect will.

I came across a paraphrase of the Lord's Prayer which goes like this: 'Your will be done in me, your bit of earth, as it is in Christ, who is my heaven!' In essence, this is what assured prayer is all about for that is the secret of prevailing prayer: it is when I open the door of my personal need to the Lord Jesus. When we lay bare our hearts before him, we have assurance and confidence that he will only do what is best for us.

The fact is, if God were to answer on any other basis, which of us would ever dare to pray again? If that were the way he handled us, I think most of us would think twice before we opened our mouths again in his presence. It is good to remind ourselves that God is neither deaf nor blind; he is familiar with every situation we find ourselves in, he sees the needs and the problems we face every day. He hears every word that falls from our lips and, even when we fail to adequately express our feelings and frustrations, he hears every sigh.

No pending tray in heaven

That should give fresh impetus to our prayer lives, it should spur us on, for as we discover in verse 15, with God, to so much as hear our prayer is to answer our prayer! This is the dramatic force of the present tense, *'we have what we asked'*. This is tremendous! There is no pending tray with God.

From our human perspective, the outworking of the answer may not be seen until some time in the future; nevertheless, our requests are granted at once. God does not need time to think the issue through, he does not need a few days to deliberate on the ramifications of his answer.

Extraterrestrial comings and goings

This is superbly illustrated in the life of Daniel in chapter 10 of his volume. The principle emerging from the experience of Daniel is that an apparent delay to the answer is not a denial from the heart and hand of God. As the prophet-cum-historian was to find out, there was a series of other mitigating circumstances, there was a battle raging in the heavenly realm and the angel who was dispatched from heaven with the answer to Daniel's prayer was delayed for three weeks!

The answer to Daniel's prayer was immediate but his experience of it was anything but that. The delay is attributed to spiritual warfare on a cosmic scale and, if that is what happened in Daniel's day, how much more likely it is to happen in our day!

It makes us realise that what is going on out there may not necessarily be what is happening!

That adds a new dimension to prayer! Where we do it, whenever we do it, we know we are 'coming to a King, and large petitions we can bring, for his grace and power are such, none can ever ask too much'. The fact is, God is more willing to bless us than we are willing to ask! Joseph Scriven's much loved hymn says it all:

Oh what peace we often forfeit,
Oh what needless pain we bear,
All because we do not carry,
Everything to God in prayer.

Prayer changes things, prayer changes people!

The leader of the 1843 Disruption in Scotland was a gentleman by the name of Thomas Chalmers. To this day it is possible to see his statue and visit his grave in Auld Reekie, Scotland's capital city of Edinburgh. He wrote in his diary, 'Make me sensible of real answers to actual requests, as evidences of an interchange between myself on earth and my Saviour in heaven.' You see, there is a man who was seeking to grow in assurance as he came to God in prayer.

Chalmers desperately wanted to know that his prayers were making a significant difference in human history. It goes without saying, they were!

And so can yours! Like him, you can be a history maker!

5:16-20

Prayer works!

All things considered, this is a fascinating section in John's epistle for he covers a fair bit of ground as he draws together the various strands of his teaching.

A new angle to prayer

These two verses (5:16,17) have over the years proven to be two of the most contentious in Scripture. They have an unenviable track record for they are incredibly difficult to interpret and that exercise is made a million times worse if they are lifted out of context and left to stand alone. Sad to say, that is what so many well-meaning expositors have done and, in some ways, they have ended up making a rod for their own back!

John puts it like this: *'If anyone sees his brother commit a sin that does not lead to death, he should pray and God will give him life. I refer to those whose sin does not lead to death. There is a sin that leads to death. I am not saying that he should pray about that. All wrongdoing is sin, and there is sin that does not lead to death.'*

One does, one doesn't!

I think the key to understanding these verses is to try to ascertain what the inspired John means when he talks about *'a sin that does not lead to death'* and *'a sin that leads to death'*. In the first instance, we are warmly encouraged to pray for a believer whom we see sinning; in the second example, we are specifically told not to pray. The niggling question is, what is the difference between the two experiences? Why pray for one and not intercede for the other?

Two brand names for sin

The traditional view of one major world religion ~ Roman Catholicism ~ is that there are two categories of sin. According to their best brains, a 'venial' sin can be pardoned whilst a 'mortal' sin automatically leads to death. However, when we take a moment and look at the Johannine text, it lends no credibility to such a school of thought; it offers no support for such a 'fine-line' division of sins, much less for a list of seven deadly 'mortal' sins. The biblical view is that every sin is a mortal sin, since every sin pays the wages of eternal death (Romans 6:23).

For some ... life is a dead-end street

Other folks have come along and they have taught that the only way the *'sin that leads to death'* can be explained is by its drastic consequences in a literal physical sense. They cite the much-trumpeted example of what happened to Ananias and Sapphira when they backtracked on their verbal commitment in Acts 5:1-11 to back up their case. They also point to the Pauline references in 1 Corinthians 5:5 and 11:30 to an immoral man being handed over to Satan 'so that the sinful nature may be destroyed' and to those who have 'fallen asleep' because of their dreadful abuses of the Lord's Supper.

If that is the correct interpretation, then there is apparent support for it in Scripture. Personally, I do not think it holds too much water; in fact, without being too unkind, it is a bit like the proverbial sieve!

We need to remember, when John's words are seen in their context, the contrast he makes is with eternal life, so that spiritual death, rather than physical death, is the most natural reading of the text. As an aside, John is discouraging prayer for such people since it would mean praying for the dead!

The unpardonable sin?

A fairly common view in some sectors of the evangelical church is to identify the *'sin that leads to death'* with the blasphemy against the Holy Spirit which the Lord Jesus referred to in Matthew 12:31,32. More often than not, people speak of this as the unpardonable or unforgivable sin. I suppose the connection depends on the distinction that is drawn between this and all other sins in that this sin, being unpardonable, results in death.

It is helpful to note that John says nothing about the Holy Spirit in this context; he does not bring him into the equation at all. I have met many dear Christian people over the years who have given themselves sleepless nights over this issue. It has caused them immense pain and anxiety, they have wrestled with the idea that somewhere down the line they may have committed the unpardonable sin!

Who is a pardoning God like thee?

The glorious truth is that in the redemptive work of Jesus, we have one whose blood can deal effectively with each and every sin; we have a gracious God who finds enormous delight in pardoning a lost sinner and restoring a Christian who has fallen on hard times. As I said at the outset, we need to keep this whole matter in context.

Saying 'no' to Jesus

The punchline in John's teaching in this final section is on knowing God. He makes it clear that it is only those who believe that Jesus is the Son of God who have eternal life. The inference is *'the sin that leads to death'* is the sin that ultimately excludes the sinner from the life of God. It can be no other than a blatant denial of that saving truth.

If this is right, and I firmly believe it is, then the *'sin that leads to death'* does so because, by its intrinsic nature, it rejects the only means by which sin may be forgiven. It says a doggedly defiant 'no' to the atoning death of the incarnate Son of God. It spurns God's offer of love and mercy in the gospel of Christ. It walks away from an opportunity to be reconciled to God.

David Jackman wraps up the idea succinctly when he writes, *'This underlines the important truth that it is not that this sin is unpardonable, but that it remains unpardoned.'*

The sin that automatically leads to death is unforgiven sin. The sole reason why it remains unforgiven is because that individual refuses to bend the knee in repentance before the Christ of the cross of Calvary.

Identification … don't pick the wrong man

When we turn back to the text, the example which is given is of a Christian brother committing a *'sin that does not lead to death'*. There is nothing, absolutely nothing, about a believer committing the sin that leads to death; there is simply the reminder that such a sin does exist. I have no doubts that the first part of verse 16 is most relevant to church life in the third millennium, it applies to every congregation of God's people in every generation for it puts a new angle on prayer.

How to make it right when we get it wrong

We have all come across the problem at one time or another: a Christian falls into sin and everyone else in the assembly is aware of it. What should we do in a situation like that? What should our response be? How should we handle it?

There are many guidelines set down in Scripture for such events and John here provides us with one that is basic and fundamental. He says we should pray for him! We should lift him up before the Lord in earnest prayer that he might be fully restored to happy fellowship with the Lord and to an enjoyment of his blessing upon his life.

When we fervently and lovingly storm the gates of glory on behalf of our backslidden brothers and sisters, the Lord in his own good time will bring them back into a close walk with himself and, as John says, he will give them life! The sinning Christian whose spiritual life is on the wane and whose relationship with Christ is wilting, even though he is not dead nor sinning unto death, will be restored by the grace of God through the prayers of the church family.

That should thrill us and it should also give us the stimulus we need to engage our hearts in believing prayer for all those who have strayed into bypath meadow. Our Father in heaven wants it to happen and coupled with our prayers on their behalf he will ensure that it takes place. That is why we watch after we pray for it is good to keep an eye open for an answer to our prayers!

Where prayer makes no difference

With regard to the sin that leads to death, John says, *'I am not saying that he should pray about that'*. This is serious, very serious. It is an extreme case. Even when things are pushed beyond the limit, even when events have overtaken us and are now hanging precariously over the edge, John is not forbidding prayer, he simply does not command it or encourage it.

To all intents and purposes, prayer in such a circumstance will make little or no difference. Basically, there is no point in us wasting our time praying for we have entered into a totally new domain, we are caught up in the Pharaoh syndrome. It is where a hardening of the heart takes place and such folks have gone well past the point of no return (Exodus 10:27).

The unambiguous reference in this verse is to all those who have become apostate in their thinking and theology; John is singling out those who have walked out on the community of God's people and openly denied the doctrines of salvation. No matter what they may once have professed to believe, they have put themselves beyond the reach of the church's prayers.

A similar line of approach is adopted by the writer of Hebrews 6:4-6 where he highlights the sheer impossibility of their current situation. They have turned their backs on God and God is left with no alternative but to turn his face away from them! That is why John does not encourage prayer or solicit prayer for such people.

Removing a name from a prayer list

Sure, there are those for whom we should pray, there are those for whom we must pray; such folks desperately need our faithful prayers and, because they are the Lord's, they deserve our prayers.

It grieves me to say it but it is equally true to say, there are some names which should be deleted from our prayer list.

They may need our prayers, but they certainly do not deserve them.

According to John, there is no point in targeting them for they have removed themselves outside the orbit of prayer, they are very much on their own and they have only themselves to blame. It is not our fault, it is theirs, and theirs alone!

A new antipathy towards sin

We know! We know! We know! Those are the opening words in the next three verses and they are a terrific shout of confidence! We are told in verse 18, *'We know that anyone born of God does not continue to sin; the one who was born of God keeps him safe, and the evil one cannot harm him.'*

We have been down this road before in our studies in 1 John and it means the Christian is a new man in Christ Jesus and because of that life-changing experience he does not go on sinning as he did before he turned to Christ. The true believer is someone who has a deep aversion to sin, he has a strong dislike of sin; he cannot stand the sight of it and it is the last thing he wants to do.

The phrase *'born of God'* is repeated a couple of times in this verse. This has caused a fair bit of uncertainty over the years because in the English translation it reads the same in both instances. However, when we read it in the Greek, it is significantly different!

Participles make a difference!

The first is the perfect participle which John uses regularly to describe the people of God. It indicates a relationship begun at a given point in the past with a continuing effect in the present. Because I was born, I am alive now! That was true in the natural realm, it is equally relevant in the spiritual world.

The second time John uses it, the word is the aorist participle which expresses a once-for-all fact. It refers to the one who was always born of God, outside of time, and who is therefore the eternal Son, the Lord Jesus Christ. One translation actually puts it like this: 'It is the Son of God who keeps him safe.'

Why do I not keep on sinning? Here is the answer! It has nothing to do with me for I could never achieve it under my own steam; it has everything to do with the Lord Jesus. He is the one who is actively working on my behalf.

Like a limpet

There is a marvellous truth tucked away at the end of the verse and we do not want to miss it. It is Christ who keeps us safe so that the devil cannot, literally, 'fasten himself' upon us like a limpet. He will attack us alright, there is no question about that but, thank God, he cannot gain a foothold. Satan can never succeed in getting us back into his grip. That is where the world is, it is in the tentacles of the evil one; he has it where he wants it to be, it is in his clutch.

Even though we may struggle against sin in our daily lives, even though we face many an onslaught from the enemy, even though he does all in the power he has at his disposal to touch us and harm us, praise God, he can never take us! The reality is, the Lord is with us, God is for us. We have total security because we are abiding in Christ. The baseline is, the new birth results in new behaviour, the new life necessitates a new lifestyle!

A new attitude to the world

John says, *'We know that we are children of God, and that the whole world is under the control of the evil one'* (5:19). This is great for it reminds us of the assurance we have because we are the Lord's own people. We are born and brought into the global family of God at the precise moment of our conversion. We have many brothers and sisters all over the place and together we share a common salvation.

We not only share a relationship with one another on a horizontal level, we also share a vertical relationship with our Father in heaven. We enjoy sweet and happy fellowship with each other because we have, first of all, experienced the delights of fellowship with the Lord. So far as the children of God are concerned, there is no question of an identity crisis; we know who we are!

The devil's playground

In the next breath, John reminds us of the status of the world in which we live. He implies that it is under the domination of the devil. He is the one who controls it, it is under his sway, he is the one who is running the show and he has an abundance of fallen stars who are more than happy to help him. No matter what he puts his hand to, it is a vain attempt to outdo the God of heaven.

But wait! The devil may see himself as the controller of the universe, the truth is, God is still in the driving seat! He is the divine supremo! The Lord reigns! Heaven rules! In a crazy, devil-inspired, topsy-turvy world, we can rejoice that our God is still on the throne and he will remember his own.

A new awareness of God

John's final assertion takes us to the penultimate verse in his first epistle. It is verse 20 where he says, *'We know also that the Son of God has come and has given us understanding, so that we may know him who is true. And we are in him who is true - even in his Son Jesus Christ. He is the true God and eternal life.'* This last great conviction echoed by John is, of course, the ground and substance of the preceding two. Your faith and mine is rooted in what God has done in history. We are followers of the historical Jesus and we are worshippers of the ascended, exalted and glorified Lord.

I think the *'understanding'* which John speaks of here is both a spiritual and an intellectual capacity to receive truth. One writer has noted, 'God's truth is addressed to the mind, through which it penetrates the heart, to activate the will.' That is not only true on an intellectual level, it is also true on a moral and spiritual level.

Knowing truth is all about knowing God and knowing God is all about fellowship with God.

Paul expressed similar aspirations in his prayer of Philippians 3:10. Graham Kendrick puts it like this: 'Knowing you, Jesus, knowing you ... there is no greater thing. You're my all, you're the best, you're my joy, my righteousness, and I love you, Lord.'

The intimacy of our communion with God is stressed by John as is the unique position we occupy! We cannot be any nearer, we could not be any closer! We are in him and he is in us; he shares with us his own indestructible life, a life which is eternal! This is fellowship at its highest level and that is what John introduced us to at the start of his letter in 1:2,3.

We have reached the top of the spiral staircase and, wonder of wonders, we have found God himself and, in him, a life without end and a life without equal!

5:21

John's parting shot

John's final word keeps our feet firmly on the ground for he issues a strong warning in verse 21, *'Dear children, keep yourselves from idols.'* On the face of it, that may seem a strange way to end a letter of love and light but, the more we think about it, the more relevant it all becomes.

- *Anything that squeezes God out of number one position in my life is an idol.*
- *Anything that relegates him to a lower rung on the ladder is an idol.*
- *Anything that moves him out to the fringes and the periphery of my life is an idol.*

Says John, look out! Be on your guard! Exercise extreme caution! Do not let it happen to you! It is a real threat in a real world. It is a subtle danger we constantly face. It is a gigantic problem we all have to grapple with. Basically, John warns us not to prostitute our faith on unworthy objects of human speculation and opinion.

If we are going to stand firm against the enemy of our souls, we need a high view of Scripture, we need a proper view of God, we need to understand who Jesus is, we need a fuller appreciation of his redemptive work on the cross at Calvary.

- *The focus of our faith is Jesus Christ.*
- *The source of our faith is the testimony of the Holy Spirit in our heart.*
- *The fruit of our faith is victory over the world!*

The ultimate challenge from John's pen is, do not live your life on substitutes, do not feed your faith on additives. Live a real life, live it in a real world, live it with a real faith in the Lord, in a God who is real!

---

2 JOHN

6

The benefits of a daily walk

Background info

I cannot remember the last time I heard a sermon on 2 John; in fact, I am not sure that I have ever heard anyone preach on it! I know for myself, this is the first time I have ever studied it, let alone ministered on it in the past! As they say, there is always a first time.

2 John is a relatively brief letter as letters go with only 13 verses to it. It can be easily read through in a couple of minutes. It has often been referred to as a postcard for it is short enough to fit on a single sheet of papyrus. It is one of five single chapter books in the Bible: we have the prophet Obadiah in the Old Testament and Philemon, 2 John, 3 John and Jude in the New Testament.

They have often been described as God's special post-it notes to his people. They are short, yet significant; they are brief, yet beneficial.

I can assure you, it may be short in terms of length, but it is long in terms of counsel and sound advice.

John is a dab hand at knowing how to pack a punch and never more so than when he picks up his quill to engage in a heart-to-heart dialogue. His second epistle has been well-described as 'a perfect gem of sacred correspondence'. I suppose this message along with the epistles of 3 John and Philemon are the nearest we approach in the New Testament to a piece of first century communication by letter.

Nom de plume

So far in our study I have assumed that the author of the letter is John. It has to be said, however, that is only an assumption on my part; the fact is, his name is not mentioned anywhere in the epistle. The opening two words in verse 1 simply identify the penman as *'the elder'*. The question is, who is meant by this pseudonym? The nameless writer obviously knows what he is talking about and it is clear from the note that he is extremely well acquainted with the recipients of his message.

The cryptic word *'elder'* is a term which comes from the Greek word *presbuteros* which has the general meaning of 'an old man'. It is a word that is frequently used in the New Testament in a technical sense to designate rank or office and, when it is used within that framework, it is normally translated 'elder' or 'presbyter'.

It hinges on whether John the apostle might not also be known as *'the elder'* and that is the area in which a lot of combustible energy in terms of scholarly debate is continuing. The fact that it speaks of *'the elder'* as a definite title obviously indicates that it was quite sufficient to identify the author to his readers; they knew exactly who was writing to them. So far as they were concerned, there was no problem, there was no identity crisis, there was not the slightest chance of mistaken identity.

We can look at it like this: if I were to say to my wife, 'I had a delicious cappuccino and cake with the minister this afternoon' …

she would (hopefully) know the person I am referring to even though I have not mentioned him by name!

Good enough for Peter!

I really do struggle to understand what all the fuss is about as Peter went down a similar track when he portrayed himself as a 'fellow elder' in 1 Peter 5:1. He did this at a time when he was already widely recognised as an apostle in the early church. That means, it is possible to be both an apostle and an elder at the same time! The dual roles are at no time seen as a potential threat to one another; instead they beautifully complement each other.

If it is good enough for Peter, I have no quibble with John adopting the same stance, particularly at a time when, as an old man, he was the last remaining member of the apostolic band left on earth. I think it is a most appropriate title especially when we realise John's relationship towards his readers is that of fatherly affection for his little children.

I have no nagging doubts in my mind that, when a comparison is made between the content and vocabulary of the three letters, the weight of evidence clearly indicates that one author is responsible for each of them. And to me, the apostle John is by far the most likely candidate to fill that editorial role.

Over the years I have seen scores of pastoral letters from a minister to his congregation. I have written hundreds myself! Some of them have been signed in the traditional fashion, many of them have signed off with the words, *'your pastor'*. Rest assured, you can take it from me, everyone in the church knows full well the identity of the anonymous correspondent!

I am inclined to think that the omission of the person's name makes it a lot less formal; if anything, it actually lends to its intimacy and warmth. So much for the author - I believe it was John!

On the receiving end

The next hurdle we have to overcome surrounds the identity of those to whom the apostle is writing. We read in verse 1 that the notelet is specifically addressed *'to the chosen lady and her children'*.

There are many eminent Bible teachers, household names, who feel that the *'chosen lady'* is the church personified. They see in her a distinct reference to the local church. When John talks about *'her children'* in the same inclusive phrase, they see them as being representative of the believers who are engaging in happy fellowship in the assembly.

The reference to the *'chosen sister'* in verse 13 is therefore seen as a figure of speech which applies to a sister church down the road that was sending Christian greetings to the said gathering of the people of God. It is a fair assessment to make that this view has a lot going for it, it has much to commend it.

Feminine focus

Having said that, I am more inclined to subscribe to the notion that sees the *'chosen lady'* as a godly mother. I think she is someone who is a devoted follower of Jesus Christ and, at the same time, she has had the joy and thrill of seeing her children come to saving faith in the Lord.

This line of interpretation tends to see her as an ordinary 'made of the same material as the rest of us' kind of individual whose radiant life has made a huge impact on her family in the home and her spiritual influence has spread out into the wider community for her testimony is respected by ever so many people. There are many who genuinely appreciate her for who she is and for what she does and, true to form, there are those who have taken advantage of her as well!

The chances are she was following in the footsteps of Philemon and many others when she made her home available for the various church meetings. It is accurate to state that John does address a group in this letter. We find the plural tense used in verses 6, 8, 10 and 12. It is equally true that John also addresses an individual, as is clear from verses 1, 4, 5, and 13.

The danger is we cannot see the forest for the trees! If we step outside into the bright light and take a look at the big picture, the most likely scenario to emerge is that of a Christian assembly which was meeting in this lady's home - they shared sweet times of enriching fellowship alongside the family of the *'chosen lady'* - therefore John had both the family and the congregation in mind when he put pen to paper.

There is nothing strange or startling about this for a similar situation existed in a handful of other places if the comments of Paul in Romans 16:5, 1 Corinthians 16:19, Colossians 4:15 and Philemon 2 are anything to go by. 'The church that meets at their house' was almost the norm in the first century, it was par for the course, that is the way it was then!

Don't throw the baby out with the bath water

The gist of John's message is: make sure your love has limits! John has a burden on his heart and it comes out very clearly in the chapter. He gives voice to many of his concerns. He makes an impassioned plea for spiritual discernment to be exercised on our part; he longs that we might exercise spiritual discretion when we throw open the doors of our homes to all and sundry. Carefully does it!

There is a grave danger that a false teacher could walk in and seriously undermine the local company of God's people. It is one thing to have a big heart and an open home but we must be wise and not allow our heart to rule our head. Caution must not be thrown to the wind! That is what John is trying to get across!

The problem was exacerbated because, back in the days of John, the church did not have the complete canon of Scripture. At best they had access to the Old Testament along with a few letters and books from the New Testament. Because of that, it meant there was a unique role for those who were specially gifted as prophets and teachers.

Preachers on the evangelical merry-go-round

Such men would travel from place to place in a much-needed peripatetic ministry. To all intents and purposes, they were travelling preachers who would spend a few days here and then move on to somewhere else. Such able men with an itinerant ministry were highly esteemed among the people of God.

The dilemma they found themselves in is a fairly obvious one: where would they stay when they were ministering in a given locality? The fact is, the likes of Holiday Inn and Travel Lodge were not around then!

The only accommodation that was generally available were public inns and these tended to be little more than brothels. That much is clear from the assessment of the rabbis in the Mishnah where innkeepers are placed on the lowest scale of human degradation. Even Roman law attests to the fact that innkeepers were untruthful, dishonest and even oppressive. Plato went a step further and labelled them pirates!

Bed and breakfast ... at your place

So what were the circuit-ridin' preachers supposed to do? What else could they do? The only viable alternative was for them to stay with some of the church people. The Christians in the local community would pool their meagre resources and provide them with a good square meal and a clean bed. These folks would show a valuable ministry of gracious hospitality to the servants of God. Sad to say, there were those who took advantage of it; the fact is, we will always get those who want to sponge off others!

A preacher's code of conduct

When we leaf through the pages of *The Didache,* which is the earliest book of church order, we notice that strict rules were laid down regarding itinerant teachers. This was an early-day version of a code of conduct that was drawn up as guidelines for them to follow.

It stated quite clearly that such a person was to stay only one or two days at a household; if he stayed longer than that or if he asked for money over and above his lodging and food, he was recognised as a false prophet. Such a person was termed a Christmonger.

There are times when we have to say 'no'

It would appear from reading between the lines in verses 9 and 10 that the dear woman John is addressing had a torridly difficult time knowing which travelling preachers to accept into her home and which to turn away. Her front door was always open and, quite honestly, she did not have the heart to say 'no' to anyone. The thought of turning somebody away from her front door was horribly repulsive to her.

The simple fact is, with all her love and keen enthusiasm to serve others, she needed to take a deep breath, put her brain into gear, and exercise a higher level of caution. In her tremendous zeal to show hospitality, it seems she lost sight of discretion.

That is the main reason why John drafted his second epistle. It was a bold attempt to strike a healthy balance between truth and love!

Many of us know from personal experience that some churches can major on truth at the expense of love, and others can swing the pendulum in the opposite direction so that they are so loving they are untruthful.

Charles Swindoll puts everything in perspective when he writes, *'The postcard of 2 John serves as a fulcrum to keep these two playmates in a happy balance so that neither gets hurt.'*

I like that and I think we will discover as we proceed to work our way through the letter how well John succeeds.

1-3

To tell you the truth

I think if someone sent me a letter like this one, it would bring more than a smile to my face, I would probably end up splitting my sides with laughter, especially when I read the introduction. This is what it says in verse 1, *'The elder, to the chosen lady and her children, whom I love in the truth - and not I only, but also all who know the truth.'*

Not the usual introduction to a letter, if I may say so! It is different, to say the least! What is happening is this: John warmly greets the anonymous woman and he uses the example of his personal relationship with her as a reference point for his teaching. There is nothing wrong with what he says, there is nothing wrong with what he does. It is all above-board. His relationship is a proper one and it is one which is marked by purity of heart and mind. The emphasis here is centred on *'truth'* for that is a word which John uses a couple of times in the space of two lines! This could mean one of two things:

* *It could mean that John's affection for her is genuine and real, there is nothing superficial about it. She occupies a special place in his heart and, for that reason, his is an authentic love for her. This places the emphasis on love.*

* *It could mean that John has a high regard for her as a member of the international family of God. He esteems her as someone who is 'in the truth' and he values her as a dear sister in the Lord. This underlines the aspect of truth.*

You can't keep a good woman down

John's eye-opener of a comment in verse 1 is hugely impressive especially when he goes on to acknowledge that he is not the only one who feels this way about her. There are others within the Christian community who see her as a shining example of godly living. There are many people, near and far, who are immensely grateful and thankful to the Lord for the consistent testimony she bears to the grace of God in her life.

I think that is a lovely touch from John; he is not afraid to give credit where it is due, he is not embarrassed to hand out floral bouquets to those who deserve them. It gives us a little idea of what makes this man tick. You see, a thoughtful word of encouragement goes a very long way, it is like oxygen for the soul.

There is no point in giving flowers to people when they are dead, it is far too late then! It is much better to give them flowers when they are alive and can really enjoy them!

John may be at the stage of life where the shadows are lengthening, but we do not find him sitting in a corner, bemoaning his lot in life; he has a wonderful ministry of encouragement and, thank God, he is willing to exercise it, he is willing to get on with it.

Truth ... the be-all and end-all

A quick glance at verse 2 shows that John pursues the theme of truth. He says, '*... because of the truth, which lives in us and will be with us for ever.*' Basically, John is writing for the sake of the truth. That is what is at stake. It is something we can know ... but it is more ... it is something which lives in us ... and it is still more ... it is something which has an eternal dimension for it will last forever!

Truth is ... timeless, dateless, unchanged, unchanging, constant!

---

* The word of God is truth (John 17:17).
* The Holy Spirit is the Spirit of truth (John 16:13).
* Jesus Christ referred to himself as 'the truth' (John 14:6).

The fact that John stresses the paramount importance of the truth would suggest that it is the solid foundation and only reasonable basis of all valid Christian fellowship. It is the premise for legitimate partnership in the gospel. We know from personal experience that a knowledge of the truth as it is in Christ Jesus produces a deep bond of love between all who share it.

When we meet someone who knows the Lord, there is an immediate affinity with that other person, we have a kindred spirit for we are one in heart and mind; we may never have met before but when we meet there is an automatic sense of togetherness; we have that feeling of belonging to each other. And in one sense, we do! It is because we are in it together and we are building our lives on the same foundation!

Where the value of our investment never falls

We discovered in John's first epistle that to know Christ is to love him and to love him is to love all those who are united to him through faith in his finished work of redemption. I was struck with these words when I read them recently, 'That special characteristic of mutual support and loving care among believers is rooted in the soil of truth. It is because Christ really is who he claimed to be that those who trust him are transformed by that relationship.'

We need to realise today that there is no substitute, there is no fall-back position, there is no Plan B. John hammers home the point that truth is primary for the Christian, it is fundamental to our faith.

The truth is said to *'live in us'* when we realise what it is, believe it and practise it. Such an investment of spiritual energy will yield an incredibly high dividend. The returns are eternal for God's truth will never be outdated or eclipsed. A commitment like this pays handsome dividends both in time and eternity. Such a lifestyle is one that John is advocating we all pursue with resolution of heart.

Greetings!

The next verse brings us to the customary salutation. It reads like this, *'Grace, mercy and peace from God the Father and from Jesus Christ, the Father's Son, will be with us in truth and love'* (verse 3). Actually, it seems more like a benediction than a greeting; be that as it may, John takes up the thought coming out of verse 2 where he says, *'the truth will be with us'* and he links it to his triple commendation of *'grace, mercy and peace'* by using the same catchphrase, *'it will be with us in truth and love'*.

John is extremely positive and upbeat in his comments. The fact that this is something that can be experienced in the here and now is a wonderful blessing and bonus for them; they do not have to wait until tomorrow for it to become a reality, they can live in the good of it now!

* *Grace* begins in the heart of our heavenly Father.
* It reaches out when it is expressed towards mankind in *mercy*.
* It is enjoyed and experienced by us as the blessing of *peace*.

This is what salvation is all about! It is a dynamic personal relationship with Jesus Christ who is here portrayed as the Father's Son. That is an unusual phrase in Scripture but it serves to underline the deity of Christ; he is one with God for he is God! These priceless blessings of salvation are channelled directly to us through the Lord Jesus Christ; the benefits which we accrue are attributed exclusively to him.

Salvation was his big idea, his bright idea, in the first place.

We must never forget it, we are only the recipients! We are beggars at the back door of his grace. We are the beneficiaries of his big hearted, magnanimous generosity. We remain forever in his debt! All that we are and all that we ever hope to be, we owe to him.

It seems to me, the truth of who Christ is and what he has done for us always exists side by side with the love we experience as we believe in him. We can summarise it like this: truth is the foundation of our faith and truth provides the basis of our love!

4-6

Getting our priorities right

The word *'truth'* is given top billing in John's opening comments in verses 1-3; in fact, it appears four times in that paragraph and he refers to it again in verse 4. This time he opens it out a little when he writes, *'It has given me great joy to find some of your children walking in the truth, just as the Father commanded us.'*

Here was a mother who had the unsurpassed joy of seeing her kids walk in her footsteps; here is someone whose life spoke volumes in the home; here is a lady who not only favoured the truth but she followed it as well. And for her the thrill and delight of seeing her children walk in the ways of God must have been the icing on the cake of her relationship with Jesus Christ.

Truth makes all the difference; we know that because John touches on it so often. It was not a theological hobby horse that John was riding; so far as he is concerned, truth is pivotal to the Christian gospel, it is a central tenet of the Christian faith.

- It is truth that drew John and *'the chosen lady'* together.
- It is truth that draws churches together.
- It is truth that draws families together.
- It is truth that draws marriages together.

Truth is the bedrock on which we build our lives, it is the solid rock on which we build our faith.

David Jackman writes, 'The truth of God, revealed supremely in the living Word and recorded unerringly in the written word, provides the route by which the Christian is travelling from earth to heaven.' For us as pilgrims, if we want to get from point A to point B and then head in the direction of point C on our spiritual journey, the best advice if we want to stay on track is to follow the recommended route. Thankfully, we find that in the Bible, it is our road map, it is route 66. Even I know, and I have no built-in sense of direction, I cannot reach the north by travelling west!

The phrase which John uses to speak of her family implies that not all of them were disciples of the Lord Jesus. He refers to *'some of your children'* and that would seem to indicate there were those who had gone their own way and done their own thing. They had either openly rebelled against the Lord and never surrendered their lives to him or they may have been sidetracked by some of the false teachers who were operating in the early church.

The glowing rhapsodic commendation which John has given to the lady in question is unfortunately coloured by a dark shade of anxiety. It is so sad for there is a strong undercurrent of pathos in that turn of phrase and it is one that must have brought a measure of deep concern to her as a mother. Her elation and joy were obviously tinged with immense sadness because she had not yet experienced household salvation. She is not alone for there are many parents today who can identify with her.

A handle on life

John moves up a gear with his stronger constraint in the closing phrase of verse 4 regarding the command of God. Walking in the ways of God, walking in the word of God, walking in the will of God, is not only a rare privilege for the believer, it can also be a profoundly happy and enriching experience as well.

The word *'command'* is another one of John's many favourites. He uses it no fewer than four times in the compass of three verses. What transpires is this, God's commandments focus the truth on specific areas of our lives. The truth can be vague and general if we are not careful, but the commandments make that truth specific and binding. If you like, they narrow it down, they deal with the nitty-gritty issues of life, they home in on the essentials, they deal with the things which really matter, they enable us to get a handle on real living in the real world!

The one who has handed the commandments down to us is none other than the Father and the thought encapsulated here is that they are for our lasting benefit. They come to us from one whose heart beats with love, they come directly from one who wants the best for his children. Our overall welfare is his utmost concern, he has our interests at heart.

Each commandment is a genuine expression of love, not law!

The poet reminds us in Psalm 33:11 that the will of God is the revelation of the heart of God, not just his mind. So when we do what he wants us to do and when we are what he wants us to be, that in itself is an outflowing of our love towards him. We obey him as his sons and daughters not because we fear him, not because we feel threatened by him, not because we see him as a kind of ogre figure hovering around us; we do it because we want to do it and we do it because we sincerely love him.

Love is ...

The implication from John's wonderful insights into life in a first century home is that what was true in the human family is equally relevant and appropriate for the wider church family. John takes a deep breath before composing the punchline in verses 5 and 6 where he writes, *'And now, dear lady, I am not writing you a new command but one we have had from the beginning. I ask that we love one another. And this is love: that we walk in obedience to his commands. As you have heard from the beginning, his command is that you walk in love.'*

There is no fading in John's voice when he calls the lady's attention to a clearly established diktat which they had from day one. This is obviously a reference back to the familiar words of Jesus where he said, 'A new command I give you: Love one another' (John 13:34).

Christians are to accept and accommodate one another not only to obey the word of Christ, but also to be a shining witness to a dark world. He wants us to love; by the same token, he wants us to be luminous! The next verse in John 13 makes that abundantly clear for we read, 'By this all men will know that you are my disciples, if you love one another.' If you like, this is John's animated appeal to one and all; he ardently longs that we might walk in love.

Walking in love means we walk in obedience to the word of God.

It is interesting to note that Jesus said in the course of his comments in the upper room that this was a 'new' command. You could be forgiven for thinking that this is one of those apparent contradictions that the cynics tell us is found in the Bible. Have Jesus and John got their wires crossed? Is there a breakdown in communication between the two of them? Has one not touched base with the other and passed on the current thinking on the issue?

It's old, yet ever new!

I think we can explain it like this: the divine directive to *'love one another'* is certainly not new in time; if the truth be told, it has been around for a very, very long time. The Jews living in the Old Testament era were instructed to love their neighbours (Leviticus 19:18). God made it clear to his people through his servant Moses that they had a solemn responsibility to those living around them in the local community.

Furthermore, they were also commanded to love the strangers within their gates, as outlined in Deuteronomy 10:19 where we read, 'And you are to love those who are aliens, for you yourselves were aliens in Egypt.' So there was nothing new about it in the sense of time.

What a difference a day makes!

The difference came about with the advent of God's Son to earth. That momentous event is what gave this commandment a newness in terms of emphasis and example. Jesus Christ gave new emphasis to brotherly love; he lifted it on to a higher plane; he gave it a fresh dimension and he exemplified it in his own life.

Jesus was the personification of love, he practised what he preached!

A new experience

We as God's children have the Holy Spirit living within us and he is the one who enables us to obey. We can do it through him! We can *only* do it through him! Walking in love means walking in truth!

The two are a couple, they walk arm in arm together. When these twin concepts are split-up, when these ideas are pulled apart, the result is an unmitigated disaster, the consequences are fatal.

'Love without truth is sentimentality; truth without love is oppression.'

What God demands of us is not a wee bit of love and a wee bit of truth blended together. He settles for nothing less than love and truth in all its fulness. The fact is, it is impossible to divorce our relationship with God from our relationship with people.

We have been down this road before in our studies in 1 John where John intimates over and over again that the proof of the pudding is in the eating! What we have here is a three-legged stool:

- *the first leg of love,*
- *the second leg of truth,*
- *the third leg of obedience.*

If we remove one leg, the stool becomes seriously lop-sided and eventually keels over; if we remove two legs, we have huge problems and so does the stool, we can pray with all the energy we can muster but it will not stand up, full stop! If we change the metaphor, we reach the same conclusion as Warren Wiersbe who writes in *Be Real,*

'Instead of living in a vicious circle, we live in a victorious circle of love, truth and obedience!'

Love equals obedience

The sharp eyed among us will have noticed a difference with distinction in verses 5 and 6. Because of this, some folks have pointed the finger at John and accused him of arguing in a circle. They say, he is like a dog running after his tail. Poor John!

Our love for the Lord is seen in our obedience to him. That will not be a selective obedience, it will not be a partial obedience. It is not a case of me doing it if or when I feel like it, or of me doing it if I happen to like it. Rather it is an obedience that accepts prima facie all that God has revealed in his word. It takes every command at face value. In the Bible, he says what he means and he means what he says! At the risk of sounding simplistic, that is a résumé of verse 6a. In that context, John equates love with obedience.

In the preceding verse, however, John has explicitly stated that the divine mandate is to love and, in case they missed it first time round, it is repeated a second time at the end of verse 6.

One letter makes a word of difference!

In verses 5 and 6b, the word *'command'* is singular which implies that walking in love is a summary of what it means to obey the Lord. In verse 6a, the word *'commands'* is plural since the outworking of love is a daily, disciplined concern to fulfil God's will as completely as possible. That is where one letter makes a word of difference!

Love is number one on God's top ten

This is why the Lord himself when asked in Mark 12:28-31, 'Of all the commandments, which is the most important?' responded by saying, 'Love the Lord your God with all your heart and with all your soul and with all your mind and with all your strength.' And then he continued in the same vein by saying, 'Love your neighbour as yourself.' His parting shot was, 'There is no commandment greater than these.' Paul comes to the same conclusion when he writes that 'love is the fulfilment of the law' (Romans 13:10).

Maintaining our spiritual glow

Love and obedience to the truth are inseparable priorities if we are to live as God requires. I imagine you will know just as well as I do that sometimes it is so incredibly difficult to do. We are inclined to separate obedience from love and when we do that it hardens into a grinding duty, it becomes nothing more than a ritualistic and mechanistic keeping of the rules. Our heart is not really in it and before too long we lose heart and we end up throwing the towel into the ring.

It is equally true to say, if we are currently in a right and healthy relationship with the Lord, if our version of Christianity is based on regular moments of intimacy with the Almighty and is primarily a matter of love for the Lord, then we will find as John did that his commands are not a burden to carry, they are a sheer joy and delight to fulfil (1 John 5:3).

We sometimes wrestle with the fact that our love is weak and faint, we feel as if we are spiritually zapped, the sparkle has gone and we are thoroughly deflated in our relationship with the Lord. On a spiritual level, our get up and go has got up and gone! The big question is, how do I recharge my battery?

When a bath is good for you!

John answered this query in his first letter. We read in 4:19 that 'we love because he first loved us.' The remedy comes when we go to the truth of God's word and soak and immerse ourselves in all that we see of God's character there, especially his great love for us! We go back to Calvary where he showed his love most clearly and we remember that 'the Son of God loved me and gave himself for me' (Galatians 2:20).

We constantly feed our hearts with the glorious assurance that God could not possibly love us any more than he does and he will never love us any less.

I often muse on the words of Jeremiah 31:3 where we are told, 'I have loved you with an everlasting love; I have drawn you with loving kindness.' That means, he will never let us down, he will never let us go, he will never give us up. He never stops loving us, not for a fraction of a milli-second.

These are great truths we need to assimilate, we need to take them on board and personalise them in our hearts and minds. We need to live in the good of them for when we do we will soon discover that our spiritual appetite returns and our love for him is firing again on every cylinder!

7-9

Sound the alarm

John is focusing attention on one of the missing elements in many people's lives. The closer we are to the second advent of Christ, the more it would appear that discernment has flown out of the Christian's wide open window. It is frighteningly hard to comprehend why so many reputedly intelligent believers are as unbelievably gullible as they are. The statistics are scary!

To many, if it looks right, they buy into it; if it sounds right, they accept it. So many are inclined to swallow hook, line and sinker all that comes their way, rarely stopping to ask the question, is this biblical? I realise John has touched on this hot potato issue before in his first epistle, but it is painfully obvious to him that it needs repeating.

Making the connection

The prevailing situation which Pastor John is addressing in this congregational letter is one that caused him considerable personal heartache and concern. It is a huge problem he could well do without! On a human level, it was the last thing he needed at this stage in his life. But such is life sometimes, even John has to take the rough with the smooth.

We can see what is happening, we watch the drama unfold as the pendulum swings incessantly and unremittingly from one end of the spectrum to the other. One minute, he is encouraging truth; the next minute, he is opposing error! He raises an alarm. And make no bones about it, it is definitely not a false one! This is what he has to say on the subject: *'Many deceivers, who do not acknowledge Jesus Christ as coming in the flesh, have gone out into the world. Any such person is the deceiver and the antichrist.'*

The original text of verse 7 actually begins with the word 'because'. That word is a link word, it joins what has gone before with what follows after. It is a connecting word.

Two wrongs never make one right

We have noticed already that failure in the realm of love is usually indicative of a failure to know and practise the truth. One cannot suffer without the other suffering too, just as each will also strengthen the other. One lives off the other, one feeds off the other. They need each other and they are essential for each other's development and survival. If you like, these are interdependent factors in the domain of faith and works. They are strategically important for they influence every area of our lives.

I think it all comes together when we realise it is because of the crisis of truth which the church family is presently facing, through the inroads of the impostors, that John wants to stir up his readers to be more determined, daring and demonstrative in their love for one another.

I agree with David Jackman's well-balanced comment when he writes, *'Love like that can be one of the church's strongest defences against heresy, just as holding to the truth is the greatest bastion against error.'*

To make matters worse

The problem was exacerbated because these folks were not just a fringe element operating on the sidelines. They made their presence felt, they tampered with the truth of God's word, they twisted it to suit their own devious ends, they turned away from the scriptural premise and, sad to say, their influence was quite remarkable for all the wrong reasons.

Mark Twain is credited with the statement, *'A lie runs around the world while truth is putting on her shoes.'*

The chilling reality is and history bears this out that fallen human nature wants to believe lies and resist God's revealed truth.

The folks who are propagating such false teaching are labelled by John as *'deceivers'*. There is more to that rigorous classification than initially meets the eye, it is more than sowing seeds of error in the soil of someone's mind, much more! It also includes leading people into wrong living!

What we believe determines how we behave. Wrong doctrine and wrong living are compatible, they are natural bedfellows, we always see them together. Similarly, the reverse is profoundly true, truth and life are extremely comfortable in each other's company, they get on very well with one another!

If at first you don't succeed … try, try, and try again!

'The two most difficult things to get straight in life,' writes Eugene Peterson of *The Message,* 'are love and God. More often than not, the mess people make of their lives can be traced to failure or stupidity or meanness in one or both of these areas.' I share his sentiments.

Is it any wonder John had to write about these topics, not once, not twice, but three times?

Dysfunctional antennae

John is seeking to correct a loving, anonymous lady whose gracious and generous hospitality may have been setting back the cause of the gospel. This dear soul had such a big warm heart for people that there were numerous well-documented occasions when, to put it simply, her heart ruled her head. There were many instances when her antennae failed to pick up the warning signal. It seems from reading between the lines that her spiritual radar was, more often than not, turned off. Or maybe it had never been switched on!

No matter who came knocking at her front door, day or night, they were always guaranteed the warmest of welcomes, the kettle was always on the boil. She would gladly put them up and give them a meal. No questions asked!

Hospitality for her was not a burden, it was always a privilege, a real delight. Precisely! And that is where the problem lay! Because of her *ceud mile fáilte* open door policy, the chances are she was unwittingly harming the progress of the gospel of Jesus Christ. Let us be clear, no way did she set out to do it deliberately, never in a month of Sundays did she do it intentionally. It just happened! And it happened because she allowed her love to spill over the boundaries of truth.

With the benefit of hindsight

We have an advantage over those who are major players in the drama for we can look in from the outside, and when we stand back and cast a critical and objective eye over the whole situation, it is fairly obvious that her discernment was flawed and her perceptive skills were weakened.

John Stott explains it so well: 'Our love is not to be so blind as to ignore the views and conduct of others. Truth should make our love discriminating; on the other hand, we must never champion the truth in a harsh or bitter spirit. So the Christian fellowship should be marked equally by love and truth, and we are to avoid the dangerous tendency to extremism, pursuing either at the expense of the other.'

'Our love grows soft if it is not strengthened by truth, and our truth grows hard if it is not softened by love.'

Stott concludes, 'We need to live according to Scripture which commands us both to love each other in the truth and to hold the truth in love.'

When we read the likes of that, it is relatively easy to see why John says what he does. In one sense, it helps to explain why John is such a realist and why he exhorts us to be vigilant at all times, in every situation. Basically, we need to rid ourselves of the ostrich mentality; we need to get our act together and stop pretending these problems do not exist, for they do!

A fly-by-night preacher's profile

John writes with candour and clarity when he highlights the seriously disruptive and divisive problem posed by these rather unsavoury and distasteful characters. The problem is this: although these teachers spoke respectfully and, at times, endearingly of the Lord Jesus Christ, they denied the truth about him as revealed in the biblical record.

Such a telltale sign is a clear indicator that they were really against him and, in spite of what they did say or did not say, they were only paying lip service to his teaching. In their heart of hearts, they did not believe a word of it! If you like, they were antichrist.

These guys went far beyond the inspired teaching of Jesus by supplementing his words with their homespun ideas and mishmash of opinions. They twisted all that he said by putting their particular spin on it. As a direct result of such contemptible arrogance and high-handed presumption, I think it is perfectly reasonable to assume these men had no part in God and God had no part in them. To me, it is a fait accompli.

They were antichrist in their thinking and theology, they were antichrist in their attitude and activity.

'*Antichrist*' is a term we have come across before; it is one we are familiar with for John used it a couple of times in his first epistle. For example, in 2:18-29 we have an entire section dedicated to exposing such nameless and shameless individuals. The folks who swelled the numbers of this sect denied the humanity of the

Lord Jesus. They held him to be merely an appearance, he was only a phantom; that means, they treated the fundamental doctrine of the incarnation with a high degree of contempt and hostile scepticism. They pooh-poohed the idea. For them, it was simply a non-starter.

The proponents of this erroneous teaching are striking at the very basis of our Lord's person and work and, in so doing, they are seriously undermining the foundation on which the Christian faith is built.

The bottom line is, the Christ they offer to their converts is not the Christ of Scripture, he is not the Christ of history, he is not the Christ of the Christian gospel.

That is why John is attempting to clear the deck and establish some ground rules so we will know how to handle such individuals when they come knocking at our front door. I think the principles which John enunciates here are not only appropriate for the Christian home, they are every bit as relevant for the Christian assembly.

A fascinating turn of phrase is employed by John when he says in verse 7 that they *'have gone out into the world'*. There are two possible meanings here, both of which make an awful lot of sense.

Hyped-up missionaries?

It could mean they have gone out as missionaries with the intention of penetrating virgin territory with the gospel. Their ambition and goal is to take their message to regions which have previously been untouched and unreached. If that is the right interpretation of the text, it suggests that these false teachers were spreading their heresies with all the zeal and enthusiasm and vigour of a racing-pulse missionary. It means they were eager to infiltrate and keen to influence new areas and, at the same time, dominate other churches.

The prediction of Jesus in Mark 13:22 was right on cue. They maybe did not realise it but it was being fulfilled right before their very eyes. In that singularly important sermon on Olivet, the Lord said that 'false Christs and false prophets will appear and perform signs and miracles to deceive the elect - if that were possible.' His earlier warning in verse 5 was very much to the point. He hit the nail on the head when he told them, 'Watch out that no-one deceives you!'

Spiritual impostors?

A second way to explore its meaning is to recognise that John normally uses the Greek word *kosmos* to refer to the non-Christian world. I think you will appreciate that it is a world which is extremely well-organised and regimented in its implacable opposition to God's rule. That premise is alluded to more fully in 1 John 2:15-19.

If that is what John is driving at here, then he is reminding us that one of the marks of a false teacher is their secession from those who hold to biblical orthodoxy. It is crystal clear these impostors cannot exist, let alone survive, in the environment of truth. It is anathema to them because they deny its essential doctrines.

So far as truth and error are concerned, the two are poles apart, they are light years away from each other. In fact, the chances of them ever coming closer together are as far fetched as you and I ever finding life on Mars. It will not happen. It cannot happen!

It is not the least bit surprising then that John reacts in the manner in which he does. He lambastes the spiritual masqueraders, he hauls them over the coals, he gives them a verbal thrashing and when he has finished with them he throws out a stirring challenge to the people of God.

20/20 vision

The wise old preacher who has seen it all before says in verse 8: *'Watch out that you do not lose what you have worked for, but that you may be rewarded fully.'* Strong language, indeed! John is urging the *'chosen lady'* and her believing children to operate at a high state of readiness. Do not be conned! This is no teddy bear's picnic, this is a battle zone; it demands that each of us be on a war footing. We need to keep our eyes and ears wide open lest the enemy creep up on us and we are caught with our guard down. This is a clarion call for every one of us to live our lives on a level of red alert.

He implores them to pull out all the stops and exercise the utmost vigilance. He is pleading with them not to succumb to the subtle and insidious wiles of the enemy. He cannot stand the thought of some of them caving in under pressure from their peers.

John knows only too well the grave danger they face, it is the danger of apathy and complacency. They are having to wrestle with these problems and, at the same time, they have to live in the real world and it is there that they need to face down the real enemy. This is especially true when error is plausibly propagated by pleasant exponents. It is all too easy to be lulled into a false sense of security and for any one of us to be taken in by extremely nice people.

Don't miss out!

But that is not the only issue at stake here. There is a much wider talking point than that which revolves around a handful of genial personalities and cultic figures. It is one that has far-reaching consequences for it sets in motion the ripple-effect syndrome. The repercussions are alarming and unthinkable.

The implication behind John's incisive comments in verse 8 is that all those who embrace error automatically forfeit their reward!

If they do not watch out, they will lose out!

That may be a neat summary of the text but the ramifications of what John is saying will come as a nasty shock to those who are within earshot of God's word. To think that they will miss out on so much will be the ultimate nightmare for them; it will be a horrifying revelation to them!

To put it simply, they were wanting the best of both worlds and, from God's perspective, they cannot run with the foxes and hunt with the hounds at the same time. It is either one or the other. They cannot have one foot in the camp of truth and the other foot in the camp of error!

It is interesting to note the variation on textual readings here. The NIV adopts second person verbs throughout the verse when it says, *'what you have worked for'*. I think the first person plural may be a more accurate rendering. It would then read, *'what we have worked for'*. When we stop and think about it, it makes very good sense.

One out, all out

This actually widens the net considerably; it means John is sharing the heavy burden on his heart that all the sheer hard work of evangelism, teaching and pastoral care to which the church leaders of his generation had given themselves so sacrificially, would in the end come to nothing if the church in the next generation turned away from the truth.

John did not want to see it coming apart at the seams. He did not want to see the whole enterprise folding up. He did not want to preside over the funeral service of a local congregation. They had invested so much, it had cost them dear, and John did not want to see it slipping through their buttery fingers.

Paul wrote on a similar vein to the churches dotted here and there throughout Galatia. This is how he expressed the concern weighing heavily on his heart when he wrote, 'I fear for you, that somehow I have wasted my efforts on you' (Galatians 4:11). You see, it would not only be the leaders who would suffer a measure of loss, such an imposition was by no stretch of the imagination restricted to them; it affected everyone in the local company of God's people, including his readers if they embraced false teaching.

Warren Wiersbe comments, *'The false teachers offer something you do not have when, in reality, they take away what you already have!'*

In the cold light of a new dawn, the devil is a thief and so too are his helpers. The aspiration on John's heart is that every believer might receive his/her reward. This is the Johannine equivalent of 2 Peter 1:11 where Peter talks about 'a rich welcome into the eternal kingdom.' At the end of the day, at the end of life's journey, there is a reward for faithful service rendered in the name of Jesus. It is John's sincere desire that his readers might receive their full pay. The word implies a proper remuneration for work conscientiously completed. He does not want them to miss out or lose out in any way!

Payday, someday

The theme of eternal rewards is expanded on by the apostle Paul in considerable detail in 1 Corinthians 3:12-15 and again in 2 Corinthians 5:10. In both these passages Paul makes it absolutely clear that our salvation is never at risk. If we know the Lord we are bound for heaven, not because of anything we have done, for it has nothing to do with us. We are there only because of the abundant mercy and amazing grace of God.

It may have nothing to do with our salvation, it may not affect our eternal destiny, that is true, but it has everything to do with our service and our faithfulness to Jesus Christ. Paul informs us in verse 14 of the above-mentioned chapter that when our life's work is tried and tested by God's stringent method of quality control, 'if what he has built survives, he will receive his reward.' You see, the glorified Lord wants to greet his servants with the bright and cheery words, 'Well done!'

One Bible commentator brings this aspect of John's message to a fitting conclusion when he writes, 'If ever we are tempted to think that matters of truth and error are marginal, we should correct our thinking by remembering the eternal perspective in which all our work and witness are carried on.'

Headfirst into error

In verse 8 we faced up to the awful, unthinkable possibility of going back. When we fast forward to verse 9 we are confronted with another equally serious hazard. It is the peril of going ahead. The threat John is warning of here is of going beyond the limits of the word of God and adding to it.

This verse, as we will see in a moment, provides both a summing up as well as a concise restatement of the basic principles on which we are to judge this issue of truth. In the same breath, John underlines the devastating consequences facing all those who walk away from the truth.

He tells it like it is when he writes, *'Anyone who runs ahead and does not continue in the teaching of Christ does not have God; whoever continues in the teaching has both the Father and the Son.'*

As it was ... so it is

Some things never change! It was true in the first century, it is uncannily true in the twenty-first. Sneering sceptics, snide comments - there will always be those who dismiss authentic biblical Christianity out of hand. They perceive it to be dull and boring and from their enlightened perch, it is out of touch with the times. The Christian faith is caricatured by many as a cultural dinosaur.

From day one in church history, false teachers of every persuasion and none have generally presented themselves as the pace setters in their day and for their generation. They have tended to place themselves in the progressive wing of religious thinking. They reckon they are forward looking and they like to see themselves as an elitist in-the-know minority who are abreast of every major development as well as ahead of their time. They passionately believe they are strategically placed to break the present mould and shape the thinking of tomorrow.

I have news for you! That is what they may think and they are certainly welcome to their airy-fairy thoughts, but if that is what they term progress, they are living in a fool's paradise in cloud-cuckoo land. It is the 'one-step-forward-two-steps-back' syndrome! If that is making an inroad, then I cannot count! It is a smokescreen of falsehood.

It has been well said, *'Novelty is always deceptively attractive, and false doctrine can thrive where it is promoted as progressive, advanced thinking.'*

The same mindset was the norm in Paul's day in the great city of Athens. This was the hallmark of the pagan philosophers. We read in Acts 17:21 that 'they spent their time doing nothing but talking about and listening to the latest ideas.' It seems to me, they would have been very much at home in the glitzy raconteur chat shows and feature columns of our contemporary mass media. Cyberspace technology with all its innovative ideas would certainly appeal to them. I can see them spending long hours surfing the net in an attempt to tap the phenomenal potential which it offers.

All that glitters is not gold

I suppose new ideas have an irresistible fascination for most of us. There is something about them which tickles our fancy, they grab us and before we realise it we have been sucked into the vacuum of all things weird and wonderful. The big problem comes when we keep moving the goal posts. It happens when we sideline God to the fringe of our lives; it emerges when we side-step the teaching of Scripture.

It does not matter how bright the idea might look, it does not matter how bold the suggestion may sound, if it does not tally with the word of God, there is no alternative, it has to be jettisoned. It has to be treated as poison and dumped. It has to be seen as disposable cargo for the man who takes it on board is a fool!

Everything must be tested by the plumbline of Scripture!

David Jackman writes, 'Our responsibility is to discover the biblical perpendicular and to judge both the new and the old by its unchanging truth. To desert the doctrine of Christ is not progress but apostasy.' In other words, our attitude to the teaching of Christ is a tell-tale sign of the state of our relationship with God. If we know him, love him, and serve him, then his word will have a central place in our lives.

10-13

Coping with a crisis

John has often been called 'the apostle of love' and I think that is a fair assessment of the man and his ministry. He is the one man we can depend upon. We always find him out there on the front line. He is a man who champions the cause of truth for he feels it is in serious danger of being sidelined to the fringes of church life, but when he does it he does it with a love which has an unusual combination of toughness and tenderness. Let me illustrate what I mean.

Legend has it that in John's day there was a well-known false teacher in Ephesus named Cerinthus; we talked about him in one of our earlier studies in John's first epistle. The story goes that one day John was at the bath house when Cerinthus arrived. Apparently, John jumped out of the water, grabbed his clothes and towel and took off running. At the same time, he was shouting, 'Let's hurry from this house, lest it fall on top of us. Cerinthus, the enemy of truth, is here!'

The other side of love

Obviously I cannot vouch for its accuracy, but it is a whacking good story! This man John is totally committed to truth and totally opposed to error.

A proper understanding of biblical love indicates that it is something which is robust and resolute, even when the opinion polls are against it.

True love remains firm even when faced with stiff unbending opposition. It stands its ground and holds its own even when the dominoes are falling all around it. It sticks by its principles when others are abandoning theirs to the winds of change and compromise.

Authentic love, real love, genuine love, spiritual love - call it what we will - such love never sells the timeless truths of Scripture down the river.

A warm welcome guaranteed ... on God's terms

That helps to explain why John says what he does in verses 10 and 11. We read, *'If anyone comes to you and does not bring this teaching, do not take him into your house or welcome him. Anyone who welcomes him shares in his wicked work.'*

The teaching which John refers to here is the *'teaching of Christ'* which he has spoken about at length in verses 7 and 9. It is also important to point out that these verses must be handled in their proper context otherwise we can read into them so much more than John ever intended, so we need to be careful and wise as to how we interpret them. It is a sad fact of life that some folks lift them completely out of context and use them to justify the most unloving behaviour.

John is not telling us to slam the door in the face of everyone who disagrees with us! Far from it! In the front of his mind are false teachers who slip furtively into our churches with their ruinous heresies about the Lord Jesus Christ. Clandestine preachers, that is what they are! He is speaking about those peddlers of error who cause people to stumble in their faith.

With the best will in the world, with the highest motive in our heart, if we receive them into our homes, we simply condone what they do and we become partners in their crime. Whether we realise it or not, whether we like it or not, we end up aiding and abetting them. Unwittingly and unintentionally, we become co-conspirators with them! According to John, the most loving thing to do, for our own sake and for the sake of those we care about, is to draw a line and stand firm in the truth.

McCarthyism revisited?

John is not advocating that we conduct a witch-hunt and go searching for reds under every bed. He is not saying that we throw the baby out with the bath water. The whole scenario needs to be set in context.

Back in the first century there was a growing number of itinerant preachers who were travelling all over the place - here a day, there a day, somewhere else a day! The problem was not so much how they put in their days, that was fine, they could handle that; the problem came when dusk fell, where would they spend the night?

To their enormous credit and they deserve a pat on the back for their sterling efforts, the local congregation of Christians were well aware of their responsibilities to show hospitality to such folks and to support them in whatever way they could.

The bottom line is, you did not invite every Tom, Dick or Harry into your home. There was a pressing need for the host to exercise a fair amount of discernment and discretion. It did not matter how nice the preacher was, it did not matter how smoothly he talked, it did not matter how well he was groomed, it all hinged on the content of his message.

I am reminded of the statement penned by Charles Swindoll when he wrote, *'Love is the hinge on which hospitality turns to open its door. But just as a door has hinges, it also has a lock. And love never opens a locked door to a wolf - even if it is dressed in sheep's clothing.'*

If it was right, then, says John, welcome him with open arms and an open heart; if it is not right and you have doubts about his credibility, then, argues John, have absolutely nothing to do with him.

The message matters more than the man

The same principle holds good for fellowship in the local church which, in John's day, was more often than not held in one of the believer's homes. To take him in would signify that we were warmly endorsing his teaching and by inference also approving his lifestyle. To welcome someone is so much more than just an expression of formal politeness to them or a casual recognition of them; it is, over a period of time, to see the relationship slowly developing into one of mutual friendship.

'If that sort of behaviour is extended to false teachers, it is not so much Christian love as spiritual suicide.'

There are three aspects of this ludicrously crazy attitude of toleration of all things which totally negates and wipes out any unlikely benefits that may have come from his stay among them.

- It does not show *agape* love to the rest of the church family for it exposes them to an insidious undermining of their faith. If we have their best interests at heart, we would be hard-pressed to justify our decision to let this purveyor of error hold the floor for a session or two.
- It is not an expression of positive love towards the religious conman for it confirms him in his error. By giving him, even so much as a guarded welcome, we have given him and his story a measure of credibility. He has got what he wanted, he has got where he wanted; the likelihood is increased that he might never be brought to admit the error and monumental folly of his ways.
- It is definitely not a serious confession of our love for the Lord for our actions show that we have consciously sided with evil in actively encouraging the spread of that which is destructive of the revealed truth.

When the doorbell rings

Let me bring it closer to home. The doorbells rings! The door knocker resonates! The question is: what should we do when we open our front door to discover a member of one of the sects standing there? What should our response be to someone from one of the cults who has come to share his faith with us?

Should we shut the door and give him the cold shoulder treatment? Should we chill him out with a stern frowned look and a snappy sentence of sarcasm? Or perhaps should we seize the moment and invite him in for coffee and biscuits and a chat?

Be nice to me, I've had a hard day!

I think we need to understand this, it does not matter who is standing on our door step - it may be the woman from across the street, the man from the Pru, the kids from next door, or the immaculately clad slimline young man from the latest cult to hit the town, they all deserve to be treated with respect. They should always be shown the utmost courtesy.

Bad manners and a harsh tone of voice achieve absolutely nothing! We let ourselves down and, apart from that, we let the Lord Jesus down. Neither does a display of hostile ignorance and an arrogant preachy 'I'm right and you're wrong' attitude do us any favours in the longer term. The man on the outside has a long memory!

We can easily decline to be drawn into a conversation and we can do it with a mixture of grace and firm politeness. There is a time and a place to talk to such folks and there is also a time and a place where it is best to remain silent.

As a rule of thumb, I think it would be most unwise and unhelpful for a new convert or someone still relatively young in their faith to be drawn into such a conversation as they could soon find themselves enmeshed in something which they know little or nothing about. Enthusiasm, combined with a big hearted generosity and a fired-up zeal to see such people brought to saving faith in Christ, could ultimately lead the new believer into a minefield of considerable difficulties, resulting in a high level of personal frustration.

I do not think for a single minute that John precludes a mature believer from inviting a door-caller into his home in order to open up the Scriptures and explain to him the error of his ways and to seek, in love, to point him to the Lord Jesus Christ.

Howard Marshall makes a perfectly valid point when he writes, *'There is a difference between giving a person love and even hospitality and providing him with a base for his work.'*

The closing paragraph is vintage John. Here is John at his best. He writes in verses 12 and 13 with typical warmth and flair as he says, *'I have much to write to you, but I do not want to use paper and ink. Instead, I hope to visit you and talk with you face to face, so that our joy may be complete. The children of your chosen sister send their greetings.'*

A man of the people

It is obvious from these final remarks that John is a people person. He loves people, he is people oriented, he would much prefer to sit down with them over a cup of tea and a few cream cakes than write them a ream of correspondence. Some things are easier said for it is not always possible to put down on a piece of paper what is on your heart. We cannot always express in words what is in our heart.

Come what may, he knows when their paths next cross, the sense of joy will be mutual and the fellowship will be rich and sweet. His parting shot is one of hope for the future; he anticipates the day after tomorrow with a feeling of joyous expectancy in his heart.

In a day of relativism and tolerance, John's briefest letter sounds the loudest wakeup call.

- Be brave!
- Be bold!
- Be alert!
- Be courageous!

Stand up for what God says is right! You know and I know, telling someone the truth may be immensely difficult, it is an incredibly hard thing to do, but in the long run, it is the most loving thing to do.

'The man who loved me the most told me the truth!' (Anon.)

In a nutshell, that is the message of 2 John.

3 JOHN

7

The power of a good example

Intro

3 John is a wonderful little book with a lot to say. It has been described as a 'postcard of candid truth'. It has not come from paradise, it has not come from some idyllic get-away-from-it-all beachfront location; rather, it comes from a church wrestling with massive difficulties and a church facing critical issues.

When we read between the lines, the people we meet in this church are the kind of people we would expect to meet anywhere for every congregation has them! The most of them are a bunch of normal well-adjusted people; a group of ordinary, decent, hard-working folks with a few worrying problems on their plate. Alongside them is the minority that we meet everywhere we go: they are the vocal ones who always have something to say, solicited or otherwise; such folks are themselves a walking time bomb of a problem!

Where we have real people, there are real problems; allied to that is the real potential for solving problems!

There are some things that never change when it comes to local assemblies of God's people. It was true then, it is no less relevant now. Each of us must honestly face the question, 'Am I a part of the problem or am I a part of the answer!'

A peep behind the scenes

While preparing this study I was interested to read that this brief note is the shortest New Testament epistle in the original Greek. In it John captures one of the most vivid pictures of the New Testament church in the first century. With the help of a few still camera shots, he gives us a glimpse into an early assembly. We have a golden opportunity to be a fly-on-the-wall and eavesdrop on all that is happening and, for what it is worth, we even encounter a smattering of early church politics.

3 John bears a striking resemblance to 2 John; in many ways, the two letters mirror each other.

- *They are about the same length.*
- *They were probably written about the same time.*
- *They address the vital issue of the church's attitude towards itinerant preachers.*
- *They are anchored to the twin themes of truth and love.*

There are many similarities between them; there is a common thread woven into the fabric of both. Having said that, 3 John is more personal and intimate than 2 John. It has a certain ambience associated with it.

---

3 John is more like a fireside chat between a couple of old friends.

By the same token, the two miniature volumes are as different as chalk and cheese, they are as different as night and day. For example,

- 2 John is a straight-from-the-shoulder warning against welcoming deceivers who are peddling their seriously flawed theology,
- 3 John is a stern warning against rejecting those who are bona fide believers and ambassadors of the true gospel.

We can look at it from another angle. John's third epistle is the positive complement to the negative prohibitions of his second epistle. He points out that just because there was a tiny minority of circuit-riding preachers who took advantage of the hospitality that was offered to them, that is no excuse for not showing hospitality to those who are genuine servants of God.

In actual fact, the contrasts between the two mini-books are just as striking as the similarities.

2 John	*3 John*
A lady was receiving the wrong kind of travellers because she had an open-door policy.	A man was shunning the right kind of travellers because he adopted a closed-shop mentality.
Hospitality was misplaced.	Hospitality was missing.
Truth was needed to bring love back in balance.	Love was needed to bring truth back in balance.
Written to a lady and her children.	Written to a man and his acquaintances.
No personal names are mentioned apart from the Lord's.	Three specific names are mentioned: Gaius, Diotrephes, and Demetrius.

Mug shots

I was quite enthralled when I read David Jackman's incisive analysis of this erstwhile trio. Within the framework of a few carefully selected words, he has provided us with a superb vignette of these colourful individuals. One word sums each of them up rather succinctly!

- Gaius ... a Christian *friend*.
- Diotrephes ... a Christian *fraud*.
- Demetrius ... a Christian *follower*.

No matter where we are coming from today, no matter where we are at in our spiritual life at this point in time, it is essential to remember that Demetrius, Diotrephes and Gaius represent the peaks and troughs in the landscape of the early church.

We cannot have a mountain without a valley. That is true not only in the world of nature, it is equally true in the life of the church of Jesus Christ. It does not make any difference whether it is a church in the first century or the twenty-first, every fellowship of God's people will have its high points and its low points.

We need to be realistic in our appraisal of our current situation. It is the height of stupidity for us to bury our heads in the sand and pretend these people are not around. They are!

We need to understand that our church, no matter how good it is, no matter how big it is, no matter how spiritual it is, no matter how mission oriented it is, no matter how faithful the leadership is ... our church - that is, your church and my church - will have those who have come from the stable of Diotrephes.

However, we can thank God that every member is not a Diotrephes the Second; our church fellowship will also have those in the ilk and mould of a Gaius and those of the statesmanlike calibre of a Demetrius. I believe that is an item for rejoicing and praise!

The Diotrepheses of this world will cause us endless hassle and a lot of heartache; the Gaiuses and Demetriuses of this world will lead us to the summit, reaching for the heavens!

A potted history

Gaius

John has a lot to say to Gaius, he has a lot to say about Gaius, and we read about it in verses 1-8. It seems to me that Gaius is a very good friend to John. Having said that, it takes two to tango and I am sure John was a trusted confidant to him as well.

He is a gracious person, he is someone who is generous in spirit. He comes across as a gregarious kind of individual. He is exceptionally kind; actually, he is the type of man who is always willing to open his arms to those going through a tough time.

Diotrephes

His rather tarnished pedigree is recorded for posterity in verses 9 and 10. It is a pot shot at a man who is a perpetual pain in the neck. Diotrephes fits into the category of being a trouble maker in the local church. He is a lay leader who specialises in causing problems.

So far as he is concerned, that is his gifting, albeit he does not see it that way! He is the kind of person who is not content unless he is throwing the spanner in the works. No matter how good the idea may be, he will always oppose it!

Demetrius

His excellent credentials are outlined in verses 11 and 12. Demetrius is a lovely brother. He is genuine, he has no hidden agenda. In computer-speak, what you see is what you get! He has a consistent walk with the Lord and his testimony is a shining example to all around him.

Rumour has it that he was the messenger who hand delivered the letter and he may even have had the important job of representing John before Gaius and Diotrephes. If the speculation is right and that was his role, then it speaks volumes about the kind of man that he is.

Whodunit?

For reasons best known to himself, John adopts the same approach when introducing himself in his two postcard epistles. He simply says, *'the elder'*. He does not mention his name but that is neither here nor there; it is nothing to get uptight about because there is no deliberate exclusion of it either. It is just the way John does things, bless him; and who knows, it may even have been the local custom as well.

The fact is, if it ain't broke, we do not need to fix it; in other words, there is no mileage gained in creating a problem, if no problem exists! The people to whom he is writing would have no problem identifying the author! They knew it was John! It could not be anyone else for he was well known around the region as *'the elder'*.

We often hear people saying, 'Oh, I meant to tell you, the pastor called in to see me today.' Or, 'I saw the minister down the street this morning.' We all know who they are talking about, and if we do not, we probably should!

It's for you … for who?

The first of the three brethren addressed by John is a gentleman named Gaius. A delightful brother! All that we know about him is contained in these eight verses but John leaves us in no doubt as to how highly he regards him. John does not necessarily place Gaius on a pedestal but he certainly looks up to him and he very definitely respects him.

There are others of the same name mentioned elsewhere in the New Testament. For example,

Gaius of Corinth

Paul referred to him in Romans 16:23 with the juicy anecdote, 'whose hospitality I and the whole church here enjoy, sends you his greetings.' This dear brother's kindness knew no bounds. You were sure of a warm welcome and a big cheery smile when you came to his house; and to round the evening off, you were pretty much guaranteed a tasty bite to eat as well. This brother was hospitality personified! I was intrigued to discover that he was one of only a handful of people Paul personally baptised (1 Corinthians 1:14).

Gaius at Ephesus

He is the poor soul who is reputed to have been caught up in the riot at Ephesus when the city was in an uproar. Unfortunately for him, he was in the right place at the wrong time! We meet him in Acts 19:29 where Dr Luke informs us, 'The people seized Gaius and Aristarchus, Paul's travelling companions from Macedonia, and rushed as one man into the theatre.'

Gaius from Derbe

Another Gaius who hails from Derbe is a valued member of an advance party for Paul's eventful trip to Troas. He is mentioned as one name in a long line of worthies in Acts 20:4. He just happens to be the same man who was delegated by his home church to convey the collection for the poor to Jerusalem.

When all is said and done, I have to be honest with you and say we have absolutely no way of knowing if any of these illustrious individuals can be identified with the Gaius of 3 John.

The dilemma is compounded by the fact that Gaius was an extremely common Roman name, a bit like Jim or Joe in today's world. I venture to suggest, if we were to conduct a straw poll of the most popular names for a boy, we would find Gaius coming out near the top; the chances are, it would be up there in the top three.

Back in the apostle John's day, it was a name handed down from generation to generation. It was a name so unbelievably run-of-the-mill, that if you or I arrived in town as a comparative stranger, we would have enormous difficulty distinguishing between the Gaiuses in the local community. Try looking for someone with the surname of Jones or Evans in a Welsh telephone directory!

1,2

The best of buddies

That may all be true but our man Gaius is one who stands out in a crowd; he is head and shoulders above the rest of his namesakes. John knows a good one when he sees one! He is proud, in the best sense of the word, to be associated with Gaius. He sees him as a valued and prized colleague.

John describes him in verse 1 as *'my dear friend'*. In fact, he speaks of Gaius in such endearing terms a further three times, in verses 2, 5 and 11. The Greek word which John employs is *agapetos* which is related to the distinctive Christian word for 'love' which is *agape*. One Bible commentator depicts it well when he says, 'This is the love that God has for us and which he creates in each of his children so that, as we are united in the truth, we are bound together in a supernatural love.'

He backs him to the hilt

We somehow get the feeling that John really likes this guy. He freely admits in verse 1 that Gaius is a man *'whom I love in the truth'*. It is worth noting that the pronoun *'I'* is in an emphatic position, perhaps because Gaius, in taking an unpopular minority stand in the church, was not greatly loved by the heretical party that was developing around Diotrephes.

John's propitious comment is then seen as a clear vote of confidence in the man. No matter what other people were saying behind his back, Gaius had John's total one hundred percent backing and John was more than happy to stand by his man and affirm him in public.

Such affirmation would be warmly welcomed by Gaius as a source of tremendous encouragement, bearing in mind the tough time he was passing through. The bond which cemented their relationship and which knit their hearts together is that of the truth of the gospel of Jesus Christ. There was a gelling of heart and mind between the two of them.

'Christian friendship, one of God's greatest gifts, expresses the divine love, grounded in truth.' (Anon.)

A get well prayer

Having bolstered the confidence of his friend, John proceeds in verse 2 to address him in the form of a prayer. I think it is thrilling to realise that when we communicate with someone else in the family of God that we can go so much further than simply saying to them, 'Hey, I hope such-and-such works out alright for you,' or, 'Bless you, pal, I wish you all the best for the future.' We can go well beyond that to saying, *'You're my friend, you're my brother, I pray for you.'* And, you know, our prayers for our friends can cover every aspect of life.

John's aspiration for Gaius is, *'I pray that you may enjoy good health and that all may go well with you, even as your soul is getting along well.'* I cannot help but wonder, has news filtered back to John through the grapevine that Gaius has been unwell and is that the prime reason why John writes to him in this way? I know it is pure conjecture but it would not surprise me if it were true.

On the other hand, this kind of a greeting was pretty common in that day, it was a standard form of words, so we must resist the temptation to build too much on it or read too much into it.

On the ball ... spiritually speaking

However, for John to pray that Gaius will prosper physically just as he is prospering spiritually is a remarkable testimony to Gaius' outstanding spiritual growth. That says something about the man, it really does, that John would want his body to be as well as his soul!

John's request for this man's health is staggeringly different from what you would expect to hear fall from the lips of a Gnostic teacher. By and large, the Gnostics tended to look down on the body and they generally frowned on material things. They viewed them, at best, as that which was trivial and, at worst, as that which was evil.

So John's down-to-earth petition for a special friend's health flies in the face of their blasé intercessory style; in reality, they are a supercilious bunch who veer towards apathy when it comes to meeting the needs of ordinary people. Basically, they and John are steering a collision course.

Holistic ministry ... first century style

I think it is helpful to notice how John's pattern of prayer is hugely similar to the standard adopted in our Lord's life. Jesus nourished people's souls with the best of teaching in the Sermon on the Mount, but he also nourished and looked after their bodies when he fed the hungry multitude of five thousand plus with a substantial square meal.

Jesus proclaimed in John 8:12 to a crowd of interested onlookers that he was 'the light of the world' but, a short time later, he also touched and healed a man born blind. He declared to a sorrowing family in John 11:25 that he was 'the resurrection and the life' but he also raised Lazarus and several others from the dead. Like Jesus his mentor, John never forgot that people have bodies as well as souls.

It is a matter of striking a balance between the physical and the spiritual in today's world. All too often in the annals of church history we read of one incident after another where the pendulum has swung from one extreme to the other.

Sometimes the emphasis has been on asceticism and this has tended to breed a spirit of heavy legalism; at other times it has gone in the opposite direction where anything goes and where everything is deemed acceptable. That has led to accusations of people taking advantage of their liberty and freedom in Christ. They have seen their salvation as a licence to do whatever they want to do and consequently they pursue their own agenda. It is an open ticket for them to go on an ego trip.

The bottom line is, physical prosperity is not a measure or a gauge of spiritual health nor is its absence a hindrance to spiritual progress. It is just as possible to be spiritually healthy and physically sick as it is to be physically healthy and spiritually sick.

David Jackman notes, 'There is no biblical wedge driven between the physical and the spiritual.' It seems to me, if the Bible does not drive a wedge between them, then neither should we!

3,4

A valued colleague

John continues with his upbeat assessment of Gaius' spiritual life when he writes in verses 3 and 4: *'It gave me great joy to have some brothers come and tell about your faithfulness to the truth and how you continue to walk in the truth. I have no greater joy than to hear that my children are walking in the truth.'*

I am sure many of us can identify firsthand with John's beautiful commendation of his friend, Gaius. We have watched our own kids take their first faltering steps; we have been excited and thrilled to see them progressing over the years. The analogy with the physical holds just as true in the spiritual realm.

It would appear, as I mentioned earlier, that Gaius was one of John's converts and what tickles John's heart more than anything else is that he has not only taken the first few steps, he has made incredible progress in his Christian life. In fact, he moved at a breathtaking pace in his ongoing walk with the Lord. He is unstoppable!

In his own inimitable way, Charles Swindoll says, *'Like a proud father, John burst a button when he heard how well Gaius was internalising his faith.'*

'This man,' in the words of the eminent American evangelist D L Moody, 'translated truth into shoe leather.' Gaius is the type of person who weighs each word, each decision, each action on the scale of Christ's higher standards. He is someone who is faithful in truth and surely that has to be seen as the first requirement of a good disciple.

The brethren who passed on the encouraging information to John about Gaius were obviously impressed with what they saw of him and heard from him. He had shown them a fair measure of love in throwing open his home to them and, at the same time, he did not scrimp on his hospitality when he got them inside! They spoke about his unswerving commitment to the truth and his unstinting loyalty to the wider family of God because that was linked to his big hearted generosity of spirit.

Truth and love are inseparable where they are genuine.

Mr Integrity

Gaius was a man whose entire life was shaped by God's truth. Not only did he passionately believe it, it became a way of life to him, it was his lifestyle. There is no greater spiritual prosperity than that. For this brother, his life was all of a whole; it is the classic example of a well-rounded character enjoying the blessings of an all-round ministry. The things he believed, he lived out. He practised what he preached.

People who met him were more than impressed with his quality of life, they were enamoured with the sharpness of his intellect, they were charmed with the warmth of his heart, they were taken aback by his consistent integrity as a fellow believer.

They may have been surprised by this man's impeccable credentials, but they should not have been, for he and all that he exemplifies should be the norm for every one of us.

Gaius is a glasshouse Christian, he is a mobile conservatory; in fact, his character is unambiguously transparent we can see right through him.

Oh that there were more like him in today's church! He is faithful in truth, he is faithful in love.

5-8

A true servant

The next paragraph deals with this essential aspect of his life, when John says, *'Dear friend, you are faithful in what you are doing for the brothers, even though they are strangers to you. They have told the church about your love. You will do well to send them on their way in a manner worthy of God. It was for the sake of the Name that they went out, receiving no help from the pagans. We ought therefore to show hospitality to such men so that we may work together for the truth.'*

I think John is focusing here on the servant heart of Gaius when he tells us that nothing is too much trouble for him. Even when Gaius does not know the travelling preacher all that well, that makes no difference to his attitude for the welcome is just as warm and the quality of service is just as good. It seems to me, this man does not make fish of one and flesh of another. He treats them all the same.

These folks may be strangers when they stand on his doorstep for the very first time, but when the time comes for them to leave after a couple of days, they are firm friends. Such is the bond we have with one another in the family of God.

Open hearts, open homes

I can testify to that on a personal level for there is barely a week goes by when I am not on the receiving end of someone's open-ended love and five-star hospitality. Like the apostle John before me, I never fail to thank God for such dear folks; these unsung heroes are worth their weight in gold.

I think most of us realise, it is not easy looking after other people in our home, there is a fair bit of hassle involved, there is a lot of expense incurred, there is a loss of privacy and it is often difficult to get on with the things which need to be done; but from what John says here and from what Gaius knows from experience, it really is well worth it!

A shared ministry

At the same time, John's extraordinarily positive comments on Gaius' sterling contribution to the work of God is a further motivation for him to keep on going. John does not want him to sit back and rest on his laurels, he does not want him to call it a day and put his feet up!

John's desire is for him to keep up the good work, to keep at it, for he must not underestimate his magnificent contribution to the extension of the kingdom of God on earth. The travelling preachers can do their part and exercise their ministry so much more effectively because Gaius and folks like him are fulfilling their God-given role and assignment.

The baseline is, we are in it together! That is what John reminds him of with his parting shot in verse 8.

A 'Name' above all other names!

F F Bruce points out that *'this letter is the only New Testament document which does not mention Christ by name, but that does not mean he is not mentioned!'*

Clearly the *'Name'* (with a capital N) in verse 7 is a reference to the Lord Jesus Christ. His is the name in which Gaius so readily received everyone who knocked at his door.

* *This is the only name in which salvation can be found, Acts 4:12.*
* *This is the name that is above every other name, and*
* *this is the name at which every knee shall bow, Philippians 2:9,10.*

We know from the record in Acts 5:41 that the early church often used *'the Name'* as a synonym for Jesus Christ. Such a turn of phrase encompasses the Hebrew tradition that the name expresses the nature. Indeed, as someone has said, 'when the Name is fully written, it is in essence the sum of the Christian creed' as implied in Romans 10:9 and 1 Corinthians 12:3.

That is the greatest spur, incentive and motivation we have to reach out to the lost in today's post-modern and post-Christian era. We go out into a world of darkness with the light of the gospel of Christ. We go forward into enemy territory taking the name of Jesus with us. We advance on our knees as we seek to fulfil the great commission.

And we do it with no help or encouragement from the pagans in today's society. We go out with the help of God and with the blessing of God and we do it in partnership with the people of God. I cannot do it on my own and you cannot do it by yourself, but together we can do it and together we can see much accomplished to the glory of his name.

John says, in your church, in my church, in the third millennium, be a Gaius!

9,10

Diotrephes ... an exposé

It does not matter where we travel in today's dog-eat-dog world, a world where puppies do not survive, we always find people who think first and foremost about number one! Me-first! They are egocentric individuals. They have their own agenda, they are ruthlessly determined to claw their way to the top rung of the professional ladder, they are in it for what they can get out of it!

This appallingly high level of self-indulgence and self-importance is rampant in the commercial sector for we see power struggles take place in the office and in the loftier echelons of the company boardroom; it is rife in many secular groups as one fringe element after another lobbies for pole position. Sadly and regrettably as many of us know from painful personal experience, narcissism is all too prevalent within the Christian church as well.

Fanning the flames

What we are (conveniently) inclined to forget is that this is not a new phenomenon to hit the church of Christ. It has been around from time immemorial; in fact, if we go back to the early days of the church, it is clear from the dusty archives of the Acts of the Apostles and many of the Pauline epistles that they had more than their fair share of life-size problems. Paul and other ministry people like him spent a lot of their valuable time in the role of a fire fighter when they were called upon to extinguish potentially dangerous blazes which flared among the people of God.

Mind you, we get one or two people in every church fellowship who will happily hijack a situation for their own ends. We always find those with nothing better to do with their time who are content to sit around in the shadows and snipe from the sidelines at those who are trying to make a go of it. Spineless cowards that they are, they tend to operate from the relative safety of the back benches; they spend their waking hours lobbing grenades into the prevailing pandemonium in a misguided attempt to create even more bedlam and confusion. Basically, such twerps are only content when they are fanning the flames.

Having said that, we need to keep the whole scenario in perspective for we get people like that everywhere: people who are spiritually warped, people who derive immense pleasure and massive satisfaction only when they are engaged in acts of spiritual terrorism.

A pain in the neck!

Many of the gargantuan problems they grappled with in the early church and which we are confronted with in the church of the twenty-first century can be attributed to the kind of person John is writing about in verses 9 and 10. I tend to call it, 'the Diotrephes syndrome!'

What a stark contrast he is to our friend Gaius! The two of them are poles apart, they are at opposite ends of the spectrum, and yet they are worshipping under the same church roof and the chances are they are both on the same leadership team.

Unlike Gaius, who was very much a people-oriented person and a genuinely charming individual with an incredibly big heart for God, this overpoweringly arrogant man Diotrephes is not the nicest of human beings. To tell you the truth, I would be hard pushed to find something good to say about him! He is a religious crank, a bit of a quirk. Quite frankly, he is more interested in furthering his own position than he is in furthering the work of God.

If you don't like it, shred it!

Just as John revealed the incandescent light in Gaius, he turns now in this chilling section to expose the jet-black darkness in Diotrephes.

'John's sketch of this man is darkly shadowed with charcoaled lines that smudge as our hands touch the verses.' (Charles Swindoll)

In a scathing statement marked by razor-sharp honesty, John writes with a heavy heart, *'I wrote to the church, but Diotrephes, who loves to be first, will have nothing to do with us. So if I come, I will call attention to what he is doing, gossiping maliciously about us. Not satisfied with that, he refuses to welcome the brothers. He also stops those who want to do so and puts them out of the church.'*
John drops a potential bombshell into their lap with what he says. It would appear from John's insider knowledge and his giveaway comment that he has corresponded with the church on a previous occasion.

- *Fact one:* whatever and whenever he wrote to the church, that letter was never read in public, it never saw the light of day in a congregational meeting, it was never shared with the other members of the eldership and/or diaconate.
- *Fact two:* that letter no longer exists, probably because Diotrephes destroyed it. It was unceremoniously dumped, ditched and discarded in his personal shredder!

Top-heavy top dog!

We can piece together a photofit picture of this man without too much difficulty. There are certain characteristics which hit us between the eyes: he was self-opinionated, he was self-appointed, he saw himself as the sole guardian of the church's interests and affairs.

I read somewhere that Diotrephes 'viewed the church as his turf'. If you like, he saw the local assembly as his patch and no-one, but no-one, would be allowed to encroach on it. If they did, it would be with his permission alone! He was the big boss! He was the chief! He was a dictator, a Hitler in miniature!

He is a man with an upside-down perspective of himself for he *'loves to be first'*. That little microchip description stores a world of information about his character. I think it is fair to say, Diotrephes is not the most likeable of people and he is not the most loveable either. As they say in the Emerald Isle, he is a hard nut to crack!

A control freak

Diotrephes has not only vehemently rejected John's teaching and flatly refused to recognise and respect his apostolic authority, he went further when he falsely accused the apostle and bolted the door against his messengers. He has even gone so far as to excommunicate anyone in the church who received them. Instead of truth, Diotrephes was a purveyor of lies; instead of love, he manufactured fear!

I appreciate the perceptive insights of Charles Swindoll on this self-styled individualist. He uses the analogy of an earthquake to describe him: *'As time passed, a fissure ran through the church, forming a hairline crack between the leadership of the local congregation and the itinerant ministers. Eventually the division became so great that a fault line formed. Tremors of resentment and refused hospitality radiated from the local church's leadership. At the epicentre was a man named Diotrephes. In a quake of rejection, he shook off John's teaching and tried to bury the apostle in a rock slide of sharp-edged words. As an aftershock, Diotrephes' refusal of*

*hospitality extended to such extremes that he not only forbade his
members to receive these visitors, but expelled them from the church
if they did so.'*

When we analyse the actions and attitude of Diotrephes, he
perfectly fits the bill of an autocrat, and when we take it a step further,
he could well be called the pioneer of the so-called heavy shepherding
movement.

This man was more concerned about calling the tune than he
was at playing second fiddle; he was more likely to throw the book
at you, rather than pick up a towel and wash your feet. He wanted to
run the show and it had to be done his way. At the end of the
assessment, there is not much evidence, if any, of a servant heart
with Diotrephes.

What alarms me, and I have seen it all too often in so many
evangelical churches, is that this man sincerely thought he was
upholding biblical standards. He felt he was maintaining the
testimony. He saw himself as the only one who had not bowed the
knee to Baal. He was seeking in his way to preserve the unity of the
local church and, when all is said and done, he really believed in his
heart that he was serving the Lord. To me, that is scary! There are
none so blind as those who refuse to see.

Such men, if they are allowed to go unchecked, can do untold
harm to a congregation of God's people. They often do irreparable
damage to the testimony of the local church. In the space of a few
hours, they can wreck a genuine work of God.

The empty can makes the most noise

In one sense, this man is his own worst enemy. One of his biggest
problems, as the biblical text informs us, is that Diotrephes cannot
keep his ideas to himself. He has a loose tongue that is exceptionally
well-oiled; he does not think twice before spreading all sorts of wild
rumours and scaremongering tales.

The juicy crumbs of information he was passing down the line
about John were nothing less than the scandalous gossip we expect
to read in the gutter press. Thankfully there was no foundation at all

for any of the ridiculous stories. It was sheer unadulterated nonsense. If it was not so serious, we could say, it was a load of drivel.

But we all know, there are people who love to hear such talk and there are people who will believe it! Media experts tell us that such stories sell newspapers! For them, the more sensational it is, the better! I often wonder, why are Christian people who ought to know better so stupidly gullible?

Apparently, Diotrephes made a series of unproven allegations and unsubstantiated accusations against John at a church meeting when John was not present to defend himself. What he failed to take into account is that God has his own way of vindicating his servants and he always does it in his own time. Diotrephes was nothing more than a coward!

I read a story the other day of one man whose fingers had been badly burned by a particular magazine editor. He described him in this way, *'He's like a blotter; he takes everything in and gets it backward.'*

I think we need to be so ultra-careful in these days. Let us not give the devil an inch for he will not be content until he takes a mile. Let us determine not to do the devil's work for him!

A legacy of pride

Diotrephes has had his followers throughout church history and such a species, it hurts me to admit it, is neither rare nor extinct in the third millennium. Too many congregations have been held in the grip of petty tyrants for us to regard this sad phenomenon as extraordinary. There are many churches today in the pocket of one person or one family dynasty. Nothing can happen without the tacit approval of Mr X or Family A because it is deemed to be his or their church!

David Jackman says of such fellowships, *'In effect, there can be no biblical plurality of eldership, no fresh or innovative ideas, no forward movement or spiritual growth. The Holy Spirit has long ago been drummed out of office in a church like that, where Diotrephes rules. What a travesty of the Christian faith and family!'*

When doing some research for this particular study, I came across an idea about the roots of Diotrephes which fascinated me. The suggestion is that his name means, 'Zeus reared, or, a nursling of Zeus'. Apparently, such a name was only to be found in noble and ancient families. It is assumed, therefore, that because of his name, he belonged to the Greek aristocracy. Whatever his pedigree, one thing is sure, he was acting like a Greek aristocrat!

His high-handed and highfalutin behaviour together with his vain pomposity combined with his arrogant nose-in-the-air attitude flew in the face of the fundamental Christian message of humility and sacrifice.

One writer even considered that Diotrephes was the first monarchical bishop of Asia! I do not know! He may have been, he may not have been, but what I do know is this: despite his apparently noble bloodline, he possessed a rather ignoble temperament!

I think we can easily trace the proud steps in his downward spiral:

* *Step one* was **resistance** when he refused to submit to authority by not accepting John's teaching, as in verse 9.
* *Step two* was **criticism** when he started pointing the finger and hurling abuse at those in leadership, as in verse 10a.
* *Step three* was **isolation** when he cut himself off from outside instruction and correction and fellowship, as in verse 10b.
* *Step four* was **control** when he would not let the people listen to any teaching except his own, as in verse 10c.

Obviously, I have no way of knowing what you think of Diotrephes. I have no way of measuring his rating in your mind. I know what I think and I can assure you, such a man needs more than pity, he needs prayer!

11

Gaius ... get it right!

Following the realistic and frightfully disturbing cameo of Diotrephes, John moves on to encourage Gaius to pursue a definite course of action which he spells out for him, *'Dear friend, do not imitate what is evil but what is good. Anyone who does what is good is from God. Anyone who does what is evil has not seen God'* (verse 11).

It is fairly obvious what John is getting at! We do not need to be rocket scientists to work this one out! We all have an innate tendency to mimic other people. We see them as potential role models and we have little or no hesitation in following in their footsteps.

Be careful! Be cautious!

If we come across a modern-day Diotrephes, do not be tempted to follow him. In the short term, he will lead us astray; in the long term, he will do us more harm than good. He is a horrendously bad example to emulate. It is much better to follow the gentleman who comes next.

12

Demetrius ... he's a jolly good fellow!

When we read what John says about this guy, we cannot help but be impressed. His credentials are impeccable. John gives him a superb testimonial when he says in verse 12, *'Demetrius is well spoken of by everyone - and even by the truth itself. We also speak well of him, and you know that our testimony is true.'* What a lovely man!

Demetrius is the kind of person I would give my right arm to meet any day, anywhere! Demetrius is everything that Diotrephes is not, he has everything that Diotrephes has not! John scores him favourably, he rates him highly. He gave him 10 out of a possible 10 on three counts.

People liked him!

It is well within the bounds of possibility to assume that Demetrius was one of the itinerating brethren who had received the cold shoulder treatment from Diotrephes. What John does here is give him the warmest endorsement possible. John pulls out all the stops as he vouches for this man's character and ministry.

There is more than a 50/50 chance that he is the same man we read of in Acts 19. Clearly he was well known as an evangelical believer and, if John was writing from Ephesus, there is a fairly robust case to be made to back that suggestion.

- *If it is true,* then he is the Demetrius who made a small fortune out of making silver shrines of Artemis.
- *If it is true,* he is also the man who initiated rent-a-mob to inflame the passions of a baying crowd against Paul.
- *If it is true,* he is the same man who orchestrated a campaign to get Paul thrown out of the city.
- *If it is true,* and this man had been soundly converted, many would have known about it and marvelled at his changed life.

At the end of the day, we do not really know, but it is worth thinking about nonetheless. What we do know for sure is this, his life is a rare example of faithful Christian living. He is a shining example to young and old alike in a dark age.

People trusted him!

Demetrius received a remarkably upbeat testimony from the apostle and his circle of friends for they all expressed total confidence in him as a man of integrity. He received a good testimony universally for people all over the place think the sun rises and sets on him.

The apostle has absolutely no qualms about commending him to the congregation; in fact, so oozing with confidence is he that he is happy to stake his own reputation on the line.

People watched him!

He also received an excellent testimony from *'the truth itself'*. In other words, if truth could talk, it would confirm that his life lined up with its teaching and practice.

My query is, when John speaks of the *'truth'*, what does he really mean? Some folks see this as a reference to the Lord Jesus Christ who is truth personified but I am not so sure that this is an accurate reflection of the text. Other folks think it applies to the Holy Spirit for he is the Spirit of truth; again I am not convinced that line of interpretation does justice to the text.

I think the most obvious meaning of the phrase in this instance is the right one. It simply says that our friend Demetrius is living his life in accord with the truth of Scripture, so that when his life was measured by that yardstick, the truth itself confirmed his quality. In that sense, it can be said rightly, Demetrius was not found lacking or wanting.

He was like his contemporary Gaius, he was walking in the truth! He was a 'see-through' Christian; there were no skeletons hanging in his closet. He was unimpeachable!

Reflections

John has pulled back the curtain and given us a look-in to life in a first century congregation. Some things we have really liked and they have blessed our hearts; other aspects have left us feeling distressed and probably a bit upset.

Such is life in any church, such is life in every church!

Every fellowship of God's people has at least one cantankerous Diotrephes on the membership roll. Quite frankly, they are worse than a real pain in the neck. We could well do without them! Having said that, they are there to keep us on our toes, they are there to drive us to our knees!

Thank God, more often than not, emerging from the dark cloud is a potential Gaius or a budding Demetrius. Church is a much better place for having them in it and church is worth it if it were only for them. I only wish every church had a few more of them!

13,14

That's it, folks!

John brings his letter to a close in much the same way as he ended his second epistle by saying, *'I have much to write to you, but I do not want to do so with pen and ink. I hope to see you soon, and we will talk face to face. Peace to you. The friends here send their greetings. Greet the friends there by name.'*

In a difficult and demanding situation, where tensions are running high, where nerves are frayed, where people are hassled and hurting, the best John can offer to them, alongside his prayerful support and fellowship and the friendship of others, is the real prospect of peace in knowing Jesus.

Study Guide
~ compiled by John White ~

<u>Chapter One</u>

Jesus ... no phantom of the divine opera!

1. '1 John is all about striking a balance between our head and our heart' (page 19). At the start of your study on John's letters, what steps can you take to make sure that what you learn goes into your heart as well as your head, and changes the way you live?

2. How do verses 1 and 2 confirm that the eternal Son of God and the man Jesus were one and the same Person?

3. What we know about *'the Word of life'* (verse 1) is based on the testimony of honest and reliable witnesses, like John, who knew Jesus intimately. How can this give us confidence in what we believe?

4. What is the difference between *'testifying'* and *'proclaiming'* (verse 2), and how was John qualified to do both?

5. We often take a passive view of our feelings believing they 'just happen'. But John expected his letter to cause joy for himself and his readers (verse 4). How did he think this would happen, and what lesson can we learn about helping ourselves to have positive emotions?

6. Based on verses 5-7, what is it about *'light'* that makes it a picture of what God is like? In what ways does this image challenge our relationship with the Lord?

7. What does it mean practically to *'walk in the light'*, and why does this result in fellowship?

8. In what ways does our society *'claim to be without sin'* (verse 8)? What about you?

9. According to verse 9, how does God's act of forgiving and cleansing show him to be *'faithful and just'*?

Chapter Two

The real McCoy believer

1. What do the words *'my dear children'* in verse 1 tell us about John's relationship with these believers? What guidance is found here for pastors today?

2. How do verses 1 and 2 point us to a right and proper balance in our attitude to sin?

3. If we are forgiven and reconciled to God, why do we need someone *'who speaks to the Father in our defence'* (verse 1)?

4. How does the title *'Jesus Christ, the Righteous One'* assure us that his advocacy will succeed?

5. Based on verses 3-6, why is it not presumptuous to say we *'know'* (or, 'are sure') that we know God?

6. John is clear about what he expects from Christians! Are our expectations about Christian behaviour (both for ourselves and for other people) the same as John's? If not, what needs to change?

7. The *'commandment'* in verse 7 implies that we have a solemn duty to love one another. How prominently does this *'commandment'* feature in our discipling of new believers?

8. Verse 8 says *'the darkness is passing'*. Yet, if anything, society seems to be plunging deeper and deeper into a bottomless chasm of darkness. What is John talking about?

9. The three groups mentioned in verses 12-14 represent the three ages of our Christian experience. From what John says here, what one word or phrase best sums up each stage? Which phase

are you in at present, and how do John's words help you?

10. John first mentions the *'world'* in verse 15. In a simple, yet concise, sentence, how would you define it?

11. What two things (at least) do verses 15-17 tell us that help us not to love the world?

12. What is the right balance between not *'loving the world'* and our being involved in the world?

13. The *'antichrists'* of verse 18 are false teachers who *'have come'*. Why is this designation an apt description of them?

14. From verse 19, does it necessarily follow that those who drift away from church are not true believers? If not, can you outline some alternative motives?

15. What is the *'anointing'* (verse 20) which we all have and what are its results in us?

16. *'You do not need anyone to teach you'* (verse 27). How does this equate with the fact that God gives to the church 'teachers' as in Ephesians 4:11?

17. How does the fact that one day the Lord will *'appear'* (verse 28) affect your behaviour today?

Chapter Three

Love ... the ultimate apologetic

1. From verse 1, what are some of the blessings, privileges and responsibilities of being a child of God?

2. Why should seeing Jesus *'as he is'* (verse 2) make us like him, and what are some of the ways in which we will be like him?

3. In verse 4, how does John's identification of sin as *'lawlessness'* add to our understanding of the seriousness of sin?

4. According to verses 5 and 8, what was the purpose of Jesus' first *'appearing'* and what evidence is there today that he succeeded?

5. Given the truth of 1:8,10 and 2:1, what does it mean that someone who is *'born of God'* does not sin and, in fact, *'cannot'* do so?

6. In verse 11, John again speaks of a message known *'from the beginning'*. In the light of this, how should we respond to new or novel Christian teaching? Should it always be rejected?

7. Someone has said, 'Loving everyone in general may be an excuse for loving no-one in particular.' Is this ever true of you or your church? If it is, what corrective steps could you take?

8. What are some of the reasons why *'our hearts condemn us'*, and what is John's antidote to this negative feeling (verses 16,18,20)?

9. Verse 22 introduces us to a great promise: 'Whatever we ask, we receive!' Is this a promise we take *carte blanche* or, in the light of other promises in Scripture, does it come to us with strings attached?

Chapter Four

Getting it right on the night

1. From what this chapter says, can you give a simple and succinct definition of love?

2. In verse 6, *'we'* refers to the apostles. What does this verse tell us about the authority of apostles? Does this add extra weight to what they wrote in the New Testament? What conclusions can we draw about those who refuse to hear what the Scripture says?

3. John's favourite theme is *'love one another'*. Within the framework of verses 7-12, what three reasons (at least) does John give why we should love? What specific thing can you do today to be more like your heavenly Father who is *'love'*?

4. What is the implication of verse 12 for our witness to the world?

5. There is a two-way abiding in verses 13-16. What is the threefold link in these verses between our experience and this abiding?

6. The consequences of *'perfect love'* are confidence (verse 17) and fearlessness (verse 18). What is this brand of love and why does it have these results?

<u>Chapter Five</u>

Winners ... every time!

1. God's *'commands are not burdensome'* (verse 3). Yet, in our lives, sometimes they seem as if they are! Why is this and how should we respond at such times?

2. If it is possible, as intimated in verses 4 and 5, to *'overcome'* and know *'victory'* in our Christian life, why do we seem to struggle so much? And why is there such an emphasis on counselling in these days?

3. Guided by verses 9 and 10, how might you respond to someone who says, 'I want to believe in Jesus, but I just can't'?

4. What important truths about eternal life are contained in verses 11 and 12?

5. Read verse 13 alongside John 20:31. What is similar and different about these verses, and how do they, in a sense, sum up John's life and ministry?

6. The expression *'the whole world'* occurs twice in John's first letter, here in verse 19 and in 2:2. How do these verses together help us understand the resistance we face and the resources we use in evangelism?

7. John's first letter ends with three glorious certainties in verses 18-20. Having working through his epistle, in what ways are you now more certain?

Chapter Six

The benefits of a daily walk

1. In verses 1 and 2, John calls himself *'the elder'*, which appears to be a title of authority. What should be our attitude to authority in the church, both as those who 'have' it and those who are 'under' it? (Note in particular the words *'love'* and *'truth'* in these verses.)

2. What do the three words *'grace, mercy and peace'* of verse 3 tell us about our relationship towards God, and his towards us?

3. In what ways are you motivated by the negative (*'that you do not lose'*) and positive (*'may be rewarded'*) challenges of verse 8?

4. The term *'runs ahead'* in verse 9 carries the inherent idea of being progressive. When is it right for our outworking of the gospel to be progressive, and when should it be conservative?

5. How do you see verse 10 working out in practice? To whom does it specifically apply?

Chapter Seven

The power of a good example

1. What underlying guidance is given in verse 2 that should enable us to pray more intelligently, and biblically, for our friends?

2. In verses 3 and 4, what principles are there to influence those who have responsibility for others' spiritual welfare?

3. How might God be calling you to practise hospitality to the *'brothers'* and *'strangers'* (verse 5)?

4. In what ways can you and your church *'work together for the truth'* (verses 5-8) with those who go out *'for the sake of the Name'* (in other words, missionaries etc.)? Can you outline some of the reasons given here which commend such a warm attitude?

5. From verses 9 and 10, what were Diotrephes' failings that caused this catastrophic breakdown in church relationships?

6. John tells us to *'imitate'* what is good (verse 11). Who are your role models, and why?